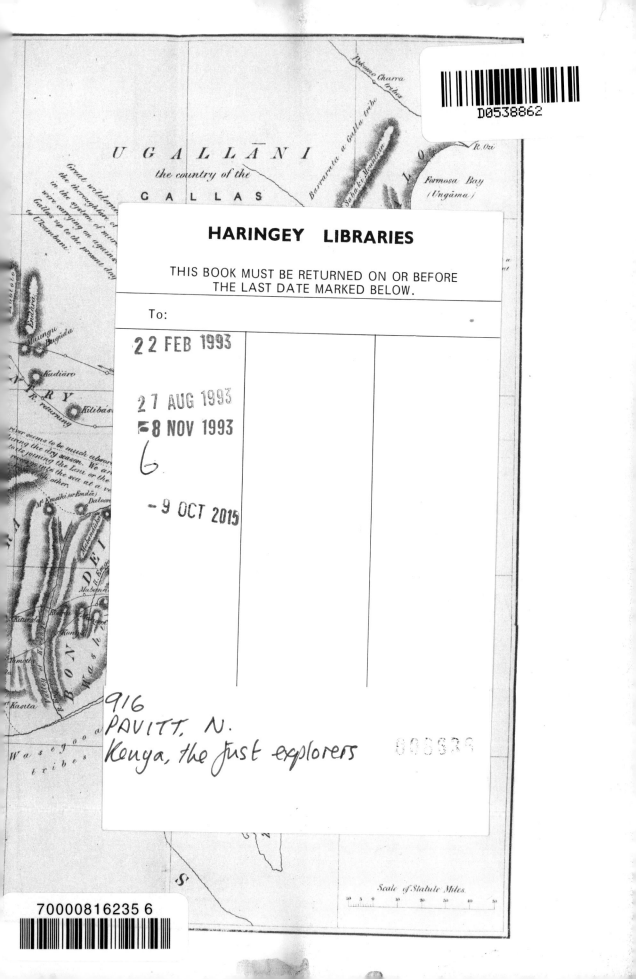

U G A L L Ā N I
the country of the
G A L L A S

Pokomo Charra tribes

Barrarata a Galla tribe

Sobaki Mountain

R. Ozi

Formosa Bay
(Ungāma)

Great wilderness or
the thoroughfare of
the system of micro
or carrying on aquires
Gallas up to the present day
to l'Kaunbani.

Kadiáro

R Y

Kilibasi

Waseyoo a tribes

Scale of Statute Miles

KENYA

THE FIRST EXPLORERS

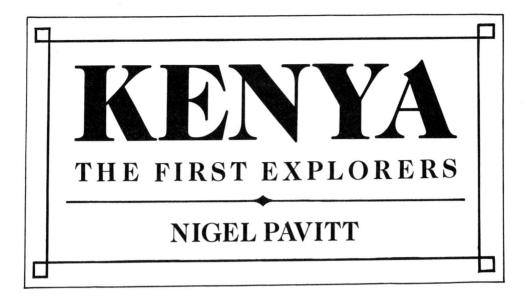

KENYA

THE FIRST EXPLORERS

NIGEL PAVITT

AURUM PRESS

To the memory of the unsung heroes of African exploration
The Porters

First published 1989 by Aurum Press Ltd,
33 Museum Street, London WC1A 1LD

Text and photographs
copyright © 1989 by Nigel Pavitt
Foreword copyright © 1989 by Wilfred Thesiger
Maps by Richard Natkiel Associates

British Library Cataloguing in Publication Data
Pavitt, Nigel
Kenya. the first explorers.
1. Africa south of the Sahara. Exploration.
Biographies. Collections
I. Title
916.7'04'0922

Typeset by Bookworm Typesetting, Manchester

Printed in Great Britain by
Butler and Tanner Ltd, Frome

CONTENTS

PART I

The Reverend Dr Johann Ludwig Krapf and The Reverend Johann Rebmann

PART II

Joseph Thomson

PART III

Count Samuel Teleki von Szek and Lieutenant Ludwig von Höhnel

AUTHOR'S NOTE

THIS BOOK IS NOT INTENDED to be a scholarly work and I make no apology for one or two deliberate mistakes for the sake of clarity.

The early explorers passing through Mombasa described the people living in the coastal hinterland as the 'Wanyika'. I have also used that name, although it is incorrect. 'Wanyika' means 'the people of the dry bush country'. They are properly the Mijikenda, a group of nine tribes of Bantu origin comprising the Wa-Choni, Wa-Digo, Wa-Duruma, Wa-Giriama, Wa-Jibana, Wa-Kambe, Wa-Kauma, Wa-Rabai and Wa-Ribe.

Joseph Thomson was mistaken in calling the friendly people he met at Lake Baringo the Njemps – instead of 'Il Chamus' – and I, too, have called them by that name for it is still in common use. However, I have corrected a number of his other errors. For instance, he named the Tugen the 'Kamasia', the Pokot the 'Suk' and the Baluyia the 'Kavirondo'. One can hardly blame him. The origin of the misnomer 'Kamasia' is a case in point. When the explorer enquired who lived in the hills overlooking Lake Baringo, the Tugen people were deliberately evasive, pointed a finger and said, 'Kamasin', meaning 'that direction'.

The Maasai belong to the Maa-speaking peoples and the spelling I have adopted is the correct one. I have referred to their homesteads or settlements as *manyattas* because it is the accepted colloquial term. In reality, *manyatta* – spelt *emanyata* in the Maa language – is a settlement for warriors only. *Enkang'* is the correct word but it is seldom used except by the Maasai themselves.

FOREWORD

NIGEL PAVITT WAS SECONDED in 1955, at his own request, during his national service to the King's African Rifles in Kenya; he subsequently became a regular officer with the KAR. He enjoyed serving with African troops and after Kenya became independent he remained with his battalion, now part of the Kenya Army, and saw active service with it against Somali outlaws in Northern Kenya, at which time he was awarded a MBE. Since then he has become a citizen of Kenya, where he takes every opportunity to visit the Maasai or to travel, sometimes with camels, in the remote desert areas of the north. Over the years he has established a close personal relationship with individuals among the Maasai, the Samburu, the Turkana and other tribes. Always interested in everything that has to do with them, he has acquired a real knowledge of their tribal histories, their customs and way of life, as well as a familiarity with the areas in which they live. He knows the mountains, the forests, the deserts, the wild animals and the vegetation of that widely differing land. His understanding of so many aspects of Kenya and its people, and a gift for writing, have enabled him to produce this most interesting book about the exploration of the country by Europeans during the last century. The remarkable photographs he has included speak for themselves.

When the Reverend Dr J.L. Krapf landed on the coast, thirty miles north of Mombasa, in 1843 to start his missionary work in East Africa, all but the coastal strip of present-day Kenya was as yet unknown to Europeans. Forty-five years later when Count Teleki von Szek arrived back on the coast in 1888, after discovering the great lake which he named Lake Rudolf, all the major geographical problems of the Kenya of today had been solved.

Nigel Pavitt describes how this was accomplished. Using as his framework the accounts written by Krapf, Joseph Thomson and Ludwig von Höhnel, who accompanied Teleki, he includes many passages from these books, thereby conveying the personalities of these very individualistic explorers. In his narrative he skilfully inserts relevant events which took place then or later, and in so doing widens its scope. He also makes use of his knowledge to amplify, for instance, descriptions of tribal ceremonies, to insert the scientific names of plants or animals and to relate the explorers' journeys to the positions of modern towns and villages.

He begins his book with a brief history of the events that had occurred along the coast and had resulted in Arab sovereignty over Zanzibar, Mombasa and other coastal towns. The Arab presence on the coast over many centuries had produced an Afro-Arab people, who had evolved Swahili as their language, and were generally known by that name. It was from them that Arab traders and European explorers usually recruited the porters on whom they depended for their journeys into the interior.

I was already acquainted with Krapf's name when Nigel Pavitt showed me the typescript of his book. I was born in Abyssinia in 1910 and for many years I had been closely associated with that country, known today as Ethiopia. I had long been collecting books about Abyssinia and East Africa, among them Krapf's *Abyssinian Journal* as well as his *Travels, Researches and Missionary Labours in Eastern Africa*. This is a formidable-looking tome and I had not read it; I shall now do so. I also owned Thomson's *Through Masai Land* and von Höhnel's *Discovery by Count Teleki of Lakes Rudolf and Stefanie*, both of which I had read several times. Reading the first part of Nigel Pavitt's typescript, I was fascinated by his description of the coast in those early days and by his account of Krapf's and Rebmann's journeys. They were the first Europeans to have seen Mounts Kilimanjaro and Kenya and were amazed by their snow-covered summits. Their report of these mountains was derided by W. Desborough Cooley of the Royal Geographical Society, who declared that it was impossible for snow to exist on the equator. I have always hoped he was still alive when their discoveries were confirmed by later explorers.

Joseph Thomson was twenty-five when he travelled through Maasailand to Lake Baringo and from there to Lake Nyanza, before returning to the coast. I was twenty-three when I explored the Danakil country of Abyssinia in 1933–4. The fact that we were about the same age when we accomplished these journeys has always given me a special interest in Thomson. Both our journeys were dangerous and both were successful. The Danakil were unadministered when I travelled among them, and rated a man's standing by the number of men he had killed and castrated. In 1875 they had wiped out an Egyptian army that attempted to invade their country, and some years later they exterminated two Italian expeditions. Just before I entered their country they killed some Greek traders who ventured into their territory, and eight months after I left they annihilated a French patrol armed with a machine gun on the French Somali border.

In 1883 when Thomson set forth on his journey, the Maasai had a fearsome reputation in East Africa; a large force of their warriors even penetrated to the outskirts of Mombasa and terrorized the town. To avoid encounters with the Maasai, Arab slave traders and the European explorers who aimed to reach the great lakes followed a route well to the south of their territory. Thomson, however, set out intending to discover a route to Lake Nyanza through Maasailand. He employed 110 porters at the coast to carry his baggage, which included the large quantities of cloth, beads and other trade goods necessary to meet frequent demands for *hongo*, or tribute, and to satisfy the rapacity of the tribesmen he encountered. Thomson gained a useful reputation as a *laibon* or magician by removing and replacing his false teeth, by making water appear to boil after adding Eno's fruit salts to it and by treating the sick. Nevertheless he was subject to repeated harassment, indignities and even physical maulings. Despite this incessant provocation he retained his patience, good temper and forbearance and felt a genuine respect for the Maasai. By using magic instead of bullets he completed this long, exacting and dangerous journey without bloodshed. It is all described in the following pages and makes fascinating reading.

Of the great African exploratory journeys in the 1880s I would sooner have discovered Lake Rudolf than the source of the Nile. Teleki's journey was undoubtedly one of the most arduous undertaken in Africa. It extended over every type of country, from the beaches on the coast to the snows on Kilimanjaro and Mount Kenya, and the lava fields on the shores of Lake Rudolf; but the tribes he encountered would have been, for me, the outstanding interest of this journey.

As a boy I had been fascinated by Major Rayne's *The Ivory Raiders* describing his adventures among the Turkana, and I had read several other books about Northern Kenya and its tribes before I went there for two years in 1960. I returned to Kenya in 1967 and have lived in the north intermittently every since. In 1960 the Northern Frontier District was a closed area to everyone, except government officials, without a special pass. I was given permission to travel there and spent most of the following two years and later years among the Samburu, the Turkana, the Rendille and the Boran. I travelled on foot, accompanied by half a dozen tribesmen. We carried everything we required, including plenty of water, on four or five camels and covered great distances on both sides of the lake. The only Europeans I met were district officers, perhaps once in six weeks. The tribesmen I encountered were either naked, like the Turkana, or wore tribal dress. They knew of no world other than their own, a world limited to the distance they could walk. British administration had largely ensured peace among them, though the Merille, known to Teleki as the Reshiat, still carried out murderous raids across the Ethiopian frontier. One such raid took place when I was near the northern end of the lake. I was interested to see that, for trophies, they had removed the navels of their victims.

Nigel Pavitt and I are fortunate to have known the Northern Frontier District as it was in the past, little changed since Teleki journeyed there in 1887, the first European to do so. Today there is a large mission station, a lodge for tourists and an air strip at Loiengalani on the east side of the lake, and at South Horr under Mount Nyiru there is another mission station and a camping site for tourist buses on their way to Loiengalani.

I had already been travelling for a month, since entering the Northern Frontier District from Isiolo, when I first saw the lake, spread out below me and stretching to the horizon. Few other sights have made a greater impact on me. This was largely due to my having travelled there on foot: the sense of achievement, such as it was, would have been lacking had I come there by car. I therefore find it easy to imagine what this sight must have meant to Teleki, as he stood there among his exhausted followers. At last, after the long and often dangerous journey from the coast, he had achieved his ambition by reaching the lake.

Teleki and von Höhnel had some 220 men with them when they set out for the lake from Baringo. Before leaving Baringo they had difficulty getting hold of enough grain to last so many men for such a long journey. Teleki was fortunately an experienced hunter. The country round Baringo teemed with wild animals, including rhino and buffalo, and he was able to shoot a large number. The men dried the meat and carried it with them. At Allia Bay on the eastern shore of the lake he found elephants and shot a number of them, and their meat helped to eke out the rations, but they suffered great hardships from hunger and thirst. On one occasion they would probably all have died, had they not found water under the sand in a dry river bed.

They explored almost the entire eastern side of the lake before they returned eighty-five days later to its southern end. From there Teleki did not retrace his steps to Baringo but travelled down the west side of the Rift among the Turkana and the Pokot. By this time his men were starving, and as he could not induce the Pokot to barter their cattle he finally authorized his men to carry out a raid; after some fighting they captured a large number of cattle and goats. This enabled them to reach Nakuru where they were well-received by the Maasai. Had Teleki been able to use camels, the northern half of his journey would have been much easier. He could have left most of his porters behind at Baringo, and would therefore have needed less food; this could have been carried, with plenty of water, on the camels. Camels, however, were only introduced by the Somalis into North-Eastern Kenya towards the end of the last century. Today the Turkana own large numbers of camels but, unlike the Rendille, Boran, Gabra and Somalis, they never load them; they still fetch water and carry the mats and framework of their huts, and their other possessions, on donkeys.

Being familiar with Northern Kenya, each time I think of Teleki's journey I am amazed at the courage and endurance of his porters, under the conditions of incredible hardship to which they were subjected: the incessant hunger and thirst, and the heavy loads they carried. Many of them died and it was with a very reduced following that Teleki and von Höhnel eventually arrived back at Mombasa. Nigel Pavitt ends his book with a tribute to such porters and the words 'without them the geographical exploration of East Africa a century ago would have been impossible'.

Wilfred Thesiger
1988

INTRODUCTION

ToDAY IT SEEMS QUITE INCREDIBLE that the wonders of East Africa were only opened to the gaze of the New World 100 years ago. As recently as 1880 the large tract of virgin country which is present-day Kenya was virtually an unknown land. There had been no effective invasion and no conquest beyond a narrow strip of coastland adjacent to the Indian Ocean. Over the centuries Arabs, Portuguese, Indians, Baluchis, Malays, Chinese and the passing vessels of European nations had all left their mark on this fertile belt, which was no more than twenty-five miles wide and perhaps 1,000 miles long. It had been the scene of bloody wars, internecine strife, a placid agriculture and the indolence of a society languishing in a sultry climate. Its trade had been based to a great extent on ivory; the white ivory from the colossal herds of elephants roaming the forests and plains of the interior – and the black, epitomized by the tortured bodies of the African people who were snatched from their homes and sold into slavery at Zanzibar.

The Reverend Dr Johann Ludwig Krapf, a brilliant linguist, was the very first European to make a permanent home in the hinterland of this region. His is not a name that is instantly known – perhaps because he was a German and in essence a missionary, whereas the majority of distinguished explorers to East and Central Africa came from England and Scotland. Like his famous contemporary, David Livingstone, Krapf was a man with vision. He had a burning desire to evangelize and to play his part in stamping out the evil trafficking in slaves. His hearsay reports of an extensive lake region fired the imagination of many geographers and early nineteenth-century explorers to Africa who were bent on finding the source of the mighty River Nile. He and his fellow-missionary, Johann Rebmann, first revealed the existence of Africa's two snowcapped mountains, the one rounded and shining like a dome of burnished silver, the other culminating in a splendid pinnacle.

Kenya is unusual in spanning an entire climatic range from these isolated alpine zones to the oppressive heat of the equatorial coast. In between lie vast open spaces studded with the flat-topped acacia trees that are such a distinctive feature of the African land scape. Before man and his deadly rifle appeared on the scene, it was a wonderland of wild animals. The nomadic cattle-owning Maasai people dominated these savannahs and the descriptive names they gave to the geographical features in their territory are the place names that we use to this day. The old Maasai maxim could well have been 'might is right'; yet tales of their naked aggression and blood lust were deliberately exaggerated by Arab merchants and their Swahili henchmen as a means of protecting their lucrative trade in ivory from foreign interference.

Despite the inherent dangers, one or two adventurers and naturalists explored the area around the Tana River and trekked inland as far as the foothills of Mount Kilimanjaro. But it was not until 1883 that Joseph Thomson, a Scot, crossed through the heart of Maasailand to the north-east shores of Lake Victoria and back. His was a remarkable journey of adventure and ingenuity which placed him at once among the greatest names of African exploration. In contrast to many travellers to the 'dark' continent in the second half of the last century, Thomson was a friendly, patient and humane man. Above all, he did not resort to force as a means of achieving his cherished goals. His motto – derived from the Italian *chi va piano va sano, chi va sano va lontano* – was his guiding principle: 'He who goes gently, goes safely, he who goes safely, goes far'. Before his historic journey, the outside world knew nothing of the Great Rift Valley, more than 4,000 miles long and in places 5,000 feet deep. Even Thomson, a geologist by profession, could not have guessed that it is the most extraordinary and dramatic feature of its kind on earth. He sighted several lakes set in the depths of the valley, some rimmed with the blinding white of naked soda, others tinged with a deep band of pink where more than a million flamingos jostled each other in the shallow waters. Along its floor in a remote area of northern Kenya lies Lake Turkana, the Jade Sea, one of the largest alkaline lakes in the world; 150 miles long and twenty to thirty miles wide, it is generally acknowledged to be the birthplace of mankind. Set against the harsh beauty of a rugged landscape, where everything that grows has prickles or thorns and where high winds constantly buffet sand and soil against bare lava rocks, it is a miracle that anything survives there.

Thomson had finally drawn aside the veil that had hidden the secrets of the interior from the outside world. The reports that he took home of a temperate and fertile land excited several European powers just when the scramble for Africa had got under way. Although the political and commercial potential of the region was of no particular interest to him, he unwittingly served the cause of British Imperialism. By the time East Africa was divided into British and German 'spheres of influence' under the Anglo-German Agreement of 1886, Britain had laid claim to all the country which Thomson had explored.

Thomson's vague report of the unknown lake and his description of the infinite variety of the animals to be found there prompted Count Samuel Teleki von Szek, a wealthy Hungarian nobleman, to lead an expedition of his own into the still-unexplored region north of Lake Baringo. Teleki was an ardent traveller with a passion for hunting big game. Since money was no object, he did himself well. He bought the finest sporting rifles from the best gunsmiths and stocked up with an incredible assortment of bric-à-brac to give away to the local chieftains. In 1886 he and his companion, Lieutenant Ludwig von Höhnel, set out on the last great expedition into the interior of East Africa. They took thirteen months to reach the southern shores of the lake and, since it was fashionable at the time to bestow the names of royalty on the discoveries of Euro-pean explorers, Teleki christened it 'Rudolf' after his friend Prince Rudolf, heir-apparent to the throne of the Austro-Hungarian Empire. The rest of their journey was a harrowing experience, with serious privations and numerous deaths among the ranks of their porters. The exped-ition eventually straggled into Mombasa on 24th October 1888 with a mere handful of survivors.

The accounts of the early travellers to East Africa fascinated me as a boy and I was thrilled to be given the opportunity of coming to Kenya thirty years ago. My twelve years as an officer in the Kenya Army took me to the far corners of the country and gave me the opportunity to acquire a knowledge of the peoples and places the explorers had described. In 1957, I spent six months on the northern shores of Lake Turkana, close to the Omo delta, where the mosquitoes were the worst I have ever come across. Every night the Dassenach people, better known as the Merille, sang and danced for hours on end until exhaustion overcame them; they could not have slept otherwise. Over the years, I have walked across most of the country north of Maralal which Count Teleki explored but, in this modern age, one tends to forget that the pioneers had to find their way there from the coast on foot. Theirs were dangerous journeys without the amenities we now take for granted; tea, salt, soap and candles were the only essentials they carried in their 'chop boxes'. They were a singular breed of men by any standards.

In Kenya, as elsewhere, the changes that have taken place this century have been immense, but the appeal remains. The graceful nomads with their herds of cattle and flocks of sheep and goats are largely untouched by the crude hand of contemporary civilization; the lovely hills and valleys, the spectacular landscape and the friendliness of the people are still there. Much, of course, has gone for ever. Great herds of wild animals have been ruthlessly destroyed; many of the wide, almost limitless, plains have been carved up into fields of crops and little homesteads; huge trees have been razed to the ground and forested river-banks laid bare; tarmac roads with roaring traffic have replaced the footpaths and game trails of the past. Yet, in the remoter areas, the sympathetic traveller can still experience something of the mystery and magic of Kenya.

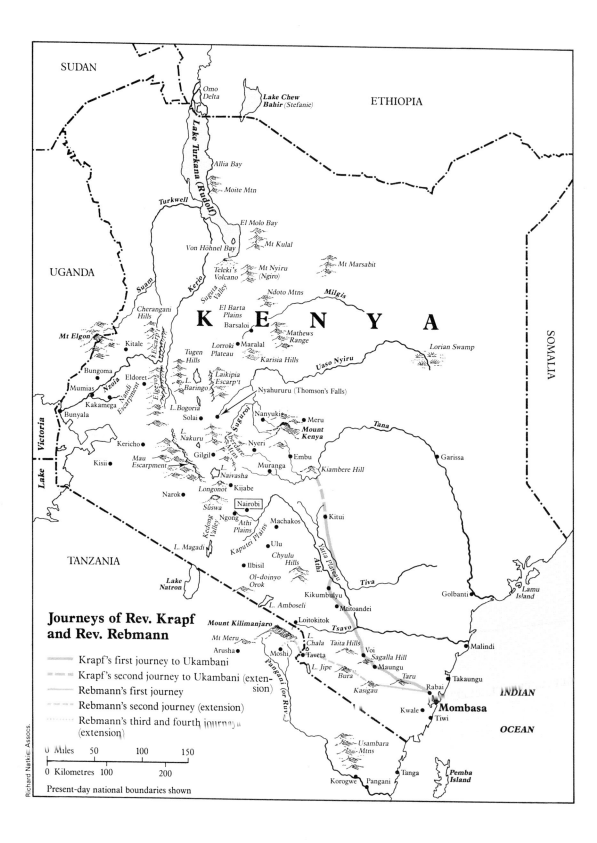

SUDAN

ETHIOPIA

Omo Delta

Lake Chew Bahir (Stefanie)

Lake Turkana (Rudolf)

Allia Bay

Turkwell

Moite Mtn

El Molo Bay

Von Höhnel Bay

Mt Kulal

UGANDA

Kerio

Suam

Teleki's Volcano

Mt Nyiru (Ngiro)

Mt Marsabit

Cherangani Hills

Sugura Valley

El Barta Plains

Mt Elgon

K   E   N   Y   A

Milgis

Kitale

Barsaloi

Mathews Range

Lorian Swamp

Tugen Hills

Lorroki Plateau

Maralal

Bungoma

Eldoret

Karisia Hills

Uaso Nyiru

Mumias

Nandi Escarpment

Nzoia

L. Baringo

Laikipia Escarp't

Kakamega

Elgeyo Escarpt

Nyahururu (Thomson's Falls)

Tana

Bunyala

L. Bogoria

Solai

Nanyuki

Meru

Garissa

Kericho

L. Nakuru

Gilgil

Aberdare Mtns

Mount Kenya

Kisii

Mau Escarpment

Nyeri

Embu

L. Naivasha

Muranga

Kiambere Hill

Narok

Longonot

Kijabe

Súswa

Nairobi

Ngong

Machakos

Kitui

Athi Plains

Kedong Valley

Kaputei Plains

Ulu

L. Magadi

Chyulu Hills

TANZANIA

Ilbisil

Yatta Plateau

Ol-doinyo Orok

Athi

Tiva

Lake Natron

L. Amboseli

Kikumbulyu

Tsavo

Mtoandei

Golbanti

Lamu Island

Loitokitok

Journeys of Rev. Krapf and Rev. Rebmann

Mount Kilimanjaro

Mt Meru

L. Chala

Taita Hills

Voi

Sagalla Hill

Malindi

Arusha

Moshi

Taveta

Maungu

L. Jipe

Bura

Taru

Takaungu

Rabai

Mombasa

━━━ Krapf's first journey to Ukambani

┅┅┅ Krapf's second journey to Ukambani (extension)

──── Rebmann's first journey

─ ─ ─ Rebmann's second journey (extension)

·········· Rebmann's third and fourth journey (extension)

Kasigau

Kwale

Tiwi

Pangani (or Ruv)

INDIAN

OCEAN

0 Miles   50   100   150

0 Kilometres 100   200

Usambara Mtns

Tanga

Pemba Island

Present-day national boundaries shown

Korogwe   Pangani

SOMALIA

Richard Natkiel Assocs.

PART I

The Reverend Dr Johann Ludwig Krapf
and The Reverend Johann Rebmann

Travels and missionary labours
in East Africa

1844–53

The end of the geographical feat is but the
commencement of missionary operations.

DAVID LIVINGSTONE

CHAPTER 1

Early days

Baada ya kisa, mkasa; baada ya chanzo, kitendo
After a reason, a happening; after a beginning, an action
Swahili proverb

THE TURBULENT HISTORY of East Africa can be traced back 2,000 years to a time when small Arab settlements were known to have existed at several ports and coastal towns from Mogadishu in the north to Maputo in the south. Due to the proximity of Arabia and India, it was only natural that the first traders should have come from there. The seasonal trade or monsoon winds blow with regularity from the north-east for three to four months a year starting in December and then, in April, change to the south-west for another six to eight months. This allowed seafarers in dhows, the sailing ships of the region, to make annual visits along the coast in search of gold, ivory, rhino horn and slaves. Egyptians, Phoenicians, Persians, Indians and even the Chinese followed in the wake of Arab merchants who were neither interested in exploration nor in discovering more about the interior than was necessary for trade. They led a listless life and their contact with the coast over the centuries was limited and sporadic. However, they built up a chain of independent city states and intermarried with the locals; this, in course of time, produced a littoral population of Afro-Arab peoples, known as Swahilis, who shared their faith and way of life. Although coconut palms, mango trees, citrus fruits and rice were introduced from the east, little effort was made to cultivate the rich productive soils of the coastal strip on a commercial scale. Indeed, much of the trade was left to Indians who, as soon as they had learned to put their trust in the reliability of the trade winds, sailed directly across the Indian Ocean from the ports of Karachi, Surat and Bombay in twenty to twenty-five days.

In the latter half of the fifteenth century the political expansion of Asia, maintained for seven centuries by the conquering forces of Islam, declined and Christian Europe moved into a new age of enterprise and development. The Portuguese applied their maritime and navigational skills to opening up alternative routes to trade with the Orient. Christopher Columbus discovered America and Bartolomeu Diaz chanced upon a passage round the southern tip of Africa. The famous sailor Vasco da Gama visited the largely unknown east coast of Africa in 1498 with three naval ships, and was astonished to come across a highly civilized society with all the trappings of material wealth. Flourishing towns had buildings of stone, well laid out streets and mosques exquisitely decorated in the Persian style. Da Gama found Malindi 'a noble city' where the ruler's palace was strewn with carpets and rugs and furnished with stools inlaid with ivory and gold. His reports of the prosperity of the region roused the covetousness of his king and countrymen. Consequently his friendly reconnaissance was quickly followed by a general assault to take advantage of the intrigue and internal strife that prevailed in the autonomous sultanates.

Kilwa and Zanzibar were swiftly subjugated, but the wily Sultan of Malindi was treated as an ally and his town was spared. Alone in resisting the invaders were the well-armed Arab and Swahili residents of Mombasa, helped by a conscript army of 'Wanyika' bowmen. The Portuguese took several years to despatch 1,500 commandos in a fleet of twenty men-o'-war and rout them. This was just the first of many occasions when the town was attacked, sacked and fired. In time, the warlike inhabitants were aided and abetted by an unexpected Moslem ally, a Turkish fleet commander by the name of Admiral Mirale Bey, who had sailed into Mombasa unannounced with his xebecs, galleys and dhows. The residents continued throughout the sixteenth century to make trouble for the European imperialists until Portugal recognized, at last, that its jurisdiction was not strong enough without the presence of a permanent garrison. As a result Fort Jesus, an historic landmark, was built between 1593 and 1596 by masons from the Portuguese colony of Goa, India and unskilled labour from Malindi. But, with Portuguese power in the eastern sector of the Indian Ocean under threat from England and Holland and soon to be in decline, it was only a matter of time before its authority in the west was challenged once more.

By the middle of the seventeenth century the Omani Arabs had regained their old energy and independence, ejecting the Portuguese invaders from Muscat and the entire Arabian seaboard. Pleas for assistance from their Arab brothers in East Africa did not fall on deaf ears. In 1652 the Portuguese settlements on Pate and Zanzibar Islands were wiped out and seventeen years later Faza, the principal port of Pate Island, and Mombasa town, except its fort, were captured. The Portuguese retaliated ruthlessly and, in a last attempt to suppress the rebellion, beheaded hundreds of leading Arab citizens and exacted a vast amount of tribute. But the growing superiority of the Omanis in the region prevailed. In 1698 they terminated 200 years of brutal Portuguese rule by capturing Fort Jesus after a siege lasting thirty-three months, during which well over 1,000 men, women and children died of disease.

The reimposition of an indolent, self-seeking Arab rule did more harm than good, however, since it failed to develop anything other than the slave trade. The Portuguese conquest had left no permanent mark on the northern part of the coast of East Africa. Their control had been purely external, forcibly maintained by a few isolated garrisons. It is true they introduced cassava, maize and pineapples but, like the Arabs whose power they had usurped, their cultivation was on a small scale. The Portuguese destroyed the historically important Arab towns of the day, which were replaced by jungle. In every way their rule was as pointless as it was profitless, both to themselves and to the inhabitants of the region. They took little interest in their surroundings and, without navigable rivers to offer them an easy passage into the interior, apparently undertook no journeys inland from the coast north of Mozambique. Perhaps they were fully occupied maintaining their authority – unless other, more compelling, reasons deterred them.

Foremost among these was the nature of the country. Beyond the coastal strip, which comprised a belt of lush tropical and semi-tropical vegetation some twelve to fifteen miles deep, lay the *nyiku*, a formidable obstacle to the movement of man. This all but limitless mass of prickly, tangled grey-brown bush with a scant rainfall stretched for eighty miles or so due west – stunted trees with thin naked branches contorted into incredible twisted shapes; short, scraggy bushes, with many stems springing up from the ground, covered with prickles and 'wait-a-bit' thorns which tear mercilessly at clothes and the skin; the hard, needle-sharp leaves of sansevieria which pierce shoe-leather as easily as paper; and the fleshy stems of euphorbias spilling out their white milky latex, a danger to the eyes, whenever they are broken or cut. For centuries, it had been an almost impenetrable barrier into the interior. Even if a traveller had managed to traverse this inimical, featureless waste with no guides to show him the way, the tribes beyond would have prevented further progress.

First to be encountered would have been the Zimba, a militant Bantu tribe akin to the Zulus but with cannibalistic tendencies, who reached the hinterland off the east coast of Africa in the sixteenth century, having fought and feasted well on a 1,000-mile journey from the south of the continent. When the Portuguese commander quelled an uprising in Mombasa for the third time in 1587, he permitted the Zimba to mop up pockets of Arab and Turkish resistance. The sequel was the ugliest incident in all the grim history of the island town, with everyone in sight being killed and many devoured. In time, the Zimba moved north to Malindi where they were virtually wiped out by the local 'Wasegeju'; those who survived the onslaught vanished inland. Centuries later the Maasai, nomadic cattle-owning people, appeared from the north to dominate the rolling grasslands of East Africa, from the Indian Ocean to the far walls of the Rift Valley and from 100 miles south of Mount Kilimanjaro to the mysterious Lorian swamp. At the zenith of their power in the middle of the last century, although barely 45,000 strong, they exercised control over an area of almost 75,000 square miles. They were fearless and courageous, relying on a well-organized age group system to produce an effective and destructive fighting machine of several thousand warriors who fought under the direction of their *ol-oiboni*, the chief soothsayer and medicine man of the tribe. They attacked their neighbours with impunity, striking even into the centre of Mombasa. Their major aspiration was the acquisition of stock, for their legend recounts how on the first day of the Creation their God, Enkai, bestowed on them all the cattle on earth; they considered, therefore, that rustling was not only an addictive and exhilarating sport but a means of recovering livestock which was rightly theirs. Before their power was broken towards the end of the last century through disease and internecine wars, the blood of Africa flowed freely on to these parched lands.

The entire East African coastline had been surveyed between 1822 and 1826 by Captain William F. Owen RN, a seaman of character, who had regarded the destruction of the slave trade as a priority task. Inland exploration of the region, however, dates from 1844 when the Reverend Dr Johann Ludwig Krapf, a pioneer among the missionary-explorers of Africa, established a little mission station at Rabai, then called Rabbai Mpia, in the hills beyond Mombasa. Almost by chance, he became the first white man to make a permanent home in the hinterland of East Africa.

Krapf, the son of a prosperous farmer, was born in 1810 at the village of Deredingen in the foothills of the German Black Forest. When eleven years old, he was so severely beaten by a neighbour that he was bedridden for six months. To while away the hours during his long convalescence, he amused himself reading the Bible. His father was not alone in thinking that he was destined to become a parson but, from an early age, the young boy's favourite subject had been geography; while other children played games, he pored over maps and read travel books. One which fired his vivid imagination was Bruce's eighteenth-century travels in Abyssinia, which he had borrowed from

a local bookseller. By the age of fourteen, he had made up his mind to become a ship's captain in order to visit the far-off lands about which he had learned and dreamed so much. However, this idea had to be abandoned when his father found out that the cost of apprenticeship was beyond his means.

A year later, a chance lecture by the rector of his school on 'the spread of Christianity amongst the heathen' turned Krapf's attention to the Church. 'Why not become a missionary and go out and convert the heathen?' he asked himself. In the Easter holidays of 1825 he walked with single-minded determination all the way to the Swiss town of Basel to apply for admission to its famous Protestant missionary college. Being under age, he was not allowed to enrol but the welcome he received made such an impression on him that, during the final year at school, he taught himself Hebrew and read the Old Testament in its original text to make absolutely certain of his place and choice of career. This was the first evidence of his remarkable linguistic talents.

He joined the Church Missionary Society (CMS) shortly after his ordination and was appointed to a vacant post on the staff of the mission in Abyssinia, the land of his youthful dreams and aspirations. His first posting was to Aduwa in the north of the country. Here, priests of the Coptic Church succeeded without much difficulty in persuading their flock to ignore his Protestant teachings; and if that was not a sufficient obstacle to his work, the arrival of openly hostile French Catholic missionaries led to his expulsion by the ruler of the province of Tigre.

We might have remained had we chosen to offer the Prince a present greater than which he had received from the Roman Catholics; but such a course we deemed an unworthy one, and after a residence of scarcely two months, I had to quit the land in which I would so willingly have striven to spread the Gospel. Many of the Bibles which I had brought to Aduwa were destroyed by the Abyssinian priests, undoubtedly at the instigation of the Roman Catholics; but many which had been distributed among the other provinces of Abyssinia it was out of their power to destroy.

It was ironical how Christianity in Africa was weakened by the religious intolerance shown by one Christian Church towards another. Their failure to work in unison retarded their pious efforts to fight the common foe.

Krapf next attempted to spread the Gospel in the kingdom of Shoa which included the subjected Galla people who lived south of the Awash River. He was initially more successful here.

By the beginning of 1842 I found that my missionary residence in Ankober [some eighty miles north-east of Addis Ababa, which did not exist at that time] *had been far from fruitful; for I had distributed 1,000 copies of the Scriptures, and many of the priests of Shoa had been awakened to a knowledge of the truth, and to a consciousness of the corrupt state of their church. My little school of ten boys, whom I fed, clothed and educated at home, was prospering. The king bestowed on me a silver sword which gave me the rank of Governor.*

Later that year, he left Abyssinia briefly in order to marry Rosine Dietrich in Egypt. The marriage was undertaken in the interests of his work; he had never set eyes on his bride, although he had every reason to believe she would be full of courage and devotion. His absence gave Monsieur Rochet, the French Consul, an opportunity to persuade the King of Shoa and his powerful mother to ban the *evil* Protestants from ever setting foot on Ethiopian soil again. By the time Krapf got back to Tajura, opposite modern Djibouti at the mouth of the Red Sea, with thirty chests full of Bibles, his way into the interior was barred. At first disbelieving that the written orders of his friend, King Sahela Selassie, applied to him, he continued his sea voyage across the gulf of Tajura – the Gubat al Karib, reputed stronghold of the King of Devils – to Zeila, a small coastal town on the north-west tip of Somalia, from where he planned another route back to Shoa through the Somali-speaking people of the region. His hopes were dashed when a message reached him from Major Harris, the British Consul, confirming the king's refusal to allow any Protestant missionaries to return. This he ascribed more charitably than did Krapf to the ruler's change of attitude due to a growing fanaticism among the Abyssinian priesthood. Instructions had also been given to close the consulate at Ankober, thus severing all direct links with the king and his Court.

The phlegmatic Krapf was depressed but not discouraged, for although his years among the Abyssinians had been relatively unproductive and frustrating, they had not been entirely wasted. He had mastered the Amharic and Galla languages and despatched a valuable collection of Ethiopian Coptic manuscripts to the University of Tübingen, for which he had received a doctorate. He had also made contact with several Galla communities; these people had shown a keen interest in learning more about the Scriptures. He

EARLY DAYS 21

felt confident that he could stem the rising tide of Islam if only he could establish a mission station in their midst. This was a noble goal which excited his restless personality. Since it was no longer possible to penetrate Galla country from Abyssinia, he decided to find a way through East Africa where, he had learned, these interesting and receptive people occupied a vast tract of country extending south to the equator.

'Having sought preparation for the long sea voyage by prayer and meditation, I set sail with my wife from Aden on 11th November 1843, our destination being Zanzibar.' Their craft was an Arabian dhow of stout wooden construction and capable of carrying 120 tons of cargo. Krapf and his wife were offered basic sleeping accommodation under a rugged awning on the open poop. Flanking the rudder on either side of the stern was a toilet – an open box affair hanging precariously over the side of the vessel with a hole in the floor. 'On an Arab vessel you must, of course, not mind living among rats and other animals. But what does it matter when you consider the great end you have in view.' Philosophical as Krapf was about rats, their presence could not be ignored. The Arab captain of one dhow in which he had voyaged admitted that 'they ran like herds of goats'! Invisible in daylight, they did not fail to annoy travellers at night, destroying beds and bedding, running over necks and faces and occasionally biting toes.

The Krapfs were unaware the dhow they had boarded was overloaded, down in the water almost to her gunwales, and the Arab captain and his fourteen-man crew were incompetent. After being nearly shipwrecked in heavy seas just two days out of Aden, they were forced to turn back. On 15th November, they set sail once more in another dhow captained by a native of Mombasa who knew the coastline intimately. In some ways the disaster of the first voyage was a blessing in disguise for, instead of going directly to Zanzibar, the second boat hugged the coast, which enabled the missionary to explore numerous mainland ports and towns between Mogadishu and *Tajura*

Pangani. His movements and decisions in the months to come might have been shaped quite differently without that initial insight of the region.

On 28th December the ship put into the winding, almost secretive creek of Takaungu, some thirty miles north of Mombasa, and Krapf gained the shore in one of the long, narrow boats hollowed out of a tree trunk which were used by the local fishermen. As he came closer to the shore, people began to run and walk down to the water's edge to see and greet him. The men, almost jet-black in colour with well developed muscles from their constant swimming and fishing in the sea, were naked but for a small loin-cloth. Many of the women wore short whirling and waving skirts like Highland kilts made from numerous strips of calico, a coarse cotton cloth imported from India, and were naked above the waist. Others, the mixed descendants of Arab land-owners and the local people, being Moslems in purdah, were shrouded in black cotton robes which all but hid them from head to toe. Occasionally, as he pushed his way through the throng, elated and excited by his friendly welcome and by what he saw, Krapf would glimpse, almost hidden by the robes, a strongly chiselled face with broad and well-defined lips and the glint of a small gold ornament in the curve of the nostril. The elders of the village were clad in *kanzus*, long traditional white cotton robes which look like nightgowns, and wore small embroidered hats on their heads. They greeted him with dignity and led him to the shade of a mango tree near a neat palm-thatched house, where they offered him the customary courtesy of cups of thick black coffee.

Krapf had at last arrived in a land to which he was to devote the most important part of his life. He looked around him with rising excitement and thanked God for calling him to such a mission. Little did he foresee the diseases, disasters and tribulations which would beset him, nor the hopes and the great moments of fulfilment which would brighten his often lonely life. These things lay ahead; for the moment satisfaction welled within him and warmed his heart.

Krapf was able to acquire a scanty and rather confused background of the geography of the area during his brief stopover at Takaungu. He was also fortunate to meet several Galla tribesmen who had come there to sell cattle and ivory. Tall, handsome people with their long fuzzy hair liberally coated with rancid butter, they wore loin-cloths wrapped carelessly round their waists or draped over one shoulder, and only a few simple ornaments round the neck or an ivory bracelet on the upper arm. In contrast, their beautiful women were elaborately dressed with numerous bracelets and necklaces set off against a crop of unruly, uncut hair. Haughty and independent, the nomadic cattle-owning Galla were more warlike than the Giriama of Takaungu who formed part of the Bantu-speaking Mijikenda peoples, known to Krapf and other early travellers as the 'Wanyika' Krapf quickly realized that the religious beliefs and political system of the southern Gallas differed from that of their kinsmen in Ethiopia, who had had a long association with people of the Coptic faith. He considered that they were more ruthless than the Gallas he had previously encountered, since they had a reputation of murdering any stranger whom they met by the wayside.

'On 3rd January 1844, I left the hospitable village of Takaungu in a small boat, called a dhow by the Swahilis, which is the smallest sea-going vessel. In it you are but a few feet above the water; but have the advantage of being able to sail over rocks and sand-banks, and always close to the shore.' Crossing the white foam of breakers splashing high above the treacherous reef, he arrived at Mombasa Island late that evening and was immediately invited to be a guest of the governor, Ali-Bin-Nassir.

[The island] *is only very partially cultivated yet mangoes and coconuts, oranges and limes, and in parts, the cinnamon tree are indigenous, whilst wild swine, introduced by the Portuguese, abound . . . The capital of the island contains 8,000 to 10,000 inhabitants who are mostly Swahilis; but there also many Arabs and some thirty or forty Banyans* [Indians of the Hindu faith], *who have in their hands the chief trade of the place. There are houses of stone, but the majority are wooden huts . . . a tolerably large fortress commands the harbour and the town, and is garrisoned by 400 Baluchis who are in the pay of the Sultan of Zanzibar.*

Krapf learned that a barter trade was conducted regularly with the Wanyika and Wakamba peoples of the hinterland; moreover, traders' caravans sometimes ventured as far as 'the mountain land of Jagga', bringing back ivory and slaves.

The Wanyika tribes are nominally dependent upon Mombasa and are governed by four Swahili Sheikhs who live in Mombasa; but the connection between the town and these tribes is extremely loose and undefined; rendered more so, indeed, by the barbarous conduct of the people of Mombasa towards these heathen tribes, especially in time of famine, when they purchase the children of the Wanyika, or make off with them as slaves, in return for provisions furnished to the parents. Things will never progress on this coast so long as the Arabian rule is maintained in its present state, as it not only makes no improvements, but often destroys what good has descended from the olden time.

Soon after Krapf's arrival, the *liwali* or governor of Mombasa travelled to England as an envoy of the sultan, where he successfully negotiated a toning-down of a British edict to outlaw slaving in the Oman-Arab East African empire. He had great personal charm yet, back home, he was a cruel man whose will was law. He was said to receive no pay for his services to the sultan, but there were always ways and means of making his post a highly lucrative one. Bribery was rife and the injustices which were perpetrated on his direct authority had to be suffered in silence by the powerless majority.

He involved himself personally in the slave trade and turned a blind eye to the nefarious activities of his motley lot of Arab and Baluchi mercenaries. They pretended to have the greatest respect for their superiors but were arrogant, overbearing, pitiless and brutal to those whom they considered their inferiors.

After an uneventful cruise south along the coast with overnight stops at the bustling mainland ports of Tanga and Pangani, Krapf completed the rest of his voyage in a *mtepe*, a quaint local dhow capable of carrying up to twenty tons of cargo. It was the only vessel of its size that was wholly indigenous to East Africa. In shape, it resembled an overgrown gondola, but its wooden hull of roughly sawn timbers was pegged and sewn together with coconut rope before being caulked with a mixture of fat and lime. No nails or screws were used in its construction. Alas, the *mtepe* is now part of history, but it was popular in its day because superstitious sailors believed that a powerful magnet lurked at the bottom of the ocean and drew out iron nails from the timbers of other types of vessels until they fell apart and foundered in deep waters. Krapf sighted Zanzibar about midday on 7th January and the first thing that struck him was that it was low and flat – a hazy, monotonous silhouette seen just above the horizon. The sea of purest lapis lazuli blue gradually turned to sapphire, then to amethyst patched with verdigris as the dhow, a determined light breeze filling its shoddy, square matting sail, drew nearer to the dangerous coral reef that protects the island. Soon, the Arab town could be made out clearly, extending one and a half miles along the sea front with several small hills covered in luxuriant vegetation rising 200 to 300 feet behind. Commanding the safe anchorage of a spacious harbour stood a square, ugly fort, fronted by an undefended battery of obsolescent brass guns that were intended more for show than use. As the dhow came to a standstill, Krapf and his wife embarked on one of the many small canoes plying for hire, and landed dry-shod amid a great deal of shouting and gesticulating by a rabble of young touts.

The newcomers were welcomed in person by Major Atkins Hamerton, a genial Irishman, in his capacity as the first British Consul. Tall and broad-shouldered with angular features, dark penetrating eyes and a beard that was prematurely snow-white, he was an old Zanzibari hand and a close confidant of the elderly sultan, His Highness Seyyid Said. Temporary accommodation was provided for them at the residence of the American Consul, Mr C.P. Waters, and a day after their arrival Hamerton arranged an audience with the ruler, whose palace was reminiscent of a double-storeyed whitewashed barrack block about 140 feet long, roofed with dingy greenish-red tiles and pierced with a few windows high above the ground – an overall appearance which prompted Krapf to liken it to a German or Swiss factory.

The Sultan accompanied by one of his sons and several grandees came forth to meet us, displaying a condescension and courtesy which I had not before met with at the hands of any Oriental ruler. He conducted us into the audience-chamber which is pretty large and paved with marble slabs; American chairs lined the walls, and a stately chandelier hung in the middle of the room. The Sultan bade us be seated, and I described to him in Arabic, his native language, my Abyssinian adventures, and plans for converting the Gallas. He listened with attention and promised every assistance, at the same time pointing out the dangers to which I might be exposed.

Krapf remained in Zanzibar for three months, hearing, seeing and learning a great deal. He estimated that the population of the island was 100,000 strong but it would seem 60,000 was nearer the mark, of whom half were slaves. Every Sunday, he conducted church services for the small Christian community of which he and his wife became popular members. In all, the Europeans numbered twenty and several of them, engaged in commerce, found it disagreeable to live in the soporific heat of this oppressive climate. On a windless day, it was positive punishment to move about and required almost too much exertion to think. Some years later Richard Burton, the famous explorer, wrote that 'No European, unless thoroughly free from organic disease, should venture to remain longer than three or four years at Zanzibar . . . lurking maladies will be brought to a crisis and severe functional derangements are liable to return.'

It did not take Krapf long to realize that Zanzibar town was more picturesque and pleasing when viewed from afar. The water-front façade

concealed a dirty, neglected interior which had been built without recourse to plans for streets or drains. The visitor needed a strong constitution to brave the open drains of fetid alleyways which literally crawled with vermin. David Livingstone called the place 'Stinkibar' and had every reason to do so, for Zanzibar looked and smelt like nothing on earth. An extensive maze, known as 'Stone town', surrounded the central or fort area, which was assigned to government offices and commerce. The flat-topped, multi-storeyed houses in this squalid residential quarter were made of rough coral and mortar but the workmanship was poor; few walls were straight, arches were never similar in form or size and floors were invariably sloping. However, beautifully carved doorways bearing massive timber doors often barred entry to the inner courtyards of the buildings. Elaborate wood-carving continues to be a feature of Swahili culture in East Africa. The popular salt market was situated in an open square beneath the eastern bastion of the fort. Here, saline sand which just passed off as salt was offered for sale by hawk-faced Muscat Arabs alongside little heaps of fruit, sugar, dried manioc (cassava), shark meat and a selection of other incongruous articles. These were laid out neatly on the ground within easy reach of their lethargic vendors, who sat with outstretched legs varying the tedium of inaction by gossiping or plaiting *makuti*, a roofing thatch made from palm fronds. Although the smells, sights and sounds of this market defied all description, it was always thronged by representatives of the different races, being situated near the customs house – the foulest of open sheds with a long, low mat roof supported by two dozen stout mangrove poles – where millions of dollars changed hands annually. Nearby shops were little more than holes in the wall raised a foot above street level, which reeked of decay. Their shrewd 'Banyan' owners sat or squatted outside all day with placid, self-satisfied countenances, their money boxes by their sides, inviting passers-by to inspect their wares.

Cloves had been introduced from Mauritius in 1818 and by the middle of the last century extensive plantations had been established. They were neglected, like so many other aspects of life on the island, and failed to produce either the crop or the return expected of them. But at least they gave the spice island an aromatic fragrance in contrast to its exports of copra, which had a nauseous smell as it dried in the sun, and the still worse stench of cowrie shells, which were spread out on mats till the molluscs decayed away. Commonly known as 'Blackamoors' teeth', the shells were widely used as money in mainland Africa. Zanzibar was the centre not only of the trade and commerce which flowed along the east coast of Africa and into the interior of what is now Tanzania, but also of the diplomatic activity in an area where European powers, in particular the British, were active in their long struggle to stop the dreadful and degrading traffic in slaves. Although some progress had been made, the Arabs were by no means ready to give up a deep-rooted custom which they regarded neither as evil nor against the teachings of their holy book, the Koran. Indeed, they viewed domestic slavery as absolutely essential because of the peculiar status of their women. So here was the main market for slaves who were captured from as far away as the countries known today as Malawi and Mozambique. Yoked neck-to-neck in the prongs of rough branches, they were herded down to the coast in agonizing forced marches without adequate food and water. It is hardly surprising that for every four people taken prisoner in the interior, only one reached the slave market alive. David Livingstone, a most careful man in his statements, estimated the survival rate was as low as one in ten on the Zambezi run. Many survivors thought those who died *en route* were the lucky ones, when they were inspected like cattle and bought and sold under the most inhuman conditions before being despatched to the lands surrounding the Arabian Gulf, the Yemen and Muscat in overcrowded and insanitary dhows. It has been said that 100,000 slaves were required annually in world markets in the 1850s, of whom 15,000 were auctioned at Zanzibar. This enormity systematically depopulated many parts of Africa and transferred her youth and manhood to work in distant lands. It continued late into the nineteenth century because it was so inordinately profitable. A child bought for less than £3 on the island fetched between £14 and £20 in Persia, thus rewarding handsomely the *nahodhas* or dhow captains, even if only one ship in two or three managed to run the gauntlet of the overstretched British Navy.

Thomas Smee, the commander of the British research ship *Ternate* which called into Zanzibar in 1811, was one of the earliest European visitors to describe the slave market.

The show commences about four o'clock in the afternoon. The slaves, set off to the best advantage by having their skins cleaned and burnished with cocoa-nut oil, their faces painted with red and white stripes, which is here esteemed elegance, and the hands, noses, ears and feet ornamented with a profusion of bracelets of gold and silver and jewels, are ranged in line, commencing with the youngest and increasing to the rear according to their size and age. At the head of this file, which is composed of all sexes and ages from 6 to 60, walks the person who owns them; behind and at each side, two or three of his domestic slaves, armed with swords and spears, serve as a guard.

Thus ordered the procession begins, and passes through the market-place and the principal streets; the owner holding forth in a kind of song the good qualities of his slaves and the high prices that have been offered for them.

When any of them strikes a spectator's fancy the line immediately stops, and a process of examination ensues, which, for minuteness, is unequalled in any cattle market in Europe. The intending purchaser having ascertained there is no defect in the faculties of speech, hearing, etc, that there is no disease present, and that the slave does not snore in sleeping, which is counted a very great fault, next proceeds to examine the person; the mouth and teeth are first inspected and afterwards every part of the body in succession, not even excepting the breasts etc. of the girls, many of whom I have seen handled in the most indecent manner in the public market by their purchasers; indeed there is every reason to believe that the slave-dealers almost universally force the young girls to submit to their lust previous to their being disposed of.

The slave is then made to walk or run a little way, to show there is no defect about the feet; and after which, if the price be agreed to, they are stripped of their finery and delivered over to their future master.

Consul Waters became 'a zealous friend of the mission' during Krapf's extended stay at the American Consulate and urged him to remain in Zanzibar to work among the 'Banyans' from India. He also wanted him to establish schools for Swahili and Arab children and compile grammars and dictionaries of the mainland languages in preparation for a missionary invasion. It was a tempting thought, 'but I could not abandon my original design of founding a mission in the Galla land ... I felt their conversion would produce the greatest impression on the whole of Eastern Africa.' Krapf left his wife behind in Zanzibar and set sail in early March with a plan to make contact with the Galla people in the hinterland adjacent to Lamu Island. He took with him a 'letter of protection' from Sultan Seyyid Said whose overall influence, if not complete jurisdiction, was a potent force all down the East African coast from Lamu in the north to Lindi in the far south.

This comes from Seyyid Said Sultan.

Greetings all our subjects, friends and Governors. This letter is written on behalf of Dr Krapf, the German, a good man who wishes to convert the world to God. Behave well to him, and be everywhere serviceable to him.

A Christian missionary could not have dared hope for a better *laissez-passer* from a Moslem ruler!

Krapf spent a day on Pemba Island, then known to the Arabs as 'Al-Akhdar', the Green. It lies forty miles north of Zanzibar and forms one of the line of coralline islands hugging the eastern seaboard of Africa. As its graceful outline emerged from the deep channel that separates it from the mainland, the dhow captain corrected his course for the complicated entrance to Chake Chake, the principal fort, port and town of this verdant isle. The air was clean and lambent in the sun; the sapphire blue wavelets tumbled and danced in a light, caressing breeze, as the dhow weaved its way past mangrove swamps towards the white walls and tall tower of the fort which was strategically sited to command an uninterrupted view across the channel.

Climbing the steep slope from the small jetty, Krapf at once entered the town which consisted of one long narrow lane sided by square huts of mud and wattle with spacious verandahs where poultry, fruit and dried fish were displayed for sale. His first call was on the *wali* or governor, who received him most cordially and offered him sliced mango, pineapple, rice and ghee while they chatted over cups of black coffee about the politics and religion of Europe. As the meeting drew to a close, the governor casually remarked that the monsoon winds had already changed. Did the missionary realize, he enquired, that he would be stuck in Lamu for eight months? Krapf was taken aback. Nobody else had bothered to tell him, so he had left Zanzibar unprepared to be away for so long. He thanked the governor most profusely for his timely caution and left hurriedly to change his plans. Instead of returning directly to Zanzibar, he decided to revisit Tanga and Mombasa.

Tanga, with its extensive orchards and abundant farm produce, had attracted him on his outward journey to Zanzibar as a possible site for a mission station whence journeys into the interior could be undertaken. Only his fascination with the Galla had nipped that idea in the bud. Now, circumstances influenced him to take a closer look. He hired a dhow for a short run across the Pemba Channel to Tanga:

a very slow [voyage] *through the ignorance and unskilfulness of the captain and the laziness of the crew who were slaves and would not obey him. The more he rated them, the more they laughed at him. It is very sad to see how obstructively slavery influences all the activity of the natives, and so long as that evil remains in those countries, there is no hope of improving their social condition. There, slaves must do everything; they till the fields, conduct trade, sail vessels, and bring up the children of the house; while the free people eat, drink and are idle, run into mosques to pray, or enjoy themselves with their many wives. No wonder that a curse rests on all they undertake. The slaves perform whatever they have to do under compulsion, lazily, unwillingly and mechanically.*

Krapf spent less than two days in Tanga before sailing on to Mombasa, where he was hospitably received once again by Ali-Bin-Nassir. Since the restoration of Arab rule more than a century earlier, European visitors to the mainland were infrequent. The residents, overcome by friendly curiosity, flocked to catch a glimpse of Krapf as he strolled through the labyrinth of narrow streets or stopped to chat here and there with those who could converse in Arabic. By chance, he met up with a small party of Wanyika who had come from the nearby hills to buy piece goods, wire and beads. All at

once the thought struck him that the hinterland beyond Mombasa would be best suited to carry out his missionary experiment, especially as the Galla people – who were fast becoming an obsession with him – lived only a few days' march to the north-west. He was strengthened in his growing conviction by the friendliness of the residents and officials of the town towards Europeans, particularly the English, for whom he was mistaken. 'The longer I remained in Mombasa, the more evident it became to me that it seemed the will of God to make the Gallas acquainted with the Gospel through the Wanyika; and that, therefore, the first missionary station on this coast should be established among the Wanyika whom I could easily reach from Mombasa.' His mind made up, he hurried back to Zanzibar to collect his pregnant wife and bid farewell to his many friends and acquaintances.

Zanzibar seen from the roof of the English mission

CHAPTER 2

The Rabai mission

Kutoa ni moyo usambe ni utajiri
Charity is a matter of the heart and not of the pocket
Swahili proverb

KRAPF RETURNED TO MAINLAND Africa at the beginning of May 1844 full of excitement and enthusiasm. The run into the spacious land-locked harbour of Mombasa's old town was truly characteristic of East Africa, with its waving fanlike fronds of coconut palms ceaselessly agitated by the trade winds; the mango trees under whose cool, shady mantels of dark green leaves people forgathered and idled away the day; and the singular appearance of obese baobabs with their bare branches pointing skywards. As all this came into view, men hailed the dhow from afar with the question 'Habari gani? How are you? What news?' Fort Jesus with its massive walls of ochre, pink and buff-coloured coral guarded the entrance to the harbour and reminded him of the violent history of conspiracy, treachery and hostility from which the town had suffered for over 500 years. The ancient baobabs, many older than the fort itself, had been the silent witnesses. Not without justification had Mombasa been known as 'Mvita', the island of wars and battles.

Krapf's remarkable ear for languages and knowledge of Arabic now stood him in good stead. He quickly mastered the Ki-Swahili tongue and reduced it to form. It is truly astonishing that within four weeks of his arrival he had

acquired a fluency of the language sufficient for him to begin translating the first book of Moses into the vernacular with the aid of the chief *khadi* or judge of Mombasa.

I always considered this day as one of the most important of my life; but scarcely had I commenced this important work, and begun to congratulate myself on the progress of my missionary labours, when myself and family were subjected to a very severe trial. The rainy season at Mombasa had been one of unusual severity, and the native inhabitants had been afflicted by all sorts of sickness, especially fever and headache. On the 1st July I was attacked by the fever; on the 4th I was somewhat better again, but the next day, my wife was attacked by it severely, and the attack was all the more serious that she was every day expecting her confinement . . .

On 6th July, she gave birth to a healthy baby girl and three days later she died. 'In these trying moments I lay on my couch beside her death-bed, so prostrated by fever that only with the greatest effort could I rise up to convince myself that she was really dead. Lying in agony I could not rightly, at the moment, estimate the extent of this great loss.' By 15th July his baby daughter was dead too. 'I was obliged by the climate to conduct this second victim of the king of terrors to the grave of my beloved Rosine as soon as possible.' The spirit of a less resolute man than Krapf would have been broken.

With a wholly inadequate knowledge of tropical diseases, especially the cause of malaria, the climate had to be grappled with and conquered. No European could live long on the coast of East Africa without being attacked by *mkunguru* or fever of the country. This is how it was described some years later by Charles New, a fellow-missionary.

It is a severe intermittent. It comes upon you, first, in a strong rigour which makes the teeth chatter in your head and shakes your whole frame with extreme violence; this, in turn, yields to an intense burning that almost consumes you. This stage is attended with severe pains in the head, tending to, and often culminating in, delirium. Lastly a profuse perspiration breaks out and you almost melt away, saturating pillow and mattress through and through. This over, you feel the fever gone but you are reduced to the weakness of a child. A similar attack, however, may be expected on the following day or in two or three or four days' time according to the type it may assume . . .

Quinine, an extract from the bark of the South American cinchona tree, was found to be the only drug capable of controlling these frequent attacks, but the illness was often fatal for those who did not have the decoction readily to hand. Twenty grains of quinine every day for the first week after an attack, ten grains every other day for the second week and five grains every other day for the third week was the recommended dosage. By then, army officers across the ocean in India had worked out their own more palatable prophylactic of Indian tonic water, which has a base of quinine, liberally laced with London dry gin!

Once Krapf had regained his health, he doggedly pursued his studies of the Swahili and Wanyika languages with fresh zeal. Before the year ended, he had translated the entire New Testament into Ki-Swahili and compiled a basic grammar and dictionary of the *lingua franca*. He had also made a number of short safaris into the interior and along the coast, when his thoughts and dreams conjured up a vision of terrestrial mission stations linking the east coast to the west coast of Africa. 'If more attention were given to the formation of a chain ... the fall of slavery and of the slave trade with America and Arabia would be quickly and thoroughly effected. Till Christianity becomes the ruling faith in Africa, however great and noble may be the exertions of the Government of Great Britain ... the slave trade will continue to flourish. Christianity and civilization ever go hand in hand.'

On 19th August 1844, Krapf visited the village of Rabbai Ku, Old Rabai, for the first time with a view to assessing its suitability as a mission station. Boarding an ungainly planked dhow, *dau la mbao*, manned by two men and a small boy, he sailed up the northern sea-arm which bounds Mombasa Island, past Kisauni (the little place of forgetfulness) and Tudor Creek, into one of the two tidal riverlike channels which extend inland for about ten miles or so. As they advanced up the nearer mangrove-fringed channel towards Rabai, it became steadily narrower and the scenery brightened till a broken line of well-wooded hills formed the backdrop. Peasant huts could be made out on the forward slopes beside the rude beginnings of plantations. Below, as the tide receded, exposing a soft bed of dark mud, clusters of rock oysters could be seen clinging to rocky outcrops, and one-clawed fiddler crabs dived into their little holes or coursed sideways among the weird forest of exposed roots thrusting upwards into a perfect maze of pointed arches. An infinite variety of birds, small and large, drab and of the most vivid plumage, lived near the swamps.

After seven hours of alternate rowing, sailing, punting and pushing they reached the 'pier' – a tree projecting from the right bank over mangrove stumps to which the boat was secured. A gun was fired and within minutes the local villagers appeared.

[They] *lifted me out of the boat and bore me on their shoulders to the land with singing, dancing, brandishing of arrows, and every possible mode of rejoicing. Ascending from the shore across a grassy soil we arrived at a wood of lofty trees. The narrow footpath in the wood led to three entrances in a triple palisade which encircled the village ... We saw only two men who beat great drums in honour of the visit, and I was sorry not to have seen the chief and the people of the village ... The Wanyika had made a favourable impression on me for they were both quick and well-behaved, but wore extremely little in the way of clothes, even the women not being sufficiently clad.*

The elders often went naked and unadorned but were never without snuff, which they carried in an indispensable cow-horn slung over one shoulder. The young men occasionally draped a tanned skin or a dirty cloth over themselves and stuck bird feathers in their ochred hair. They hung metal chains, beads and talismen sewn in leather pouches around their necks while small earrings of brass or iron wire dangled from their elongated earlobes. Strips of hairy cowhide were bound like garters below each knee and the tiny bells they strapped to their ankles made a tinkling sound as they walked. Their women wrapped a tanned skin round their loins, which was held in place by numerous strands of coloured beads. They dressed decoratively in thick brass or heavy beaded necklaces, and bracelets and anklets embellished with red and white beads. Polished coils of brass wire were wound tightly round their forearms and over their calves to form broad bands of armour for warding off thorns. The Wanyika dwelling house can be seen in Giriama and Duruma country to this day and is beautifully constructed. It is an oblong-shaped hut some eight feet high at the ridge pole and from twelve to eighteen feet long and eight to ten feet wide. It is thatched from top to bottom with hay and looks exactly like a small haystack. There are no windows, nor any means of ventilation except an entrance in the centre of one side, yet it is surprisingly cool in the heat of the day. However, if goats and chickens are accommodated with the family and a small wood fire is kept alight in the hearth all day, the atmosphere inside can be suffocating.

Although Krapf was encouraged by what he saw, he was not entirely convinced that the village suited his missionary needs, so two weeks later he took another look at the Rabai Hills.

Towards noon [we] *reached the outermost gate of the village of Ribe, where we were to await the chiefs and their retinue. They arrived, welcomed me, and conducted us through three entrances in the palisades into the village, amid cries of rejoicing, dancing and brandishing of swords and bows. In the village the noise was still greater as young and old, men and women, streamed forth to pay the European the same honours which are paid to a great man from Mombasa ... When I declared to the chiefs that I was not a soldier, nor a merchant who had come to trade, but a Christian teacher who wished to instruct the Wanyika and the Galla in the true knowledge of God, they looked at me with something of a stupefied expression.*

One can certainly understand their amazement!

Krapf continued his journey east through fine stands of rice and maize until he arrived at the large village of Kambe where the chief met him in 'his holiday clothes and ostrich feathers on his head'. His reception was even noisier than at Ribe but he was a little saddened by the licentious behaviour of the villagers – palm toddy being their favourite beverage and the groves of lofty coconut palms surrounding their village serving, so to speak, as their immediate and inexhaustible wine cellar. Krapf had no compunction in ruling out the two villages as mission sites because he felt their inaccessibility would inevitably expose missionaries to unnecessary danger. What he wanted was a more direct transport and communication link with Mombasa; this narrowed his options to a location within easy reach of the navigable channel to the sea. On his way back to Mombasa, he passed through forests teeming with beautiful birds and butterflies 'but in the Wanyika territories there are no longer any elephants to be found ... If it be true that yearly about 6,000 elephants' tusks are brought to the Swahili coast, it can easily be understood how quickly these animals diminish and why they recede even further into the interior of Africa.'

His first contact with the Wakamba tribe came in early 1845 when he visited the small village of Endile, consisting of a dozen or so circular huts built of short stakes with grass roofs supported by stout centre poles. The doorways were so low and narrow that a visitor had to bend double to enter. The elders were sitting under a tree, completely naked, and took not the slightest notice of the strange European, which caused him to wonder. High in the branches above their heads he noticed a *mzinga*, a beehive, made from a hollowed log of wood some four feet long and twelve inches in diameter with a

tiny hole at one end, whence bees could be seen flying to and fro collecting nectar from the nearby acacia woods, 'The chief went at last into his hut and fetched a bowl of milk, mixed with blood as I afterwards found; for they believe that thus taken, blood helps to nourish their natural strength . . . [The Wakamba] are very fond of ornaments, especially beads and copper wire. Their legs, arms, necks and hair were covered with white and blue beads which in combination with their nudity gave them a striking and singular appearance.'

The women, surrounded by naked children, busied themselves grinding corn between two stones, tipping the coarse flour into small baskets beautifully woven from the fibres of a wide selection of local plants. Krapf gained the impression that the Wakamba were a finer and more powerful people than the Wanyika. '[They] go in caravans of from 200 to 300 persons into the interior to fetch ivory, and form in a general way the commercial medium between the coast and the interior, into which they journey a distance of from 200 to 250 leagues [275 to 350 miles]. I therefore regarded this people as an important element in relation to future designs in Eastern Africa.'

The ensuing twelve months were a period of varied experience and suffering for Krapf, who was constantly on the move. He revisited Takaungu and stayed with Major Hamerton in Zanzibar; he made an excursion to Likoni and several other villages to the south of Mombasa; he went north and 'explored among other places the ruined and deserted town of Malindi which might again be a populous and flourishing port'; he visited another Mkamba village where his shoes, which were thought to be iron, his hair, which was compared to that of a baboon, and his spectacles were viewed with astonishment and ridicule; he returned to Rabbai Ku and visited Rabbai Mpia, a village of some twenty to twenty-five huts built in a coconut grove on a hill which commanded a magnificent view of Mombasa and the bright blue waters of the Indian Ocean beyond.

At first our way lay through a wood, upwards, by means of the bed of a mountain stream, then along a well-trodden footpath, to the right and left of which the ground was covered by thorn-bushes and tall grass; till having ascended for several hundred yards, we came to the hill itself on which the village of New Rabbai is built, and where the more abrupt ascent really began; for the village, with the cocoa-nut [sic] wood in which it stands, seemed to lie straight up above our heads, so steep was the rock which we had to mount . . . Before the rain came on we had found shelter in a hut, and it was a favourable circumstance that it rained just

when the white man entered the village for the first time. The Wanyika imagined that it was my foot which brought the welcome rain . . . I felt at once the impression that this would be just the place for a missionary station . . . The elders were very friendly and, what pleased me very much, did not beg. I explained to them that the object of my visit was to teach them the words of the book (the Bible) which I held in my hand . . . On the whole, I could not avoid seeing that the people were somewhat shy of me for fear that I should convert them to Mohammedism; for they could not draw any distinction between Christianity and Islamism. Mothers removed their children as soon as they saw me in the streets of the village, a practice not uncommon among the Wanyika, arising out of the apprehension that strangers merely come to steal the children to sell them into slavery.

At times children were simply abducted but on other occasions they were plied with presents of sweetmeats by heartless *tende-halua* men, pedlars of dates and Turkish delight who, like the Pied Piper of Hamelin, enticed gullible youngsters on board their vessels and promptly set sail for Arabia.

At long last Krapf had identified the perfect place to establish his little mission, but he was unwilling to undertake the daunting task single-handed. It was common for missionaries to work in pairs and soon after his wife died he had urged the Church Missionary Society to send out a volunteer to assist him. Though his request had quickly been approved, unavoidable delays had ensued. It was not until 10th June 1846 that he was overjoyed to learn 'my dear, and long-expected, fellow-labourer, Rebmann' had arrived at Mombasa.

Johann Rebmann was ten years younger than Krapf and had been trained at Basel and later ordained at the CMS college in Islington near London, though he was a fellow-Württemberger. He immediately fell under the spell of the older man's compelling personality and restless zeal to spread the Gospel of Christ throughout these mysterious lands. He worked loyally and incessantly with Krapf until he established himself as a full and trusted partner in the great endeavour they had both undertaken. Amid all the trials of disease, the attacks of malaria and the disagreeable climate, Rebmann learned that nature was far less hospitable than the natives. Within days of his arrival he was struck down by fever, barely recovering in time to accompany his colleague on their crucial journey to seek approval from the Wanyika chiefs for the Rabai station. The missionaries sat on the ground surrounded by twelve wise old men while Krapf outlined his aims. He stressed the suitability of their village for the mission and the kindness he had received there.

Immediately and without any stipulation, even without asking after African fashion for a present, they responded 'Yes!' and truly with one heart and mouth. They gave us the strongest assurances of friendship; the whole country should be open to us; we might journey whither-so-ever we pleased; they would defend us to the uttermost; we should be the kings of the land etc. When we spoke about dwelling places, they replied 'The birds have nests and the Wazungu [Europeans] too, must have houses.

'It was wonderful,' Rebmann wrote later to the committee of the Church Missionary Society, 'to see how Krapf's labours have not been in vain; for this willingness, though little less than a direct manifestation of God in the wilderness, must also, in some measure, be considered as the fruits of his exertions.'

The missionaries were elated by the unequivocal response of the Wanyika elders and hastened back to Mombasa where, in less than no time, another severe and debilitating attack of fever laid them both low. A whole month elapsed before the invalids were back on their feet again, and their departure for Rabai on 25th August should have been postponed but 'whether the result be life or death, I said to myself, the mission must be begun; and with this resolve, and an inward prayer for succour, I tottered along by the side of Rebmann, who was likewise very weak and could scarcely walk. We therefore determined to ride by turns on our single ass, but after some time I was quite unable to go on foot and obliged to monopolize the beast. With much pain I ascended the steep hill, which even without a rider the ass could scarcely have mounted, and Rebmann, also, could only clamber by the most painful exertion.' Never before had a mission been founded in such a state of weakness.

Their health quickly improved at their new home which lay 1,000 feet above sea-level, away from the sultry heat and the worst of the mosquitoes. The chiefs had promised to build them a house on repayment terms, but the workers were diffident. The missionaries ended up doing most of the work with their own hands.

We had ourselves first to dig a foundation, breaking up the ground for nearly two feet, that we might fix the poles more firmly. As in places there were blocks of stone under the slight soil, these had first to be dug out or broken into pieces, and in the heat of the sun, in our weak state of health, this was no slight toil. The house was twenty-four feet long and eighteen feet in width and height; the walls were plastered with mud within and without, the roof being covered with makuti [the plaited fronds of coconut trees] . . . If anyone had seen us then and there in dirty and tattered clothes, bleeding from wounds caused by the thorns and stones, flinging mud on the walls in the native fashion and plastering it with the palm of our hands, he would scarcely have looked upon us as clergymen . . . After the erection of the house we had to attend to many other little building matters – kitchen, stable, store-house, oven and especially a hut for public worship, were all to be provided. All this went on slowly for the elders were very dilatory in bringing the materials, although well paid.

We can imagine with what relief these two devoted men settled into their new house, a cool protection from the hot tropical sun and a haven from the fierce monsoon squalls of the rainy season. It was their home for over four years until Rebmann decided the time had come to build a storeyed house in the Arab style out of more permanent materials. Time and the restless destructive force of the African climate have, alas, removed all trace of the original fountain-head for the spread of Christianity in East Africa. The monument of Krapf's work which can be seen today is a fine church built in 1887 and the neat stone buildings of the mission school which still dominate the small village of Rabai.

Some twelve to fifteen Wanyika assembled in their unpretentious little church on the first Sunday after it had been completed to hear Krapf explain its purpose. 'When I had finished my address a Mnyika, Abbe Kondi by name, from Jembeni asked what we would give the Wanyika to eat if they were to come here every *sikuku* [holiday or Sunday]. If the Wanyika received rice and a cow, they would always come; but if not, they would stay away for

no Mnyika went to a *maneno* [a discussion] without eating and drinking. This was rather a humbling experience for the day of our little church's consecration.' Another elder stood up to echo the theme of Krapf's address that God truly loved all men, for he gave the Wanyika rain, liquor and clothes! On a previous occasion the chief of Kambe had openly declared his disbelief in God since he was invisible. 'The Mohammedans,' he added, 'were fools to pray and fast so much.' These were just the first of many such incidents which made the missionaries realize the magnitude of their task. Even the introduction of the Sabbath day had its difficulties.

Insistent begging was another problem which taxed the missionaries' patience. The Wanyika abhorred stealing but begging was considered highly proper. They coveted everything they saw and never lost anything for want of asking for it. Undaunted by the most positive refusals, they pressed their suit. 'It often came about that our house was like a shop where there were customers in abundance, except in our case they were customers who wished to have everything for nothing.' In an air of transparent cunning, a man who had fixed his mind on getting a length of cloth would appear before Krapf in the most miserable rags. He would assure Krapf that he was the greatest man on earth. He was Krapf's servant, his slave, he would do anything for him, if only he would help him. The man would be a perfect master of flattery and his obsequiousness knew no bounds. He gained his objective and snapped his fingers at his dupe! Krapf's philosophy was to bear this persecution patiently and give as much as he could afford, letting prudence be his guide.

Once all the mission buildings had been constructed, Krapf went out into the villages to spread the word of God to unresponsive audiences, while Rebmann stayed behind to learn the Swahili and Wanyika languages before starting up a small school for boys. The devout Christians were disappointed at the way the Wanyika clung to their old superstitions. The *muansa*, an instrument made from a hollowed-out tree-trunk, was used in all important ceremonies and was treated reverently. Women and children were not

allowed to look at it for fear of dying, yet no one was permitted to be absent from a gathering, at the risk of being fined a goat or a sheep. When rubbed, the *muansa* made a fearful sound like a wounded animal roaring in the bush. As an evening's festivities wore on, a cacophony of shrieking, dancing, singing and shouting filled the night air. 'We were often awakened from our sleep when the blind and mad servants of the *muansa* passed the house,' Krapf lamented. 'As may be expected they fortified themselves from time to time with large draughts of palm wine which re-kindled their flagging powers and rendered them more uproarious.'

These traditional ceremonies formed a strong bulwark against Christianity but Krapf was not easily discouraged. In next to no time another twelve months had slipped by and, on 25th August 1847, he wrote in his diary:

It is a year today since we arrived here. How much grace and mercy has the Lord shown to His servants during this year! How mightily has He preserved us within and without! By His aid we have had access to this people; have built a habitation to dwell in, and above all, have raised a humble fane [church], though but a poor hut, for worship; have laid out a small garden, and opened a school. We have made tolerable proficiency in the language, prepared books for the people, preached the Gospel to the Wanyika, Wakamba and Swahili, and become acquainted with the manners and customs, the prejudices, and, in short, with the good and evil qualities, as well as the geographical relations of these tribes, by which means our allotted task in Eastern Africa has become clearer to us, and in our hearts, too, we have had many blessed experiences. Viewing all these things, we are full of thankfulness, and take courage for the future!

As the year drew to a close, the school children dispersed to their villages fancying that they should be paid to attend lessons and Krapf, for the first time, began to despair of converting the Wanyika. His spirits were buoyed up, however, by the belief that other inland tribes might be less intractable.

CHAPTER 3

The snows of Kilimanjaro

Kipya kinyemi, ingawa kidonda
A new thing is a source of joy even if it be a sore

Swahili proverb

KRAPF HAD ALWAYS VIEWED the establishment of the Rabai mission as a stepping-stone to the interior. That the next step would be dangerous was obvious enough. The Arab and Swahili traders in Mombasa were a rich fund of information and scandal, and had regaled the missionaries with all manner of disquieting tales about the obstacles that would be encountered from wild animals and marauding bands of robbers beyond the hinterland. These stories were grossly exaggerated, of course, but Krapf knew there had to be a semblance of truth in them, for it was common knowledge that Monsieur Maizan, a French naval ensign, had been brutally murdered only two years earlier less than 100 miles from the coast in what is now Tanzania. There is no question that the missionaries acted courageously in planning to visit Kasigau, commonly known to the Wanyika as Kadiaro, at the invitation of the residents there, who occasionally called at Rabai on their way to sell ivory in Mombasa.

Kasigau had been singled out as a solitary mountain mass which can be seen on a clear day from the high ground above Rabai, standing out in dark, frowning majesty from the undulating plains that surround it. They had been told that it formed the southern apex of a large triangle in which the amiable Taita people lived, and could be reached in four to five days. Rebmann was chosen to undertake this potentially perilous, but relatively unambitious, journey along with two Swahili guides and six Wanyika porters. The Arab merchants had orchestrated stiff opposition to the trip behind the scenes in the belief that it would threaten their lucrative sources of ivory. It would also expose them as the monstrous liars they were, for spreading rumours that all white men were cannibals and should be assiduously avoided. Rebmann was not altogether surprised when two pliant chiefs from Rabbai Ku called at the mission the evening before his departure to declare that the house of every Mnyika who went to Kasigau would be burnt to the ground. Without porters to shoulder his loads, Rebmann had to resign himself to staying put for a while. Instead of striding out into unknown lands, he accompanied Krapf the following morning on a quick trip to Mombasa to iron out the *shauri* or problem. Ali-Bin-Nassir was himself apprehensive of the plan but realized that it would be fruitless to dissuade such determined men; in any case, he was under orders from the sultan to give them every possible assistance. He promised, therefore, to provide an escort of soldiers as far as Rabai with an ultimatum to the capricious chiefs. His command was seldom disobeyed since he had the ruthless Baluchis at his beck and call.

Rebmann, after the bitter disappointment of his false start, prayed for God's blessings before setting out from Rabai on 14th October 1847 just as the moon appeared over the distant horizon. Within a day he had left the Wanyika grazing grounds behind him to face the dense, inhospitable *nyika* or wilderness which, up till then, had kept strangers firmly out of the region. His party forced a passage for three weary days through featureless, barren

country on narrow, overhung footpaths where hostile tribesmen were reputed to lie in wait for unsuspecting travellers. Despite strong protests, the missionary refused to allow his Wanyika to take with them two magic staves as protection against these dangers. 'They told me what my Bible was to me, the staves would be to them ... but I was determined that whilst the men served me they should use none of these magic *uganga* [charms].' Rebmann was lucky. They saw nothing of the Galla or Maasai, only large herds of wild animals disporting themselves in this appalling no-man's-land. He was received warmly by the Wataita who viewed the first European they had ever seen in their midst with equanimity. After learning a little of their customs and struggling 5,383 feet up the steep-sided rocky hill to acquaint himself with the geography of the area, the missionary turned for home. He suffered from lack of water, the fierceness of the midday sun and ill-fitting shoes which made him long to walk back, like his porters, in bare feet. Otherwise, his had been an easy and uneventful safari of exactly ten days, which would not have been noteworthy but for the fact that it was the first recorded journey of a

European into the interior of the land that was to become Kenya.

The following year Rebmann's second excursion inland was a more ambitious undertaking lasting six weeks. Ali-Bin-Nassir was unwilling at first to give Krapf permission for the journey, on the grounds that it would expose the missionary to too many dangers. In the end he relented but 'I forbid Rebmann to climb Mount Kilimanjaro because it is full of evil spirits,' he warned Krapf. 'People who have tried to climb it in the past have been killed by the spirits, their feet and hands have stiffened, their powder has hung fire and all kinds of disasters have befallen them.' Krapf was sceptical of Arab superstitions; he had already been told of a 'silver matter' on top of the mountain but he had no idea, of course, that it was snow. So he merely warned Rebmann to avoid shifting sands if he came across any on the way.

About noon on 27th April 1848, Rebmann and his party of nine started out for the unknown in the company of Krapf, who turned back a short distance down the path having committed his fellow-missionary to the protection of the Almighty. They retraced their steps to Kasigau, then struck north-west towards 'Jagga' (Chagga country, occupying the southern slopes of Kilimanjaro):

through the most luxuriant grass and undergrowth, alternating with noble trees, first ascending and then descending the mountain at the foot of which we had encamped ... How splendid the whole landscape, with its rich variety of mountain, hill and dale, covered by the most luxurious vegetation. I could have fancied myself on the Jura Mountains near Basel ... so beautiful was the country, so delightful was the climate. Our way was across the bed of a mountain stream, over hill and dale, through plantations of Indian corn and beans, past small herds of cattle belonging to the Taita, then along fields of sugar-cane and banana, till we descended into the valley, with its rich pasture-lands. What a pity that this luxuriant growth of grass year after year must perish unused! An immeasurable tract of the richest land stands here open to the church of Christ.

Rebmann was most fortunate to have undertaken this journey after a month of heavy rain when the countryside was looking its best. The uninhabited district ahead of them was infested with big game and they had to stop frequently to avert danger. On one occasion, they bivouacked under a large acacia tree shortly after sunset. 'Here my guide looked at me with astonishment saying, "You are here with nothing but an umbrella, and formerly we needed five hundred muskets, so dangerous was the spot where we are; for this was one of the chief encampments of the plundering Wakwafi." I replied, "It is the work of God; He has opened a way for His Gospel." ' The events of two days later were to emblazon Rebmann's name on the great record of African exploration and discovery. Possibly overcome by his emotions, his account imparts a lack of excitement to what must have been, and still is, a scene of outstanding beauty. Here is his diary entry for 11th May 1848, as published in the very first edition of the *Church Missionary Intelligencer* a year later:

We continued our journey at daybreak. When we had proceeded for about half an hour, we saw to our right two men, who, terrified on seeing that we exceeded them far in number, began to flee from us as fast as they could. Some of the Taitas, who supposed the fugitives to be their countrymen, went some distance after them to make them stop, but without success. I sighed within me, 'Oh God, preserve us!'

To the north-east we saw a single mountain as high as the Boora [Bura, south of the Taita Hills], *at a distance of about two days' journey, called Ongolia* [Ngulia in the Tsavo West National Park, now the site of a lodge], *which already forms part of Ukamba, bordering on the Galla and the Taita country.*

The mountains of Jagga gradually rose more distinctly to our sight. At about ten o'clock (I had no watch with me) I observed something remarkably white on the top of a high mountain, and first supposed that it was a very white cloud, in which supposition my guide also confirmed me; but having gone a few paces more I could no more rest satisfied with that explanation; and while I was asking my guide a second time whether that white thing was indeed cloud, and scarcely listening to his answer that yonder was [not] *a cloud, but what that white was he did not know, but supposed it was 'coldness', the most delightful recognition took place in my mind of an old well-known European guest called 'snow'. All the strange stories we had so often heard about the gold and silver mountain Kilimanjaro in Jagga, supposed to be inaccessible on account of evil spirits, which had killed a great many of those who had attempted to ascend it, were now at once rendered intelligible to me, as of course the extreme cold, to which the poor natives are perfect strangers, would soon chill and kill the half-naked visitors.*

As if to confirm his judgment, Bwana Kheri, his guide, told him that many years ago the Paramount Chief of the Chagga had sent a large expedition to explore the mountain, hoping that the white dome might prove to be silver or something else equally valuable; only one of the party survived and he, poor man, returned with his feet and hands bent inwards. He had undoubtedly suffered from severe frost-bite without knowing the cause of his wounds.

So Rebmann had the honour of being the first white man ever to set eyes on the snows of Kilimanjaro. Inevitably, there were many who treated his account with incredulity and suspicion. Foremost of the critics was the eminent English geographer W. Desborough Cooley, an expert on Central South Africa, who dismissed Rebmann's discovery as a fireside tale from someone gifted with a strong imagination. 'With respect to those eternal snows on the discovery of which Messrs Krapf and Rebmann have set their hearts,' Cooley wrote, 'they have so little of shape or substance, and appear so severed from realities, that they take quite a spectral character. No one has yet witnessed their eternity: dogmatic assertion proves nothing; of reasonable evidence of perpetual snow there is not a tittle offered.' The French, however, were more prepared to believe the story and, in 1850, the Paris Geographical Society awarded Rebmann and Krapf medals for their discoveries. Likewise, at Berlin, King Friedrich Wilhelm invested Krapf with a gold medal. Only the Royal Geographical Society, so it seems, remained aloof. The controversy was frustrating for the missionaries, but it did make East Africa the centre of interest for a while, thereby setting the seal on several important geographical expeditions into the region.

Rebmann moved on to Kilema before turning his back on the mountain.

I gazed on the lovely country which seemed to be bursting with plenteousness, and presented in a comparatively small extent the most striking contrasts. In our immediate vicinity was the beautiful River Gona; and on its banks, as well as on the foot of the mountains around, the richest vegetation of a perfect dark green of perpetual summer; and when I raised my eyes I beheld, apparently only a few leagues distant, but in reality from one to two days' journey, Kilimanjaro, covered with perpetual snow and ice.

Chief Masaki, a lively young man, ruled over a small Chagga community in the foothills. He and his warriors wore tanned hides with fringed edges which hung loosely about them. They were attracted to everything Rebmann had on, even his trouser buttons which they inspected minutely. After a sheep was slaughtered as a token of friendship, food was brought in return for his gifts of calico, beads, a knife, fork, scissors, needles and thread plus a few other knick-knacks. Later, Rebmann noticed the chief with the fork stuck in his hair as an ornament. 'I explained to him the use of it; he laughed but did not seem to understand.' Rebmann had problems with his feet again; they were so dreadfully blistered that it took a full week's convalescence before he was fit enough to bid his host farewell and hobble painfully into the unrelenting African bush. The snows of Kilimanjaro lay untrodden for another decade until Charles New, the English missionary, reached the snowline in 1857. It was forty-one more years before the German scientist, Dr Hans Meyer, conquered the summit of Africa's highest mountain, whose true height of 19,321 feet was not finally fixed until 1921.

Rebmann visited the Kilimanjaro region for a second time in November 1848 with a party of fifteen, some armed with muskets and others with bows and arrows. The debate raging over the 'discovery' of a snowcapped mountain on the equator prompted him to give the world a more detailed account of its appearance, although – possibly being a little too close for accurate assessment – he misjudged its massive dimensions and underestimated its height by 5,000 feet.

A Chagga house

There are two principal summits placed upon a base some ten leagues [14 miles] *long and as many broad, so that the space between them forms, as it were, a saddle, which extends three or four leagues* [4 to 5 miles] *from east to west. The eastern summit is lower and pointed, whilst the western and higher one presents a fine crown which, even in the hot season, when its western and lowlier neighbour can no longer support its snowy roof, remains covered by a mass of snow.*

It took the professional eye of Joseph Thomson thirty-five years later to recognize Kilimanjaro's volcanic origins. Rebmann was misled into thinking the main peak, 'kibo', meant 'snow' in the Chagga language; in fact the word 'kibo' is unknown to the Chagga. In the Taveta tongue, however, it is used as a word of exclamation similar to 'Good heavens!' The word 'njaro' literally means something shining white and now has the added meaning of snow. Hence Kilima-Njaro was aptly named by the Chagga 'white' or 'snow mountain'.

Masaki was delighted to play host to Rebmann again but his shameless greed was irksome. He probably would have prevented his visitor moving on to another of the nine or ten petty states which were ruled over by the *mangi* or chiefs of the Chagga, had not soldiers of the Paramount Chief Mamkinga been staying with him at the time. Mamkinga held sway over several thousand of his subjects in the little 'kingdom' of Majame which was situated close to modern Moshi. Escorted by Kilewo, Mamkinga's brother, the missionary crossed over the high foothills of Kilimanjaro before descending to the fertile land below. The majestic snow-clad mountain was so near that he could see it clearly in the moonlight. He found the people living in fortified villages for fear of an attack by the warlike Wakwafi of Arusha who were said to be close relatives of the Maasai. He was kept waiting five days for Muigno Wessiri, a cunning Mswahili who was Mamkinga's vizier, medicine man and rainmaker, to make arrangements for the chief to see him. It was customary for a goat to be killed before audience was granted to a stranger, and no sooner had this been done on the threshold of his hut than he was called outside and spattered with its blood using a fly whisk made from the tail of a cow. 'It was as well my leave had not been asked,' Rebmann commented ruefully, 'for I should have absolutely refused it.' The chief was in one of his more benign moods and concealed his disappointment that the missionary was not a sorcerer by assuring him frequently of his great affection towards him. '[He] would have kept me much longer with him, had I not entreated him to allow me to return. Indeed, he would have been well pleased if I had at once settled down at Majame, in which event he would have given me his own son for a pupil.'

Rebmann got back to Rabai on 16th February 1849 where his favourable report encouraged the missionaries to take advantage of Mamkinga's friendship and organize a return visit with the minimum of delay. An idea was even mooted to extend their travels beyond Kilimanjaro in an ambitious attempt to penetrate Unyamwezi country – reputedly the land of the legendary *Lunae Montes* – to form another link in the chain of fanciful mission stations spreading the word of God across the breadth of Africa. By 6th April Rebmann had purchased a wide selection of trade goods and assembled a modest caravan of thirty porters in readiness for his hazardous journey. In his rush to leave, however, he unwisely set out just as the long rains broke. It rained all day and sometimes all night. No tents had been carried so his only protection against the elements was his umbrella. Mire, swollen rivers and wild animals hindered his progress and by the time he reached Majame again on 16th May he was cold, wet and exhausted. In making his plans known to the insidious Muigno Wessiri, Rebmann fell into a trap. In no time the chief became aware that most of the tantalizing trade goods the missionary had brought with him were destined for the chiefs of Unyamwezi and not for himself. He took instant umbrage at the meanness of a visitor whom he had made so welcome only two months before and steadfastly ignored him for nine days. When he did deign to see him, it was obvious his mood had changed. Gone were his flattering expressions of affection and friendship; in their place he made a series of insincere promises, each followed by extortionate demands for presents. Anxious as always to avoid trouble, Rebmann bore this churlish behaviour without complaint until:

I saw the stock of goods which I had intended for Unyamwezi gradually melting away, and when by order of the king I was obliged to part with piece after piece of the calico which I had reserved for my further journey, I could not suppress my tears . . . Other persecutions were added to robbery, and my health as well as my spirits gave way under the influence of the cold and wet weather, and the smoke with which my miserable hut was filled. I was attacked both by fever and dysentery; so now I wished, of course, to return to the coast as soon as possible, a wish which my people shared with me; for they as well as myself were plundered and threatened.

Despite these humiliations, *desturi*, the custom of the day, did not permit Rebmann to walk out on the chief without first taking his formal leave. He cut a forlorn little figure as he waited for Mamkinga, the very personification of avarice, to grant him audience. Only when he had been robbed of all his valuables did the chief's cronies have no further use for him and let him go.

Their greed was displayed even at the moment of our leave-taking, which was accompanied by the usual ceremony of expectorating upon the departing stranger, and repeating the words 'Go in peace'. For this dirty expectoration with which, first the Wanyika, then the Swahili, and last of all myself, were favoured, a special payment was exacted from each. My Wanyika had nothing but a handful of beads which I had given them for the purchase of their daily food; but one of the Swahili wore a rather better garment, as is the custom of Mohammedans, and this was demanded of him in the rudest manner, and so he was obliged to take it off, and pay with it the price of the saliva of peace.

After this harrowing treatment, Rebmann's porters were only too thankful to take to the bush rather than run the risk of a chance encounter with the rapacious Masaki. However, they accidentally strayed into virgin forest which reduced their speed to a snail's pace. Tall trees had to be felled to cross swollen rivers and paths had to be hacked out of the dense undergrowth. They took seven days to re-emerge, despondent and half-starved, on to the open plains beyond. Valuable days had been lost, which gave rise to severe food shortages and their dwindling stocks of dried beans would not have lasted the journey home had they not foraged in the countryside for wild honey and fledgelings. They were assisted in finding honey by the persistent, harsh 'ke, ke, ke, ke, ke' call of the Greater Honeyguide, *Indicator indicator*, which is a member of a family of small parasitic birds of sombre brown, olive, grey and white plumage. They have developed a remarkable habit of guiding humans and ratels – honey badgers – to the nests of wild bees. Once the honeycomb has been chopped out, they delight in feeding on the beeswax and larvae that are left behind. It is still generally believed that misfortune will follow anyone who does not leave the Honeyguide its share of the nest.

Rebmann's strength began to fail him and by the time he regained Rabai on 26th June, he was a sick and disillusioned man. Though he lived at the coast for another twenty-six years, he never ventured into the interior of East Africa again.

CHAPTER 4

Ukambani

Kivuli cha fimbo hakimfichi mtu jua
The shadow of a walking stick cannot protect one from the sun

Swahili proverb

T WO MORE MISSIONARIES had arrived to reinforce the Rabai station in Rebmann's absence. Intelligent, noble-minded men fresh out from Europe, they came to survive under the faith of God or die in the great endeavour. Both were seized within days of landing at Mombasa with virulent fever, which in the case of Johann Wagner proved fatal. Reverend J.J. Erhardt was prostrated for weeks hovering between life and death, as the attacks returned again and again with increased severity. In the end, he was lucky to pull through and take his rightful place as an important member of the little Christian community. It was a sad and worrying time for Krapf, who delayed plans for further missionary exploration until late 1849. He had already completed a six-week expedition to the Usambara Mountains in what is now north-east Tanzania between Rebmann's first and second journeys to Kilimanjaro. Yet he yearned for a more adventurous trip through Ukambani with the ultimate aim of setting foot in Galla country and finding a route to 'the source of the Nile and to those surviving Christian remnants at the equator, of whom I had heard at Shoa'. These ambitious objectives could not be attained at once, but he vowed to make a start by surveying the unknown regions north-east of Mount Kilimanjaro as far as the Tana River.

He had learned that the Tana formed the northern and eastern boundaries of Ukambani from Chief Kivoi, a prominent senior chief, who had visited Mombasa a year earlier on one of his regular pilgrimages to sell ivory. Krapf had nurtured the thought for a long time that the key to a large inland region of Eastern Africa was the Wakamba, so he had gone out of his way to befriend the chief whose jurisdiction covered the important central area of Kitui. In return, Kivoi had extended an open invitation to the missionaries to stay with him. This was precisely what Krapf now had in mind having studiously mastered the vernacular in readiness for a journey which he expected to be the most important and dangerous to date.

He set out on 1st November 1849 with a party of eleven Swahili and Wanyika porters, leaving Rebmann and Erhardt behind to run the mission station. His footpath followed almost exactly the same route as the main Nairobi to Mombasa highway and railway line of today, over which the destiny of much of Kenya has ebbed and flowed. As he moved away from the tropical coast belt, he fell in with a small caravan of Wakamba returning from Mombasa. Together, they pushed through the *nyika* and scenery remarkable only for its want of the attractive or picturesque. For nine days the dense thorn scrub proved an unyielding frustration. Often they were forced to crawl long distances on their hands and knees under a waist-high canopy of vicious barbs and spikes, yet whichever way they turned it ensnared them. No one was more relieved than Krapf to reach Maungu where the country opened out and the nearby hills afforded weary travellers a permanent water supply, at the same time giving them an uninterrupted view of the surrounding countryside for the first time since leaving the coast.

To the east lay Galla-land; to the north-west the Endara [Sagalla Hills] *and Bura* [the Taita Hills]; *to the south-east Kadiaro* [Kasigau] *and the mountains of Pare* [just across the Kenya border in Tanzania] ... *We had a beautiful view of the snow-mountain Kilimanjaro in 'Jagga'. It was high above Endara and Bura, yet even at this distance I could discern that its white crown must be snow. All the arguments which Mr Cooley has adduced against the existence of such a snow-mountain, and against the accuracy of Rebmann's report, dwindle into nothing when one has the evidence of one's own eyes of the fact before one so that they are scarcely worth refuting.*

The important staging posts of Maungu, Ndara and Tsavo on the up-country trade route are now insignificant mainline railway stations abutting the Tsavo National Park. Alarming news awaited Krapf at Maungu that Maasai warriors had raided as far as the Tsavo River a few days earlier and had murdered several Wakamba herdsmen before making off with their livestock. Undeterred, he pressed on bravely, but the very mention of the dreaded Maasai instilled fear and panic in his porters; the slightest excuse for turning back would have been seized upon immediately. Dry water pans and rock catchment areas beyond Voi almost gave them that excuse, had Krapf not exhorted them to use their last reserves of energy and cover the remaining twenty odd miles to the permanent waters of the Tsavo River before nightfall. As they hesitated, he strode out, calling for volunteers to follow him.

The sun was just setting when we perceived some trees of the palm family, called mikoma [doum palms], *in the Wanyika language. I redoubled my pace in the sure conviction that the trees seen must be on the banks of the Tsavo; and so it proved; for after a brief interval, we were standing on the bank of that noble river, and refreshing ourselves with its cool water. On the soft soil we observed fresh footprints of men and goats, and also the remains of fires which my people took to be the traces of the savage Maasai.*

Tsavo achieved notoriety exactly fifty years later when it became a temporary railhead camp-site for the construction of a railway line to Uganda. Nicknamed the 'Lunatic Line' by an outspoken member of the British Parliament, the main purpose of the £5 million project was to strengthen the administration of the insecure British Protectorate. As secondary objectives, the railway was intended to give Britain control of the headwaters of the Upper Nile, to suppress slavery and replace the inefficient system of porterage which had become far too costly in human lives.

Hardly had plate-laying begun on the far bank of the Tsavo River than a labourer disappeared, followed several days later by another. Search parties were sent out and returned almost immediately with the grisly evidence that both men had been devoured by lions. The two ferocious 'man-eaters of Tsavo' delayed construction of a bridge spanning the river for nearly eight months during an unprecedented reign of terror which lasted from March until December 1898. At the height of their depredations, the entire workforce of 2,000 indentured workers and artisans from India threatened to strike, for they had volunteered to come to East Africa on an agreement to work for the government, they argued, and not to supply food for the lions! By the time the marauders were shot dead by Lieutenant-Colonel J.H. Paterson, an Indian army officer experienced in hunting tigers who was in charge of railway construction, twenty-eight railwaymen had been eaten and many Wakamba besides. Although the man-eaters were huge, they were in no sense sporting trophies. However, their bloody exploits have earned them a lasting place of rest in the Field Museum of Chicago.

With danger averted for the time being, Krapf moved quickly on to Kikumbulyu, where 'the Wakamba soon surrounded me and looked at me as if I were a being from another world. Hair, hat, shoes and umbrella excited their liveliest attention, and they hopped about me like children. They often asked if rain would fall, and whether I could not make it come, as I was a *mundu wa manzi manene*, a man from the great ocean, and had with me *niumba ya mbua*, an umbrella.' Paradoxically, his umbrella was about the most useful thing he had ever bought. Two days later the first rain for many months fell, bringing an end to the unusually long dry season. This placed him in great favour with the locals – much to his embarrassment. After spending a night out in the drenching rain, Krapf gave orders to break camp at dawn. His party waded the Athi River with its deep pools and alternately swift and slow-moving waters, then climbed to the top of the narrow Yatta Plateau, which is characterized by an abrupt wall of lava that stretches, as far as the eye can see, 1,000 feet above the surrounding plains.

We took up our quarters for the night in one of the many little villages of the Wakamba, who were very friendly towards us, and offered us the meat of giraffes and elephants, as well as fowls for sale. I enjoyed my giraffe steak very much; but I found the flesh of the elephant too hard and tough, and although roasted, it had a peculiar and unpalatable flavour. My Mohammedans were most indignant at this meat of the 'unbelievers', as they called it, and asked for beads with which to buy fowls. For the sake of peace I did not refuse them.

The Wakamba had a reputation for being fearless hunters, but they had made absolutely no impression on the size of the animal kingdom; Krapf travelled through countryside abounding in game. Today, alas, an ever-increasing human population, sophisticated weapons and high world prices for ivory have changed all that. The district is no longer 'more beautiful and richer in grass and trees than any we had seen during our journey' and elephants can no longer be seen digging for water with their tusks in the Tiva sand river over which the missionary crossed on his way to modern Kitui.

Krapf reached Kivoi's village five days after leaving Kikumbulyu and seated himself under a shady tree to await the chief.

He came at last out of his little village, accompanied by his chief wife who carried in her hand a magic staff which was coloured black. The chief gave me a friendly greeting, and said that when I spoke to him at Rabai about a journey to Ukambani, he had thought I was not speaking the truth, us he could not imagine that I should ever perform so distant a journey; but now he saw that I had spoken the truth I was very welcome to his country. He then ordered a lodging to be prepared for me in the hut of one of his wives, who was forced to leave it, whilst the Wakamba ran together in crowds to see and wonder at the Mzungu or European.

Kivoi was a man of medium height, a little paunchy in keeping with his status, yet still lithe of body. He had a merry, but sincere, countenance and his features were finer than those of the Wanyika. When he laughed, Krapf

noticed that all his front teeth had been neatly filed away to sharp, almost needlelike points. He had a spare, thin beard and neat arrowhead markings tattooed on each cheek. His hair was braided in endless tassels, mop-fashion but not long, in which a single white ostrich feather danced in the breeze. His body was smeared with red ochre mixed with animal fat, giving him a glistening, dark brick-red complexion. As with many Bantu peoples of East Africa, Kivoi was circumcized in the neat and tidy Mohammedan way. His only clothing was a light cotton cloth with long fringes, of a burnt umber hue, which was knotted on the right shoulder and fell loosely across his chest. Looking round, Krapf saw that most of the village elders were naked except for their ornaments.

The lobes of Kivoi's ears extended into great loops, in each of which dangled a copper earring in the form of a down-turned lyre. His amulets and bracelets were fashioned from a variety of metals and his imposing necklace from twisted strands of copper wire. Krapf noticed that the younger generation preferred the less traditional but more garish ornaments of red, white and blue beads backed with leather. Kivoi also used white beads to embellish his leather gaiters, which were bound tightly round his ankles to the instep and upwards to the calf. A short sword in a leather sheath was strapped to his waist by means of a soft rawhide belt and in his right hand he carried a club of polished ebony as a symbol of office. Every warrior was armed with a fine tempered iron spear forged by Wakamba smiths and a bow, four to five feet in length, which was so stiff that the uninitiated could hardly draw the string back one foot. In a leather quiver slung across their backs they kept superbly flighted arrows with metal tips dipped in a deadly black vegetable poison.

The women wore a small leather apron decorated with brass or beads and, covering their buttocks, a long V-shaped strip of leather which ended in a point and was split up the centre. This rear garment reached down to the back of their knees or lower and made a rustling sound as they walked. They adorned themselves with heavy beaded necklaces while their legs, from the ankles to the knees, were encircled with thick iron wire, wound round and round in the form of a continuous bracelet; like the gaiters of their menfolk, these acted as a protection against the wicked thorns of the acacia trees and the long upright bayonet leaves of the sansevieria which barred their way.

The sudden arrival of a strange *Mzungu* gave Kivoi *heshima*, honour and respect, among his sub-chiefs and relatives. Krapf was put on display the day after he arrived, while Kivoi boasted, 'Did I not tell you that I would bring a *Mzungu* to you? Now he is here, am I not a man of note since a *Mzungu* has come to me, into my country?' Krapf commented that the villagers 'took delight in inspecting my shoes, hair, hat, clothes and especially my umbrella which was often opened and shut up. They then began to quaff *uki*, a drink prepared out of sugar-cane.'

The chief was delighted to learn of Krapf's plan to explore the Tana River, for he was quick to realize the many advantages of the white man's presence in dealing with his neighbours, who would mistake Krapf for a magician. 'Stay with me till next month when I am going to Mwea and Kikuyu country to fetch ivory,' he pleaded. 'You can accompany me and we will then make the return journey to the coast together in four or five months' time. However, there is only one thing I must insist you do now and that is to send your Wanyika away. I do not like them because every time I travel through their country, they rob me of my ivory.' Having said this, he ordered a bullock to be slaughtered and shared between his family and guests but not among the Wanyika.

By this time Krapf was feeling unwell, having eaten very little nourishing food beyond Kikumbulyu. He was also in a dilemma. Since the rains had set in, any chances he may have had of journeying alone to the Tana were thwarted. Furthermore, if he sent his Wanyika porters away, he would be wholly dependent on Kivoi for his return to Rabai 'and I had reason to trust the Wakamba even less than the Wanyika'. Later that day he made up his mind to return home. Kivoi and the village elders sat in a circle on their small three-legged stools listening intently to his speech, which was delivered in halting Ki-Kamba. In reply Kivoi said:

I wished the Mzungu *to remain with me, and go next month with me to Kikuyu where the River Tana can be crossed. But the* Mzungu *wishes to return to the coast. He can go if he pleases; I will not prevent him. I wished to bestow on him one elephant's tusk four feet long, another three feet and a half in length for what he has is mine and what I have is his. But here I have no ivory, it is at Kikuyu. I will go and fetch it, and then I will travel to the coast, and bring with me two elephants' tusks for the* Mzungu *... I am a man of note; I do not use many words but I will keep my promise.*

He did not!

Krapf first learnt of the existence of a second snowcapped mountain at Kivoi's village. It was known to the Wakamba as 'Ki-nyaa', not 'Kegnia' as Krapf had supposed, and was said to lie six days' journey north of Kitui. Kivoi had assured him that it could be seen when visibility was good from the high ground a few minutes' walk from his village; but with the advent of the short rains, the highlands were swathed in a perpetual blanket of pewter-coloured clouds. Just as Krapf was on the point of bidding his host farewell on 3rd December 1849, a light breeze sprang up and the clouds rolled back miraculously. 'I could see the Kegnia most distinctly and observed two large horns or pillars, as it were, rising over an enormous mountain to the north-west of the Kilimanjaro, covered with a white substance.' This description is somewhat confusing. He can be forgiven for mistaking the direction of the mountain, which actually lies due north of Kilimanjaro, but the reference to two snow-clad peaks is inexplicable. Mount Kenya has, very obviously, only one pinnacle when viewed from afar. It is of interest to note that 'Ki-nyaa,' or more correctly 'Kiima Nyaa', was the word from which early British administrators contrived the name 'Kenya'. 'Kiima Nyaa' in Ki-Kamba literally means 'Mountain of ostriches', as does the loose translation of 'Kirinyaga' (Kiri-nyaga) – the Kikuyu name for this mountain. Many ostriches roamed the plains adjacent to the mountain a long time ago, and it is probable that the shimmering snowcapped peak reminded the local people of the white tail feathers of adult cocks, which were once much sought-after for tribal finery.

Kivoi took leave of his honoured guest with one last parting shot at the Wanyika. 'You Wanyika listen to me; I have a word to say to you also. You are not to give an annoyance on the road to the *Mzungu* for he is my friend. You are to take him in safety to his house at Rabai that my anger may not be provoked against you.' Krapf rejoined his fellow-missionaries at Rabai just four days before Christmas after an absence of fifty-one days.

He was too preoccupied planning his next trip to give his slight setback in Ukambani more than a passing thought. He decided the time had come to reconnoitre the entire coastline as far south as Cape Delgado 'and thus become better acquainted with the various routes by which messengers of the Gospel may press forward to some common centre which in my opinion is Unyamwezi, the great country of the interior, towards which missionaries from east, west and south should converge; as from Unyamwezi they can reach the innumerable tribes of Central Africa by water in all directions'. Cape Delgado is situated on the north-eastern tip of Mozambique and, in those days, marked the boundary where Arab rule ceased and that of Portugal began. Krapf hired a Swahili dhow for the voyage and, in the company of Erhardt, sailed to all the little ports and coastal towns from Tiwi in the north to Lindi in the south. Six weeks later he arrived back in Mombasa full of ideas as to how the interior of East Africa could be opened up to missionaries. Like his contemporary, Dr David Livingstone, his underlying aim was to provide geographical knowledge of the region which would serve to bring the slave trade to an end and foster the spread of Christianity. Both men had a similar

Mombasa

philosophy and Livingstone's famous journeys into the interior of Eastern and Central Africa eight years later must have been influenced in part by Krapf's first-hand reports.

Towards the end of 1849, Krapf began to realize that he was in need of a complete break from his missionary labours. His health had suffered badly after thirteen years in the tropics and he believed a change of air would reinvigorate him for the challenging tasks that lay ahead. Less than a month after returning from Cape Delgado, he set sail for Europe, where he stayed the best part of a year.

CHAPTER 5

Robbers at the Tana

Mwanzo kokochi, mwisho nazi
The beginning is a bud, the end is a coconut

Swahili proverb

WHILE IN EUROPE, Krapf took the opportunity to appear in person before the committee of the Church Missionary Society at their London headquarters. In particular, he wished to put forward his grand design of a chain of mission stations stretching across Africa. He argued his case eloquently in front of a sceptical body of men. Secretary Vern and his committee were on their guard against expensive and grandiose schemes which could have led to unnecessary loss of life. In these circumstances it was a remarkable tribute to Krapf that he got his way. He received permission and immediate financial aid to found two inland stations, one in the Usambara Mountains and the other in Ukambani. He was also given the authority to set up others when circumstances allowed. With that in mind, two more missionaries and three lay-brothers travelled back to Africa with him at the beginning of 1851. Although all were volunteers, one of the missionaries absconded in Aden on the voyage out. Scarcely had the other four newcomers been fourteen days at Rabai when one after another they were struck down by fever. Within weeks, Missionary Pfefferle, who had endeared himself to the others by his devotion and humility, was dead. Two of the three lay-brothers would have assuredly suffered the same fate had they not been sent back promptly to Europe; only Brother Hagerman, a carpenter, recovered sufficiently to justify the risk of his remaining in Rabai. Mosquitoes, those minstrels of misery, had taken their toll of human life yet again; not without good reason had some irreverent people called the hapless mission 'God's waiting room'.

Missionary Pfefferle had been earmarked to help Krapf establish the Ukambani station. Now that he was dead, Krapf had to undertake this momentous task single-handed. He had already decided to site the mission in the little village headed by Mtangi wa Nzuki, who was a man of great influence. His home was strategically situated, astride the main up-country trade route, some 200 miles north-west of Rabai on the high ground of the Yatta plateau. Krapf reasoned that the location afforded comparatively quick and easy communication with the mission at Rabai, and that Wakamba would be most unlikely to mistreat missionaries for fear of reprisals being taken against their relatives and friends living near the coast.

This was to be Krapf's last major expedition into the interior of East Africa and his most difficult. In anticipation that he would be away for some months, he bought in extra trade goods requiring more porters than had hitherto been needed to shoulder the loads. In all, thirty Wanyika were hired and, much to Krapf's chagrin, they turned out to be a disobedient, greedy and drunken rabble. Shortly after leaving Rabai on 11th July 1851, his party joined forces with about 100 Wakamba who were homeward-bound, having exchanged their ivory with Arab and Hindu merchants in Mombasa for loads of unbleached *merikani* (a cheap American cotton), blue calico, glass beads, copper and brass wire, salt, ruddle (red ochre) and blue vitriol (copper sulphate). They crossed the uninhabited *nyika* wastelands in convoy, passing, by the wayside, another group of hunters carrying ivory to the coast. Dozens of caravans trekked down to Mombasa in an annual routine at the end of the long rains and this was common knowledge to bandits and highway robbers alike.

Krapf was told that a large armed gang of Galla tribesmen, evidently bent on plunder, had been seen in the vicinity of Maungu. Since he felt reasonably confident that his little party would not be a worthwhile target, he pressed on regardless. Less than a full day's march from the Tsavo River, however, the Galla ambushed the heavily laden Wakamba in the rear of his column.

Just as I had entered with my Wanyika a large thicket where it was difficult to move to the right or to the left, we heard suddenly a loud cry which proceeded from the Wakamba . . . Aendi! *Robbers! Robbers! Robbers! A frightful confusion now arose among my people; they threw down their loads, and would have fled into the wood but found it difficult to penetrate the bushes. One called out this, another that; several shouted, 'Fire off the guns, fire off the guns!' I wished to do so, but the man who carried my double-barrelled one had fled and I was quite unarmed. I got hold of him and it at last and fired in the air, on which the Wanyika set up a dreadful war-cry, and the others who had guns then fired three or four shots in succession. Whilst this firing was going on at our front, the Wakamba were discharging their poisoned arrows at the* Aendi *. . . The Wakamba who were furthest behind threw down their loads at the sight of the enemy, allowing them to come and put them on their shoulders, whereupon the Wakamba fired and shot three of the robbers dead; and we had one Mkamba wounded. When the enemy saw that the Wakamba made a stand and heard our firing, they retreated . . . Had the conflict lasted any longer we should have been in a very perilous plight as, in the confusion, I lost my powder-horn and one of my people burst the barrel of his gun by putting too large a charge into it. The ramrod of another was broken through his being knocked over by a Mnyika in the confusion, just as he was going to load; whilst the gun of another missed fire [sic] altogether. I saw clearly that it was God who had preserved us and not our own sword and bow.*

That seems a little uncharitable to the Wakamba whose courage undoubtedly saved the day! Nevertheless, Krapf did admit that it was fortunate the Wakamba were attacked first 'for they defended their property while my people cared neither for me nor for my baggage, but were anxious about their own lives alone'.

His Wanyika porters were badly shaken by the clash and had to be coaxed into moving forward again; but there were no further incidents on the march. They reached the safety of Mtangi wa Nzuki's village atop the Yatta plateau on 26th July and waited patiently for the chiefs to assemble. At length, Krapf expounded the purpose of his journey, whereupon the chiefs assured him of their protection and declared that he would be very welcome to live among them, build a house and proceed however he pleased. Krapf was delighted, bearing in mind the indignities from which Rebmann had suffered on his second visit to Chief Mamkinga. The formalities over, 'I delivered to them my present which consisted of eight ells [ten yards] of calico and some four pounds of beads for which they presented me in return with a goat. I made a special present to Mtangi wa Nzuki as it was within his enclosure that I was to erect my hut and as he had offered me his particular protection.'

Nothing ever went quite according to plan in those early days of African travel and Krapf's journeys were no exception. After he had spent a bitterly cold night in the open and a scorching hot day crouched in the shade of his black umbrella, his Wanyika porters blithely announced that they were hell-bent on returning home. He looked aggrieved by this unexpected turn of events and reminded them, almost apologetically, of their undertaking to build him a house. 'In a few hours they had put together, with stakes fetched from the wood, a miserable hencoop scarcely six feet high and about as many feet broad and long, but which I was fain to be content as my things were lying in the open.' It was a very makeshift affair with its roof improperly thatched but, somehow, it gave him the illusion of protection. Just as the Wanyika were about to decamp the next morning, he learnt that his lone servant had taken fright in the night and run away. This could have signified the end of his safari, so Krapf was desperate enough to hold out an incentive of high wages to anyone who would volunteer to remain behind. At the last moment, two Wanyika porters offered their services on condition that the period of their engagement did not exceed two months.

In my hencoop, I could neither write, nor read, nor sleep and was continually besieged by the Wakamba who by day, even before dawn, did not leave me a moment alone. If I wished to read, they asked if I was trying to spy into their hearts, or whether I was looking for rain, and inquiring after diseases; when I wrote, they wanted to know what I had written and whether it contained sorcery. Every one of my movements was sharply observed. Many came to beg this or that, to see new things, or to buy wares as they took me for a merchant; others brought a few eggs or a little meal and then asked for twice or three times as much as their presents were worth. My hut had not even a door so that I could not close it, and by night I was safe neither from thieves nor wild beasts.

With a diary entry such as this for 28th July 1851, one can understand why Krapf had written, 'Our friends in Europe can scarcely conceive what obstacles a missionary has to meet and to overcome who wishes to travel into the interior.'

Krapf was once more in a sorry plight. Everything seemed to hinge on the loyalty of his servants and, somewhat despondently, he came to the conclusion that it would be unwise of him to stay in Yatta more than a couple of months. He resolved, therefore, to make full use of the interval by revisiting his 'old friend' Kivoi in the hope of reviving plans for their safari to the Tana River. If he could win his way through, he would be consoled to some extent for having to leave Ukambani yet again with his work unfinished. Kivoi seemed genuinely delighted to see 'his *Mzungu*' again and expressed his willingness to make the arrangements just as soon as he had cleared up a feud with a neighbouring clan which threatened to disturb the peace. While Kivoi attended to his affairs of state, Krapf waited patiently at Kitui, a virtual prisoner, all the while having to parade before a gaping audience 'like an ape or a bear in Europe', with his precious days dwindling. In Kivoi's absence the village was reduced to women and children who lived in constant terror of a surprise attack. They came trembling to the white man's hut at night, beseeching him to look through his telescope to tell them whether friends or foes were approaching. Three days later the chief and his warriors returned from a satisfactory settlement of their dispute, which was followed by a week of drunken revelry, with Krapf's patience being taxed to the full.

Eventually Kivoi announced that he was ready to undertake the belated journey. Gathering together the bare necessities of life, including basic foodstuffs, cooking pots and Krapf's simple belongings, they set out in the late afternoon of 24th August in a party thirty strong. The missionary must have looked a strange sight with his rolled umbrella and pith helmet – shaped like an ethereal halo round the head of a saint – surrounded by the Wakamba with ostrich plumes fluttering in the breeze from their shocks of ochred hair, some naked except for their ornaments, others with a light cotton cloth knotted and thrown over one shoulder. The warriors, their lithe, dark bodies patterned in red ochre, fanned out to protect their chief and his important guest, a few armed with spears and oval-shaped shields painted with designs in red and white, the rest with bows and arrows carried in quivers at the ready. The latter were not merely for defence against sudden attack but to secure, if possible, an addition to their food supplies from the innumerable herds of antelope which dotted the plains, watching the travellers suspiciously or darting off with snorts and whistles and clicking of hoofs as they distanced themselves from the unknown intruders. Kivoi and Krapf were the only members of the little party armed with ancient muzzle-loaders. They were followed discreetly by a bevy of the chief's wives, each with a few sundries strapped to their backs in square leather bags.

Their route took them in a north to north-westerly direction through fine uninhabited country well suited for agriculture or grazing; and so it proved when the tsetse flies were driven out. Krapf could clearly make out the mountains that form the south-east aspect of the Kenya highlands far away beyond the Tana, but Mount Kenya was hidden permanently in clouds. Not a single tree broke the vista of pale yellow, copper and straw-coloured grasses which waved endlessly before them. Kivoi, in readiness for the short rains, deliberately fired the grass to improve the grazing; it turned out to be a mistake for which he paid dearly.

Progress by the fourth day was infuriatingly slow. Early on, Kivoi lost the handle of Krapf's umbrella and insisted on back-tracking to find it. This resulted in a delay of several hours. Then one of his wives picked up an ostrich feather lying in the long grass beside the footpath, whereupon he again commanded a halt and sat on the ground until the whole area had been finely combed. With delays such as these commonplace, twenty-five of Kivoi's kinsmen and a small group of Mbere traders caught up the expedition, having left Kitui a day or so later. More time was wasted in needless greetings before the parties got under way again, to come within a mile and a half of the Tana River, where the golden grass of the plains converged on the clear-cut demarcation line of a dark green riverine forest. As they neared the forest edge, groups of armed men, some ten, others twenty strong, came out of hiding and made a determined beeline for Kivoi's rag tag column. 'Our whole caravan was panic-stricken and the cry "Meida", they are robbers, ran through our ranks upon which Kivoi fired off his gun and bade me to do the same.' In his hurry to load, Krapf fired his gun with the ramrod in the barrel. The gun survived the blast but a makeshift ramrod had to be fashioned from a sapling during a lull in the scuffle. Poorly aimed bullets only caused the robbers to relax their pace, but they stopped momentarily dead in their tracks when a porter suddenly unfurled Krapf's secret new weapon and opened it with a flourish! As they came within bow-shot, Kivoi called on them all to halt and ran bravely forward to defuse the potentially dangerous confrontation. Several minutes elapsed before he managed to persuade three spokesmen to come over to the place where his own people were squatting on the ground; after they had seated themselves opposite, he told them who he was and whither he was going. When Krapf had finished one of the strangers stood up and laughed. 'You need not be afraid,' he said. 'We have no hostile design. We saw the grass on fire and only wished to know who the travellers were that had set it on fire. You can now go forward to the river; we will follow at once.'

Kivoi strongly suspected treachery and urged his men to get under way again immediately. He personally took up a position at the exposed rear of the column to protect it with his muzzle-loader. His apprehension was soon confirmed, for just as his forward elements entered the riverine forest on a narrow footpath in single file, the robbers wheeled round and closed in purposefully. All of a sudden shrill war cries filled the still air and a shower of poisoned arrows was loosed off into their midst. Kivoi was quickly surrounded, then fatally wounded alongside one of his wives. Meantime, Krapf fought it out in the middle of the caravan.

A great confusion arose; our people threw away their burdens and discharged their arrows at the enemy, begging me imploringly to fire as quickly as I could. I fired twice but in the air for I could not bring myself to shed the blood of man. Whilst I was re-loading a Mkamba rushed past me wounded in the hip, a stream of blood flowing from him. Right and left fell the arrows at my feet but without touching me. When our people saw that they could not cope with an enemy 120 strong they took to flight.

Krapf also took off in the general direction of the Mbere traders, since he was unable to distinguish friend from foe and truthfully had no stomach for a fight. As he rushed headlong through the forest, he came to a deep gulley which he tried to leap over; in the attempt, he lost his footing and fell right into it, breaking a nasty fall with the butt of his rifle, which splintered on impact. By the time he had pulled himself together and made sure no bones were broken, he found himself all alone. The Wakamba and Mbere people had vanished and the robbers were too preoccupied carrying off their booty to worry about stragglers. To his lasting credit, he kept calm. Driven by thirst – he had not had a drink all day – he headed straight for the Tana River and drank deeply. 'After my thirst was satisfied, for the want of water bottles I filled the leather case of my telescope as well as the barrels of my gun which was now useless to me; and I stopped up the mouths of the gun barrels with grass and with bits of cloth cut off my trousers.'

Clear evidence of Krapf's tenacious character was shown in his decision to explore the Tana River before lying up in thick cover for the rest of the day. He noted its serpentine course eastwards and calculated that it was 150 feet wide and some six to seven deep. This, he reasoned, was unusual in dry weather, for he distinctly remembered being told that the Wakamba crossed the river on rafts only in the rainy season. He was the first European to gain the upper reaches of the Tana, Kenya's largest river, at a point barely sixty miles north-east of modern Nairobi. So far as one can make out, he must have been in the vicinity of Kindaruma and Kamburu where most of the country's hydroelectric power is now generated. The mountain he christened 'Mount Albert', in honour of the audience accorded him by the Prince Consort at Windsor Castle earlier that year, was probably Nduni Hill, which rises 4,398 feet above sea-level on the far side of the river in Embu district.

To while away the hours, Krapf reflected on the highlights and frustrations of his outward journey. He remembered the acrid grass smoke from Kivoi's pyromania, which was in large measure the cause of all the trouble – and, in the end, had cost the old man his life. 'The wind was strong and blew unerringly on my back,' he mused. 'If I now walk with it full in my face, it could help me to retrace my steps.' He came out of hiding as darkness fell.

Once he had emerged from the deep shadows of the forest into open country, a ghostly silver-grey in the moonlight, his pulse unconsciously quickened for a moment as he felt a light breeze ruffle his hair. He changed course to face it and set off at a steady pace over broken ground. Sometimes he gained the impression that he was heading in the right direction and sometimes not. 'It often seemed as if an invisible hand guided my steps for I had invariably a strong sensation that I was going wrong whenever, by chance, I deviated from the right direction.' Around midnight, he reached a hill that he definitely recognized and began to feel more relaxed; this would almost certainly have been Kwamathumba Hill which rises 4,302 feet above sea-level and served as a landmark for caravans journeying to Kikuyu and Embu country. Krapf named it 'Mount William' in memory of the audience granted to him by His Majesty Friedrich Wilhelm IV of Prussia a year earlier. Since he never took bearings to pinpoint the positions of the geographical features he described and no further exploration of the region took place for more than a quarter of a century, it is quite understandable why these unimportant hills have never been known by their foreign names. Krapf slumped down at the foot of Kwamathumba Hill and slept fitfully for two to three hours under a panoply of twinkling stars. It was so cold that he had to cover himself with grass to ward off the worst of the biting wind. He arose well before dawn and started out once more along a barrier line of burning grass, which warmed him, besides making the going a little easier. 'I felt the pangs of hunger and thirst; the water in my telescope case had run out and that in the barrels of my gun, which I had not drunk, had been lost on my way to Mount William as the bushes had torn out the grass stoppers ... My hunger was so great that I tried to chew leaves, roots and elephant's excrement to stay it, and when day broke to break my fast on ants. The roar of a lion would have been music in my ears.'

He got well beyond the Tana River by sunrise, still heading in the right direction though on a different track to that of his outward journey. 'Soon after daybreak I saw four immense rhinoceroses feeding behind some bushes ahead; they stared at me but did not move and I naturally made no attempt to disturb them. On the whole I was no longer afraid of wild beasts and the only thought that occupied me was how to reach Kitui as soon as possible.' Later that day by pure chance, he fell in with a Mkamba and his wife, who, like himself, were fugitives from the affray. They travelled together for thirty-six hours, stopping to snatch a few hours' sleep here and there, until they finally staggered into the village of one of Kivoi's relatives. Krapf was completely done in; his tongue cleaved to the roof of his mouth and hunger gnawed at his stomach. He ate a few bananas and almost immediately collapsed into a deep

sleep, heedless of the bitterly cold wind as dusk fell.

Next morning he realized that his problems were far from over. The news of Kivoi's death had spread throughout the land and retribution had been swift. Fifteen traders from Mbere, who happened to be in Kitui at the time, had been murdered in cold blood for the atrocity committed by their fellow-countrymen. The villagers openly accused Krapf of causing their chief's death and his New Testament, notebook and pencil, and telescope were all regarded as connected with witchcraft. He was kept a prisoner for three days while Kivoi's relatives decided what to do with him. 'I heard from some Wakamba that Kivoi's relations intended to kill me, asking why I had gone to the Tana since, as a magician, for which they took me, I ought to have known that the robbers were there. In any case, they said, I ought to have died along with Kivoi.' Since Krapf believed this might well be his fate, he decided to escape. When no one was looking, he hid a little food and a calabash of water in readiness for flight. He awoke in the early hours of 5th September and stealthily removed some of the logs barring the entrance to his hut. Then, covering this hole with the cowhide on which he had been sleeping, to prevent the cold night air from waking his guards, he slipped silently out of the village and made good his escape. He dared not travel by day for he was in a well-populated neighbourhood, but his progress at night was pathetically slow. Tall grass, gullies, rocky outcrops, dense undergrowth and thorns – 'those relentless tyrants of the wilderness' – obstructed his path and ripped his clothes. He even lost his gun which, though useless as a weapon, had served to boost his flagging morale. He advanced barely eight miles in the direction of Yatta in three agonizing nights, having covered a much greater distance in a roundabout way. Sensing the hopelessness of the situation, he gave himself up, fully expecting to be put to death.

Muinde, Kivoi's eldest brother, listened attentively to Krapf's story and showed apparent compassion for the disasters which had befallen him. He

A coastal dhow built at Lamu. Krapf sailed to Takaungu in a much larger vessel
that had been built in Arabia.

(Right) The old town of Mombasa. Its tall buildings and narrow streets signify its historic links with Arabia.

(Left) A typical Swahili village. Buildings have walls of coral rock and are thatched with *makuti*.

(Opposite) A Swahili woman from the coast. The *buibui* denotes that she is a Moslem in purdah.

(Right) Ruins of the palace at the coastal town of Gedi, one of many Arab settlements that were either destroyed by the Portuguese or fell into decay.

(Below) The cradle of Christianity in East Africa – the church at Rabai, although rebuilt since Krapf's day, still has the original bell.

(Above) Giriama girls pounding corn. These were the people described by Krapf as the 'Wanyika'.

(Left) A Giriama girl carrying a gourd full of water. Her traditional skirt is made from strips of printed cotton.

A Mtaita with an array of musical instruments. He is wearing ear ornaments and goggles made from calabashes.

(*Right*) Mount Kilimanjaro seen from Lake Jipe.

(*Above*) The Galla
village of Tulu,
north of Malindi.

A Galla girl wearing
traditional necklaces.

denied that there was a plot to kill him, claiming that Krapf's detention had been an arbitary act perpetrated by greed. Krapf deduced from these remarks that his life was out of danger, but in case he had mistaken the relatives' forgiving mood he warned Muinde of the consequences likely to befall the Wakamba in the event of his violent death. If, on the other hand, they would remain friends and escort him to Yatta, he would reward them with a portion of the trade goods he had left there. For as long as he stayed at the village recovering from his ordeal and fighting a high fever, no one would come near him; he was left an outcast to beg for food and fetch his own water. Only Kivoi's senior wife, who now belonged to Muinde by custom, showed pity on him in sickness and gave him a bowl of fresh milk.

After an indeterminate wait, the escort showed up and Krapf was unceremoniously bundled off to Yatta. He was given nothing to eat for three days except dried mealies which he found impossible to masticate; thus he arrived at Mtangi wa Nzuki's village half-starved and exhausted. After days of mental anguish and physical suffering he was most thankful to be among friends again. Only his own servants appeared somewhat reticent in their welcome, for they had confidently expected to inherit all the property he had left in their care. It was a foregone conclusion that an argument would develop over the gift he proffered to Kivoi's kinsmen, and no sooner had a settlement been reached than both his servants insisted on returning home.

[As] *I could not trust the Wakamba either as servants or burden-bearers on a journey, no choice was left me but to return in the company of the Wanyika if I did not desire to place myself entirely in the hands of the capricious and uncertain Wakamba. Kivoi, the only influential Mkamba who had been my friend, was dead; Mtangi wa Nzuki of Yatta had not yet been tested; my knowledge of the Wakamba dialect was very defective; I could not dwell in a strawhut without injury to my health; and what was to become of me in sickness without a faithful servant? Can I be blamed if I renounced for the time the Ukambani mission and returned to the coast whilst an opportunity was still afforded me?*

Mtangi wa Nzuki seemed genuinely upset by Krapf's decision, as he would have wished him to remain longer. But he let the missionary go in peace and with honour, even giving him a goat as a token of friendship. On 17th September 1851 Krapf set out with a heavy heart to return to the coast. Though it was a comparatively trouble-free journey, the usual shortages of food and water and the rigours of the terrain necessitated several forced marches which, in his emaciated condition, almost overwhelmed him. By the time he reached Rabai on 28th September, to dispel the rumours of his death which had preceded him on the 'bush telegraph', he was so worn out that he could barely stand. However, the joyous welcome he received from his devoted fellowers was a far better tonic to the restoration of his health than any medicine could possibly have been. Within days he felt strong enough to start planning future strategy, his spirit of adventure and his vision of a chain of inland mission stations in no way diminished by this second disappointment in Ukambani. For the time being, he accepted that a permanent station at Yatta was an unsafe and doubtful enterprise unless an intermediate station could be first established at Kasigau or Ndara. Until more missionaries could be recruited to join the Rabai station he avowed to postpone, but not to abandon, this project.

Indefatigable, Krapf next turned his attention to the Usambara Mountains where he had been well received by 'King' Kimeri three years earlier. The chief administered an orderly region whose people were less prone to witchcraft, superstition and lawlessness than the Wakamba. He had implored the missionary to return quickly and open up a mission school but the tragedies at Rabai had prevented this. The more Krapf now thought about it, the more convinced he became that the first link in the chain would have to be forged in Usambara. He went there in early February 1852 to confirm his judgment. 'I saw at once that I was in a country where much better order reigns than in the lawless republics of Wanyika and Wakamba . . . Never have I travelled anywhere so comfortably . . . I do not believe that one could be safer in any European country than in Usambara.' Kimeri welcomed him with open arms and repeated his personal assurances of full cooperation in the establishment of a mission. With this cordial relationship restored Krapf had no misgivings. Here, at last, his vision would be transformed into reality.

But he was not destined to take any further part in the vision. Though only forty-three years old, his health had deteriorated to such an extent that it became self-evident he would not survive if he remained in Africa much longer. He was persuaded against his will to return home to Europe in the summer of 1853, leaving Rebmann in charge of Rabai and Erhardt responsible for the new station at Usambara.

When he finally sailed from Mombasa scores of friends – Arabs, Wanyika, 'Banyan' traders and fellow-missionaries – came down to the old harbour to wish him Godspeed. A solitary fisherman, naked but for a loin-cloth, was paddling his dugout canoe towards the harbour, a square wicker fish-trap straddled across its bows. As Krapf's ship put out into the Indian Ocean and

he waved goodbye, it was with mixed feelings that he watched the baobab trees on the verdant African shore glide past him. The boat headed round the northern point of the old harbour and he looked back at the little cluster of whitewashed Arab houses, the palm trees waving in the monsoon breeze and the sun scintillating on the waves as if someone had bedecked them with faceted diamonds – a scene, he thought, which had remained almost unchanged for centuries. His satisfaction in what he had achieved was tempered by the knowledge that his vision of a great chain of mission stations, harbouring and spreading the word of Christianity across the beckoning continent of Africa, was still largely a dream. He had come to accept that the weakness of his body through incessant illness was no match for his mental zeal and the ardour of his soul.

Within months of his departure, ill-health forced Erhardt to abandon the Usambara experiment and return to Rabai. Here he remained for a further eighteen months until severe illness drove him out of Africa for good. Even though a link in the chain had snapped, Krapf, ever the optimist, would not accept defeat. He returned to East Africa on a short visit in 1861 with the intention of helping the United Methodist Free Churches re-establish those tenuous links. However, life in Africa did not suit the two Swiss missionaries, who had not foreseen the risks. The wail of the muezzin calling the faithful to prayer took on a baleful significance as they lay prostrate with fever within days of arriving in Mombasa. While they tossed and turned in their delirium, a stray bullet from a lively skirmish between the British Navy and Arab slavers lodged in the wall of their bedroom. Besieged on all sides, they decided that they had mistaken their calling and quickly returned to Europe. That left Krapf with two English missionaries whose destination was to have been Usambara. Notwithstanding a formal 'passport' signed personally by the Sultan of Zanzibar, they were treated roughly and had to turn back for the coast barely two days' journey up the Pangani River. On their return to Mombasa, one of them became so ill that he had to be sent home, a physical wreck, to save his life. Had the Reverend Thomas Wakefield also succumbed, the proposed Methodist mission would have died with him. But he survived the usual debilitating bouts of fever to found the Ribe station, a short distance away from Rabai on the same range of hills.

'Bwana Wakifili' – as he became known to the locals – was a remarkable personality. Above all he was a man of God; yet his contribution to the development of the region during his twenty-seven years at Ribe and Mombasa was not confined to his missionary pursuits. In his spare time, he was a man of many parts: an amateur botanist, lepidopterist, ornithologist, astronomer and artist. He painstakingly recorded all the known trade routes into the interior of East Africa by interviewing numerous caravan leaders and ivory traders. This almost unique contribution to geography was published in a paper entitled 'Caravan routes from the coast to the interior', which earned him the Murchison Grant for 1882 – an annual award by the British Geographical Society to recognize important achievements in the field of geography.

Wakefield was an itinerant traveller and succeeded in Galla country where his predecessors had failed. At the outset of his missionary work, Krapf had left him in no doubt that the Ribe station should be viewed merely as a stepping-stone to the Galla people. To begin with, his porters shied away. 'If you are going to Ukambani or Maasai country or even beyond,' they used to tell the missionary, 'we will willingly go with you but no – oh no! – not to the Gallas. That is utterly impossible.' Their horror was in part due to the well-known Galla practice of emasculation. Wakefield persevered and, in the end, persuaded ten brave men to accompany him. Their first attempt in August 1865 failed but their second journey a month later met with success.

They came across several Galla settlements where the people were friendly but exceedingly avaricious. The way into their country was open at last to those who could afford the price. 'I could throw up my hat and shout for very joy!' Wakefield wrote in a letter to the General Secretary of the United Free Methodists.

It took Wakefield another twenty years, however, to fulfil his and Krapf's dream of a mission station in their midst. Golbanti was chosen as the site. It was an obscure village some twenty-five miles from the coast up the mosquito-infested Tana River. Wakefield was full of enthusiasm as usual.

Here we are at Golbanti, on a station, and fairly established in one of the most promising, if not the most promising, position for mission work in East Africa, on the banks of the River Tana, with a waterway of several hundreds of miles, leading to numerous races in the interior. We must be up and doing, and promptly strengthen this grand beginning with all the force we can possibly command. Men and women of the Free Churches, rally round Golbanti! Send us the best of your sons and daughters to push on the conquest of the Redeemer far and wide amongst the races of the Dark Continent.

One day after Wakefield had returned from a visit to Golbanti, a small group of missionaries met in the mission house at Ribe and dined together. Within a year three of them were dead. Bishop James Hannington, a broad-minded man, warm and generous, was murdered in Uganda on the orders of the *kabaka* or ruler of Buganda; John and Annie Houghton, who had taken charge of the Golbanti mission, were speared to death by Maasai warriors outside the little chapel they were building there. Wakefield was the sole survivor until failing health drove him home to England a year later. Yet again, the East African missions had suffered a severe setback, but there was no longer any question of failure. From Krapf's humble beginnings, Christianity had taken firm root.

The two founders of the first Christian community in East Africa devoted the rest of their lives to the region of Africa they loved. Rebmann stayed on at Rabai for another quarter of a century, bearing the cross of Christ until finally, blind and broken – in health, not in spirit – he was forced to return home to his native Germany in 1875 where he died inside a year. Meantime, Krapf continued to apply his energy and talents for the advancement of Christianity. He laboriously revised the Amharic version of the Bible: translated the Scriptures into no less than six vernacular languages; added a comprehensive Ki-Swahili dictionary to his grammar which had been published in 1850; and prepared basic vocabularies of the Maasai, Ki-Nyika, Pokomo and Galla languages. This brilliant linguist and dedicated Christian died in prayer on 26th November 1881 at the age of seventy-one.

To Krapf must go the honour of pioneering the inland exploration of East Africa in ways which bore no resemblance to the elaborate, well-armed expeditions of the travellers and explorers who followed in his footsteps. In the days when the picture of Africa was a dark one, he walked a perilous tightrope. He was possessed of an irresistible will to crusade, as he penetrated mysterious and hostile lands armed only with his faith in God and a black umbrella. Krapf's and Rebmann's journeys proved conclusively the existence of two snowcapped mountains in tropical Africa. Their reports of a large lake region also acted as a catalyst for further exploration, and fired the imagination of other travellers who were determined to trace the source of the River Nile. While their geographical discoveries were accidental to their work as zealous missionaries, their inaccurate maps were at once open to criticism and at the same time attracted expert attention.

As early as 1844, Krapf had collected a whole mass of geographical information from local sources, which included reports of large 'inland seas'. His headman, Bwana Kheri, had been adamant in his assertion that Lakes Nyasa and Tanganyika were quite separate, which called into question another strongly held view of the geographer and critic, W. Desborough Cooley. When travelling in Ukambani in 1851, Krapf had been told of 'a mighty inland sea, the end of which was not to be reached even after a journey of 100 days'. Lake Ukerewe had been mentioned as its name. Maps embodying this information were drawn up and presented to those members of the public in the countries of Western Europe who had become fascinated and enthralled by these glimpses, however inaccurate, of what lay beyond the coastal veil of East Africa. Geographers were taken by surprise. Beautiful lakes and fertile lands now took the place of scorching sands and desert wastes!

By 1855 Rebmann and Erhardt had unravelled the problem of how these 'inland seas' had been formed – 'by the simple supposition that, where geographical hypotheses had hitherto supposed an enormous mountain land, we must now look for an enormous valley and an inland sea . . .' More than thirty years elapsed before Professor J.W. Gregory of the British Museum mapped out the extent of one of the most amazing geological faults in the world, which we know today as the Great Rift Valley – a system of deep trenches and troughs stretching from the Lebanon in the north to Mozambique in the south.

Heated discussions succeeded the missionaries' exciting reports – discussions which did not end in mere words. Something had to be done and something was. In 1856 the Royal Geographical Society, spurred on by a promise of financial backing from the British Government, resolved to send out an expedition under Major (later Sir Richard) Burton, 'a man well

experienced in Eastern travel', to test the accuracy of the geographical data. He arrived in Zanzibar on 20th December 1856, accompanied by Captain John Hanning Speke of the Indian Army, and at the first opportunity repaired to Rabai, where Rebmann gave them valuable advice while his charming English wife prepared a meal from 'all the delicacies of a dry Wanyika season'. Their visit happened to coincide with a devastating raid by some 800 Maasai warriors who swept right through Wanyika country like a hurricane to the outskirts of Mombasa. Here, twenty-five Baluchi and Arab soldiers armed with matchlocks were quickly despatched by exploiting the known weaknesses of muzzle-loaders, particularly the time taken to reload them. Perhaps this bloody massacre put paid to any thought Burton may have had of exploring the Kenya region, for he was still very nervous of conflict, having almost been killed by Somali robbers on his previous journey to eastern Africa. Whatever the case, it is somewhat surprising that no serious attempt was made to verify the existence of the snowcapped mountains, for the acrimonious controversy raging over them must have placed them exceptionally high on his list of possible and tempting avenues of exploration.

Burton and Speke, armed with Rebmann's sketch maps of the region, set out in June 1857 from the beautiful coastal town of Bagamoyo with its magnificent flamboyant trees ablaze in a riot of colour. Their destination was the important inland town of Tabora, known then as Kazeh, some 500 miles from the sea. They followed a well-beaten path, since most of the trade routes from the stretch of coast opposite Zanzibar converged on Tabora which, over the years, had become a main centre for ivory as well as for slaves. Twenty-five Arab slave dealers had set up shop in the town and gave the weary explorers a dignified welcome as their men straggled in after a five-month journey. Speke had been rarely free from illness and neither man had had a moment's peace, as the local people flocked to gawk at the first white men who had ever ventured into their land. Burton was foremost an Arabist and delighted in the company of Sheikh Snay Bin Amir and the slavers, even though he had witnessed the misery of their trade. Never for a moment did it seem to worry him that their principal preoccupation was the capture and sale of human beings. During their long talks he gleaned a great deal of valuable information on the lake district. For the very first time he and Speke were made aware of three distinct lakes – Lake Ukerewe in the north, Lake Tanganyika in the centre and Lake Nyasa in the south.

By early December, the explorers had recovered sufficiently to start out for Lake Tanganyika, and on 13th February 1858 they reached the Arab slaving post of Ujiji. 'Here you may picture to yourself my bitter disappointment when, after toiling through so many miles of savage life, all the time emaciated by divers sicknesses and weakened by great privations of food and rest, I found, on approaching the zenith of my ambitions, the Great Lake in question nothing but mist and glare before my eyes,' Speke wrote. 'From the summit of the eastern horn the lovely Lake Tanganyika could be seen in all its glory by everybody but myself.' Speke was suffering from ophthalmia, while Burton had an ulcerated mouth and could not eat solid food. Their moment of triumph was marred by serious illness, yet it did not prevent them hiring two native canoes in their determination to find a north-flowing river which might be identified as the source of the Nile. In this they failed and turned back to Tabora, having satisfied themselves by questioning the local people that no river actually flowed north out of the lake. Burton regained the town exhausted and dejected, with no intention of moving on for a while. He willingly allowed Speke, six years his junior, to investigate the Arabs' reports of a much larger lake to the north.

It was Speke, therefore, who became the first white man to shed light on the second largest lake in the world. With a poorly equipped party of porters and Baluchi guards, he touched its southern shores near Mwanza on 3rd August 1858 and renamed it Victoria Nyanza. The locals firmly believed the lake extended to the end of the world, but the explorer had his own ideas. Relying heavily on the word of merchants who had never actually seen the Nile, he announced, 'I no longer feel any doubt that the lake at my feet gave birth to that interesting river, the source of which has been the subject of so much speculation, and the object of so many explorers. The Arabs' tale was proved to the letter. This is a far more extensive lake than the Tanganyika; so broad that you could not see across it, and so long that nobody knew its length.' This was inspired guesswork. It was a foolish claim to make without the geographical data to support it. Burton was quick to decry Speke for his recklessness and sometime later openly accused him of propounding a theory on the Nile basin which was based on 'an amount of fable unknown to the days of Ptolomey'. Unfortunately, the two had got on each other's nerves and were by now bitter opponents. They took good care to have as little as possible to do with each other on their journey back home.

The success of the RGS expedition – in geographical terms – can be attributed in no small measure to the missionaries, and Speke was magnanimous enough to acknowledge this. 'I must call attention to the marked fact that the church missionaries residing for many years at Zanzibar [he must have meant Rabai] are the prime and first promoters of the discovery.'

Burton had likened Africa to a coconut 'hard to penetrate from without and soft within'. Joseph Thomson and other late nineteenth-century travellers were left to crack the Kenyan nut which Krapf and Rebmann had dislodged so tantalizingly from the tree that had been shrouded in mystery over the millennia.

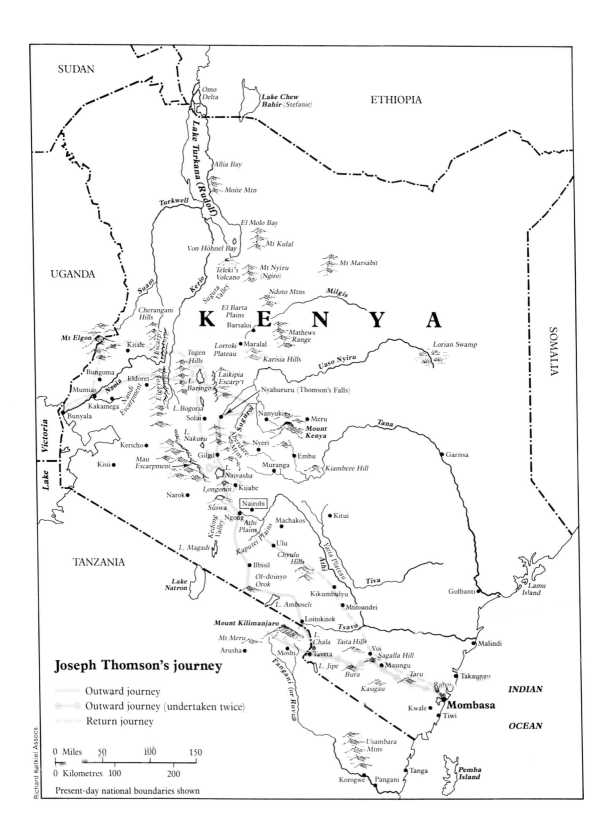

SUDAN

ETHIOPIA

*Omo
Delta*

**Lake Chew
Bahir** *(Stefanie)*

Allia Bay

Lake Turkana (Rudolf)

Turkwell

Moite Mtn

El Molo Bay

Von Höhnel Bay

Mt Kulal

UGANDA

Suam

Kerio

Suguta Valley

*Teleki's
Volcano*

*Mt Nyiru
(Ngiro)*

Mt Marsabit

*Cherangani
Hills*

Mt Elgon

Kitale

*Tugen
Hills*

*El Barta
Plains*

Barsaloi

Ndoto Mtns

Milgis

K E N Y A

Lorian Swamp

Bungoma

Eldoret

*Lorroki
Plateau*

Maralal

*Mathews
Range*

Nandi Escarpment

Elgeyo Escarp't

Karisia Hills

Uaso Nyiru

Mumias

Kakamega

*L.
Baringo*

*Laikipia
Escarp't*

Nyahururu (Thomson's Falls)

Tana

Bunyala

L.Bogoria

Solai

Nanyuki

Meru

Sugutu

**Mount
Kenya**

Garissa

Kericho

*L.
Nakuru*

Gilgil

Nyeri

Lake Victoria

*Mau
Escarpment*

*Aberdare
Mtns*

Embu

Kisii

*L.
Naivasha*

Muranga

Kiambere Hill

Narok

Longonot

Kijabe

Nairobi

Kitui

Suswa

Ngong

*Athi
Plains*

Machakos

Kedong Valley

Kaputei Plains

L. Magadi

Ulu

*Chyulu
Hills*

Athi

Yatta Plateau

TANZANIA

Ilbisil

*Ol-doinyo
Orok*

Tiva

Tiwa

**Lake
Natron**

L. Amboseli

Kikumbulyu

Mtitoandei

Golbanti

*Lamu
Island*

Loitokitok

Tsavo

Mount Kilimanjaro

Mt Meru

*L.
Chala*

Taita Hills

Voi

Malindi

Arusha

Moshi

Taveta

Sagalla Hill

Maungu

Taru

Takaungu

L. Jipe

Bura

Kasigau

INDIAN

Pangani (or Ruvu)

Kwale

Mombasa

Tiwi

OCEAN

SOMALIA

Joseph Thomson's journey

——— Outward journey

——— Outward journey (undertaken twice)

– – – Return journey

*Usambara
Mtns*

**Pemba
Island**

Tanga

Korogwe

Pangani

| 0 Miles | 50 | 100 | 150 |

| 0 Kilometres | 100 | 200 |

Present-day national boundaries shown

Richard Natkiel Assocs.

PART II

Joseph Thomson

*A journey through Maasailand
to Lake Victoria*

1883-4

*He who goes gently, goes safely;
He who goes safely, goes far.*

THOMSON'S MOTTO

CHAPTER 6

Safari preparations

Anayetaka hachoki, hata akichoka keshapata
There is no tiredness in desire; tiredness is only desire realized
Swahili proverb

THE MAASAI, PROUD PASTORALISTS of the East African plains, are renowned throughout the world. More books have been written about them and more photographs taken of them than any other people in Africa. Slender, fine-featured warriors resplendent with their long, ochred hair and flashing spears, bead-bedecked maidens and blanket-clad elders, they cling to traditional values and their old ways of life in this modern age. Their fame dates back more than a century to the period when European travellers and explorers were bent on exposing the manifold secrets of a mysterious continent to the outside world.

'Aggressive', 'bloodthirsty', 'warlike', 'treacherous', 'ferocious' and 'savage' were some of the adjectives used to describe the dreaded Maasai by nineteenth-century visitors to East Africa. Tales of their valour and ruthlessness were legion. Sir Charles Eliot, the commissioner or governor of the East African Protectorate at the turn of the century, wrote of them, 'They resemble the lion and the leopard, strong and beautiful beasts of prey that please the artistic sense, but are never any use, and often a very serious danger.' Few Arab or Swahili traders had dared to trespass into their vast territory for fear of being slain and, at a time when the golden age of African exploration and discovery was on the wane, no European had been bold or reckless enough to enter Maasai country. Kenya, as we know it today, remained concealed from foreign eyes – the last, and one of the most important, regions in tropical Africa to be explored.

While David Livingstone was preparing to return to Africa as Her Majesty's Consul for the east coast of Africa, and Richard Burton and John Speke were researching Lake Tanganyika and the Victoria Nyanza, Joseph Thomson was born in a tiny hamlet in the lowlands of Scotland. The year was 1858. Twenty-five years later, as an old Africa hand, he led a Royal Geographical Society expedition through the heart of Maasailand to Lake Victoria and back, a journey of adventure which was to place him among the greatest European travellers. Gentle and humane, his demeanour in Africa gave him a stature that was unique among the many successors of his schoolboy idol, David Livingstone.

Thomson was a born leader and a first-rate scholar who performed brilliantly in his university examinations in 1878, receiving medals in natural history and geology. In his formative years at school he had read avidly the narratives of the early explorers. Like Krapf before him, one of the first books which had excited his fertile imagination was *Bruce's Travels*, an account of journeys and adventures in Abyssinia written in 1790 by a fellow-Scot. The search for David Livingstone, and Henry Morton Stanley's account of how he found the great man, also influenced him enormously. Determined to explore Africa for himself, Thomson prepared for the hardships that lay ahead by sleeping on bare boards at home and by taking long walks in the rolling hills and lonely moors of the Scottish lowlands.

His chance to join an expedition came immediately after he left Edinburgh University. In April 1878 Alexander Keith Johnston offered his services to the Royal Geographical Society with a plan to open up a route from the East African coast to Victoria Nyanza (Lake Victoria) past the snowcapped mountains of Kilimanjaro and Kenya. However, his proposals were turned down as too dangerous, since only the previous year Dr J. M. Hildebrandt, a German botanist, had been prevented from travelling beyond Ukambani by truculent Maasai warriors. Instead, Johnston was asked to find a route from Dar-es-Salaam, now the main seaport of Tanzania, to Lake Nyasa and 'to make all practicable observations in meteorology, natural history and ethnology with a view to rendering as exact as circumstances permit, the information obtained regarding the region, its inhabitants and products'.

Thomson applied to join the expedition and was appointed the geologist-cum-naturalist, in effect becoming right-hand man to Johnston, who was a distinguished cartographer. They reached Zanzibar on 6th January 1879 but unusually heavy rains prevented their departure until the middle of May. Even then, the mainland was waterlogged and fever was rife. Within six weeks Johnston had died of dysentery and Thomson, at the tender age of twenty-one, assumed command. Three thousand miles and fourteen months later he returned to the coast in good health and excellent spirits. In carrying out the society's objectives, he became the first white man to visit Lake Nyasa from the north and to reach Lake Rukwa, then called Lake Leopold, from the east. He had crossed an immense tract of unknown country, throwing light on a variety of geographical subjects. The expedition had been unusual in many ways – there had been no major disasters which, hitherto, were considered an inevitable adjunct of African exploration; none of his porters had defected; no shots had been fired in anger; and only Johnston and one porter had died during the long arduous journey. Thomson had gone out as a boy and returned a man. In his maturity, he had gained qualities of common sense, courage and leadership which were to stand him in good stead in later years. He was modest about his scientific achievements but the experts were delighted. He had collected with remarkable judgment 200 species of flora, many of which were related to the known South African and Ethiopian genera, and forty-seven different species of freshwater and land shells, of which fifteen were new to science. This conchological collection was one of the most exciting ever to have been made and it enabled scientists to conclude that, before the upheavals which formed the Great Rift Valley sixteen million years ago, Lake Tanganyika had been a hollow in the bed of the sea. This they deduced from the fact that several of the freshwater shells he had collected there were exactly the same as their marine forms, or had developed only slight mutations from their counterparts in the sea.

The expedition had cost a thrifty £2,911 and was considered to have been one of the most successful to date. 'My fondest boast is not that I have travelled over hundreds of miles hitherto untrodden by the foot of a white man, but I have been able to do so as a Christian and Scotchman [sic] carrying everywhere goodwill and friendship, finding that a gentle word was more potent than gunpowder, and it was not necessary, even in Central Africa, to sacrifice the lives of men in order to throw light upon its dark corners.' Thomson returned to his native Scotland a hero, but found himself at a loose end there. The African exploration fund of the Royal Geographical Society had been wound up and no further opportunities to travel presented themselves until early in 1881. Then he received and accepted an unexpected invitation from the Sultan of Zanzibar, Sultan Seyyid Barghash, to investigate the commercial potential of coal and other mineral resources in the sultan's mainland territories along the coast of East Africa. There was reputed to be a coal-bearing region up the Rovuma River (the present border between

Tanzania and Mozambique), which had first been brought to light by David Livingstone in 1862. Subsequent reports by an Arab prospector of an abundance of high-quality coal excited the cupidity of Sultan Barghash, who greedily longed for the day when palace coffers would be filled to overflowing from mining royalties.

Thomson spent a boring fortnight in Zanzibar while 'the somewhat eccentric machinery of an Oriental government' decided what to do with him.

Just when he was settling down for a long wait, the sultan issued orders requiring him to leave the island within three days. He hurriedly recruited seventy-four men, most of whom had accompanied him on his journey the previous year, and set sail for Mikandani, an important entrepôt with a large community of Asian and Arab merchants where slaving was still very much in evidence. For two weeks, his party had to force its way inland through a barrier of dense tropical undergrowth to the upper reaches of the Rovuma River where, 120 miles from the sea, the country opened out, with tamarind and palm trees lining the banks of the three-quarter-mile wide river. Grotesque baobab trees of enormous girth, some 500 to 1,000 years old, dotted the landscape like gigantic inverted root vegetables of a prehistoric era; the hard outer shell of the pendulous fruits made excellent calabashes which were widely used as water buckets. The district was sparsely populated by the Makonde people – famous in more recent times for their fine abstract carvings – whose faces and bodies were heavily tattooed and whose women distended their upper lips in childhood by implanting a circular ring of wood. As a girl grew up, larger rings were inserted until, at the age of eighteen, the lip stood out at right-angles to the face in a manner which reminded the traveller of a duck-billed platypus.

The so-called coalfields that Thomson came across in a fairly restricted area near the confluence of the Rovuma and Luganda Rivers turned out to be a few irregular layers of bituminous shale, which would neither burn on its own nor decrease its bulk. An anthracite-like deposit found with the shale was combustible with great difficulty. Since the geological structure of the area did not point to rich coal-bearing seams, Thomson felt that there was no need to search further afield; so he turned back for the coast to complete a leisurely and uneventful journey of about 700 miles in barely eight weeks.

Sultan Barghash was furious to learn of Thomson's abortive attempt to find his El Dorado. He was convinced that Thomson was lying – deliberately concealing the truth from him for his own personal gain – though subsequent prospectors proved the geologist right. Failure had never been considered by the sultan; now he would lose both income, on which he had relied, and prestige with his court. In a fit of pique, he refused to send a boat to collect the expedition from Mikandani and when Thomson did eventually regain Zanzibar on board an overcrowded dhow, the sultan steadfastly ignored him for three months. Unwanted and unappreciated, with no prospect of being sent to assess the potential of other mineral deposits, Thomson decided to negotiate the abrogation of his two-year contract through Colonel Samuel Barrett Miles, the acting political agent and British Consul-General, in return for one half of the remaining salary to which he was entitled. The sultan rejected the proposal out-of-hand and countered by offering him no more than a return passage to England. The disillusioned Scot capitulated and returned home towards the end of December 1881 to another period of frustrating inactivity and uncertainty in a Victorian society from which he had largely become alienated.

In June 1882 Thomson was overjoyed to receive an invitation from the Royal Geographical Society to lead an expedition to East Africa whose aims were 'the ascertaining if a practicable direct route for European travellers exists through the Maasai country from any one of the East African ports to Victoria Nyanza, and to examine Mount Kenya; to gather data for constructing as complete a map as possible in a preliminary survey; and to make all practicable observations regarding the meteorology, geology, natural history, and ethnology of the regions traversed'. This was the country Johnston had longed to explore; it was also the opportunity for which Thomson had been praying. For him and the Royal Geographical Society it was the last unexplored region of Eastern Africa, promising a rich reward of interesting discovery. Doubtless, other expedition sponsors had in mind much broader imperial and commercial objectives than these.

Thomson was firmly of the opinion that penetration of Maasailand would not be too dangerous if normal precautions and care were exercised. As far as he knew, the Kilimanjaro region was in its normal state of tribal rivalry and slight insecurity, with no special conflicts in progress. Several East African missionaries shared his view. They believed a traveller of the right calibre – brave but not bullying, gentle but not cringing, with a knowledge of the Maa and Swahili languages – would succeed where others had failed. Although the Maasai may have been unprincipled and treacherous, the missionaries felt such conclusions had been drawn from traders who feared the Maasai too much for their reports to be entirely truthful. In any case, the Maasai were not so brave, or so foolhardy, as to attack a well-armed caravan without provocation. Nevertheless, there was a strong body of opinion in Britain and elsewhere that disagreed with Thomson. Stanley, for example, characterized the Maasai as a tribe that specially delighted in blood – and he was not thinking of their habit of drinking blood drawn from the jugular of their cattle! On one occasion he had stated publicly, 'I do not know in all my list of travels where you could become martyrs so quickly as in Maasai.'

While the Maasai can be said to have inconvenienced and delayed foreign exploration of that part of East Africa known today as Kenya, their unbridled supremacy had kept commercial slave trafficking in check prior to the signing of the rather ineffective Anglo-Zanzibari treaty of 1873, which made illegal the export of slaves from mainland Africa to the islands of Zanzibar and Pemba or elsewhere. The Maasai themselves never bought or sold slaves; their custom was to adopt women and children whom they abducted in battle into their own families and to treat them well. When boys grew up, they were allowed to inter-marry and acquire cattle, but they never gained the social status of a true Maasai elder. This humane approach is one reason why there are not too many pure Maasai left today.

The Royal Geographical Society was surprisingly mean with its funding for such an important expedition. Thomson estimated that it would cost £4,000 to sponsor, despite his willingness to forgo a salary – whereupon the society allocated half that sum. He argued that he would be unable to enhance geographical or scientific knowledge significantly unless more monies were voted for the purpose. 'All I expect to be able to do is to penetrate up the River Pangani to Kilimanjaro and then without any delay straight to the Lake, returning very much the same way.' Perhaps a warning that German scientists coveted the important geographical prizes of the region swayed the society for, in November 1882, a further £600 was approved on condition that Thomson promised to explore, and report on, Mount Kenya; it subsequently disbursed another £400 when he was forced to seek additional funds in Zanzibar. Some sixteen months later the society was clearly delighted that the expedition had overspent by a mere £188, thanks to Thomson's frugality.

Thomson was confronted with two pieces of bad news when he reached Zanzibar on 26th January 1883. First, he learned that Dr Gustav Fischer, a

German naturalist sponsored by the Hamburg Geographical Society, had left secretly for Kilimanjaro and Maasailand. '[The report] took me not a little aback as I thought of the ground being cut away from my feet in this unexpected manner. I had to console myself with the reflection that the field was large and some pickings might after all fall to my share.' Second, he learned with sadness of the death of Chuma, his outstanding headman, who had done so much to make his previous safaris relatively trouble-free. 'My first business was to secure my headman on whom so much depends for the success of an African expedition.' Makatubu, one of his assistant headman in Central Africa, was available and Thomson was delighted to sign him on again. However, Makatubu lacked tact in dealing with the men under him and was considered unsuitable for promotion. Thomson also recruited Brahim – nicknamed 'Ali Ngombe', Ali the Bull – who had been one of his best porters, albeit a troublemaker. Thomson reasoned that if he promoted Brahim to a position of responsibility, he might turn both his good and bad traits in his master's favour. It was a calculated risk which proved an unqualified success. 'He had a remarkable influence over the men. They were afraid of him, yet they loved him for his jolly, rollicking disposition. Where formerly he delighted to raise trouble and mutiny, he now became the terror of all cantankerous individuals.' Looking round for a headman, Thomson was very pleased to secure the services of the experienced Muinyi Sera, Stanley's headman during his journey across Africa in 1875–6. Only much later did he realize that Muinyi was incompetent; he was also woefully lazy and seemed content 'to be looked upon as purely ornamental'.

Thomson had been influenced not to take another European on the expedition, partly on account of the size of the society's budget and partly by his own quest for fame. However, his attitude changed in Zanzibar when he was introduced to a 26-year-old Maltese by the name of James Martin. Baptized Antonio Martini, Martin was a sail-maker by profession who had travelled to the far corners of the globe. Six years earlier at Bombay, he had signed up as crew on an American ship bound for East Africa. Close to Zanzibar it ran aground and, by good fortune, he was rescued by a British naval frigate, HMS *London*, which was at the time on one of her regular anti-slavery patrols off the island. He quickly attracted the attention of Lieutenant Lloyd Mathews, the ship's captain, who was later seconded from the Royal Navy in the rank of major-general to train a regular army of local people for the sultan. Mathews personally arranged for him to be employed as a handyman by the Church Missionary Society at Frere Town, Mombasa – a centre for runaway slaves. Martin was a man of great natural ability, a gifted linguist and, seemingly, a perfect second-in-command for the ex-pedition, even though he was unable to read or write. Thomson employed him on the spur of the moment for the princely sum of £4 a week. 'I am happy to say that I had never reason to regret my decision ... from first to last [he] was most respectful, had no opinions of his own as to what should be done or not done, was ever prompt to carry out orders, and always anxious to do something ... I cannot speak too highly in Martin's praise, and if it were ever my lot to go back to Africa, I would seek for no better assistant,' The importance of Martin's role in the expedition was great, though it can never be estimated exactly; it is true, however, that Thomson would have been hard-pressed to accomplish his objectives without the support of a competent assistant whose skill as a caravan leader became legendary in his own lifetime. In later years, Martin was appointed district commissioner, Ravine – then within the jurisdiction of Uganda – until he was transferred under a cloud for trading in ivory. When war broke out in East Africa, he served with distinction in the intelligence section of the British Army. He died in Lisbon in 1924.

Thomson was in a hurry to get organized; he was more upset than he cared to admit about Fischer's expedition, which had pre-empted his own. First, though, he had to seek advice on the least dangerous routes through Maasailand, the type of trade goods he should take with him and the best place from which to leave. This information was available only on the mainland, to which he set sail with Martin and his headman on 1st February. Luck was on his side at Pangani, a coastal town which lies north of Dar-es-Salaam. He met Fischer's headman by chance and learned of the problems involved in recruiting porters there. This had been his own intention, for the porters of Pangani were well acquainted with the languages, manners and customs of up-country tribes. Moreover, they were accustomed to a meat diet, and to carrying loads and undertaking marches which would have made the pampered and spoiled Zanzibaris look aghast. For all that, they were thoroughly unreliable – as Fischer found out to his cost. He had suffered from mass desertions, with no less than fifty porters in chains at the time. It seems he was partly to blame for this predicament, having unwisely recruited an undisciplined rag-tag by advancing barter materials in return for a percentage of the ivory they were expected to purchase inland.

Thomson gleaned other useful information during his short visit. 'That evening was spent among the Indian merchants who received me hospitably and gave me most valuable information regarding the goods required up-country.' Sultan Seyyid Said, Sultan of Muscat from 1806 to 1856 and hereditary ruler of the East African coast, had transferred his court to Zanzibar in 1840. No immigrants were more welcome to his new capital than the Hindu 'Banyans' from India. They were loathed and resented by the established Arab traders of the island, who quickly realized that their hitherto undisputed hold over the economy of the region would be under serious threat. By the time Thomson appeared on the scene 100 years ago, the Indian merchants had a stranglehold over the Swahili traders, who spent what money they earned without a care for the morrow. In return for financial support, the traders had to part with most of their hard-won profits to the Indian moneylenders, whose policy it was to demand payment in ivory at the end of each trip on highly unfavourable terms.

Thomson decided to walk from Pangani to Mombasa along the coast 'as much to acquaint myself with the general appearance of the country, as in the hope of adding to my knowledge of the requirements of my expedition'. At Tanga, 'charmingly situated on the upper raised beach among groves of coconuts and with a pretty creek running into land which forms a capacious harbour', he reluctantly agreed to give up walking any further, in deference to Martin who had badly blistered his heels and was in no fit state to continue on foot. A delay of twenty-four hours ensued while Thomson negotiated the hire of a number of different dhows from reluctant and evasive Arab captains.

I have now at one time or another had a considerable amount of experience in dhow-sailing; but this trip, though by no means the longest, was by far the most awful in its varied combination of miseries. I am by no means fastidious; I have not a very delicate sense of smell, and my African experiences have not made me over squeamish; but in this case I must confess neither my senses nor my feelings were proof against the experiences of that dhow voyage. Imagine a curiously-shaped boat capable of carrying about thirty tons, partially decked aft, high in the stern and low in the bow, suggesting to the nervous mind a suicidal tendency in the shape of a determined purpose of diving beneath the first advancing wave. A single mast, fifteen to twenty feet high, supports an unwieldy lateen sail of dimensions enormous compared with the size of the craft, and held by rotten coconut fibre ropes which not infrequently startle the crew and passengers – if they do no worse – by breaking and letting their whole burden crash down on deck. The water leaks at innumerable points, continually requiring several men to bale night and day. Then, from stern to stem, there rises a combination of abominable smells truly sickening.

Rotting wood, rancid coconut oil, stinking bilge water and an all-pervasive stench of stale sweat turned Thomson's stomach and, as night fell, a horde of tenacious little creatures – lice, bugs and rats – made a bee-line for an unfamiliar pale-skinned subject. He cursed his misfortune the following morning when high seas brought on an instant bout of seasickness. This added greatly to his suffering, as their dhow tossed and wallowed in a storm for twelve hours. Had it not been for Martin's navigational skills they would almost certainly have struck a reef, bringing the explorer's life to an abrupt end, for he was a non-swimmer. As it was, Brahim, his trusted headman, still had to save Thomson from drowning because the leaky canoe they commandeered to bring him ashore, 'in shape not unlike a dog's hind-leg', capsized in the surf. Thomson reached *terra firma* and vowed never to set foot

in a dhow again. True to form, he completed the rest of his journey to Mombasa on foot.

For many years [Mombasa] *has gradually dwindled away in size and importance till now it occupies but a second-rate position among the coast towns. Even as a trading centre for caravans to the Maasai country and the tribes beyond, it has fallen far behind Pangani, Tanga and Vanga chiefly owing to a series of disasters – caravans almost annihilated, and bad returns for their investments ... The island of Mombasa is formed by the division of the picturesque creek which here runs deep into the land terminating at the base of the Rabai Hills ... the northern branch of the Mombasa creek forms a splendid harbour, which is protected from the swell of the north-east monsoon by the coral-line bar on which Vasco da Gama was so nearly lost ... Except for the fort and some wells, there is little left to tell of the Portuguese occupation. Everywhere ruins of houses and mosques tell the tale of decayed grandeur, of the loss of former spirit, energy and enterprise. Mud huts are replacing the well-built dwellings of the Mazrui period. The Arabs are leaving the town as rats leave a sinking ship, and a general want of life characterized the aspect of this ancient and interesting city.*

Mombasa was still innocent of the steam age and the white man's telegraph poles when Thomson wove his way through the labyrinth of narrow streets on 8th February 1883. The succeeding century has turned the sleepy old-world place into a bustling gateway to the interior of Kenya and the land-locked countries beyond. The change in its fortunes began with the building of the Uganda railway in 1895 – barely a year after the last lion hunt had taken place on the outskirts of the old town. The pace of development gathered momentum after the country gained independence from Britain in 1963 when the picturesque coastline, with its golden beaches and safe bathing in the warm waters of the Indian Ocean, became a popular tourist resort.

Thomson's first call was on the *liwali* or governor, the sultan's personal representative, who plied him with coffee and sherbet, the indispensable accompaniments of all meetings with Arabs, enquired about his health, as if he had known him all his life, and glibly promised full cooperation and whatever assistance was needed. After these shallow pleasantries, Thomson visited the missionaries and found in the Reverend Thomas Wakefield 'a lively companion, boiling over with good spirits, full of hearty laughter, puns and genial stories – in fact, the very prince of African good fellows'.

Thomson formulated plans in Zanzibar to make Mombasa his point of departure, despite hearing of the havoc wreaked on the last three caravans that had set out to the Victoria Nyanza; in consequence, none had ventured forth from Mombasa into Maasailand for eighteen months. This was a challenge he eagerly accepted. Moreover, the route was far enough removed from Fischer's for him to explore new country and not be seen following in another's footsteps. He also decided to recruit his porters at Zanzibar, although this proved extremely difficult. Several large caravans had just left for the Congo, now Zaire, taking most of the good men with them; in any case, the very idea of travelling through Maasailand frightened most Zanzibaris.

The out-look was not encouraging but I was determined not to be beat. Not a man having presented himself, I offered as an inducement a dollar a month extra for those who gave satisfaction by their behaviour. This brought a few men to my standard; but little progress was made till it became noised abroad that I was prepared to receive whoever offered, no questions asked or certificates required – medical or otherwise. Then and only then, a flood of vagabondage let itself loose upon me – the blind and the lame, the very refuse of Zanzibar rascaldom . . .

Within a fortnight the party was ready – 110 men, two white Muscat donkeys (his ambulance corps, named 'Nil desperandum' and 'Excelsior'), one dark half-breed donkey, goods and stores. His cook, a mission boy named Mark Wellington, was well-intentioned and honest but atrociously slow: 'he spoiled more of my meals than I care to think of now'. In contrast Thomson's personal servant, Songoro, was 'simply perfection'.

Exactly five weeks after he had first arrived on the island, Thomson had the satisfaction of watching the Victoria Nyanza and Mount Kenya expedition clear harbour under the command of Martin for the full day-and-night sail to Mombasa. He himself remained behind for three more days in a futile attempt to recruit a few more reliable men and to gather up those who had failed to embark on the appointed day. Now, with his round of farewells over, he boarded HM Steam Tug No. 11, otherwise known as the *Suez*, accompanied by Colonel Samuel Miles. Thomson was a dreadful sailor at the best of times and the motion of the small tug in monsoon weather made him violently seasick; but he sought comfort in the fact that he was not alone in his misery. The august representative of Her Britannic Majesty in East Africa was anything but a dignified spectacle by the time they entered Mombasa harbour twenty-four hours later; his face had blistered and peeled as he sat, drenched and nauseous, braving the mountainous seas.

Thomson completed the preparations for his departure in next to no time. There were only one or two loose ends to tie up and one important member of the expedition still to be recruited. At first sight, the Reverend Wakefield introduced him to just the right man. Muhinna, an experienced ivory trader, was taken on as guide and interpreter. He apparently had all the right attributes, with a fluency in the Maa and Kamba languages and a thorough knowledge of up-country trading routes, having penetrated Maasailand on at least twenty occasions. 'Without some such man it would have been impossible to have gone six marches from the coast, so utterly unacquainted were my men with this tract of country, and so different were the manners and customs from those prevalent further south. I had, therefore, as it seemed to me, much reason for self-congratulation.' However, the seeds of doubt were soon sown in his mind. Reports reached him that Muhinna was exercising an unhealthy influence over his Zanzibari porters, which necessitated a hurried return from a visit he was making to the missionaries at Rabai to put matters right. Muhinna remained a thorn in Thomson's side for most of the journey and, at the end of it, was put on trial for treason.

CHAPTER 7

Rebuff at the border

Mwenda mbio hujikwaa dole
A person who is in (too much of) a hurry stubs his toe

Swahili proverb

O N 15TH MARCH 1883, the expedition was ready. 'The signal was given. There was a wild rush and scramble for the head of the caravan, the customary incentive shouts to "hurry up" and a running fire of farewells as, headed by our flag, the long file of men passed through Rabai village, leaving behind the cocoa-crowned [*sic*] heights, the verdant ridges with their stern, sentinel-like fan palms and the cultivated outer slopes, and away into the *nyika* or "wilderness" beyond.'

Taking his men according to rank, first and foremost came Thomson's caravan assistant, James Martin. Comparatively short of limb, though stout, he had the somewhat ungraceful gait of a sailor. His dark hair and eyes and swarthy complexion indicated at once that he came from a Mediterranean race. Next came Muhinna, on whose honesty Thomson depended for a successful attempt to penetrate Maasai country. Then followed Muinyi Sera, short and advancing in years; Makatubu, tall and muscular; Kacheche, 'the detective', of below-average height and characterized by a sly expression; Brahim, 'the bullock', as faithful as a bulldog and almost as unprepossessing in appearance; and Mzee Mauledi, the last of the headmen, quiet and steady with tell-tale traces of Arab blood in his veins. Bedue, bold and strong but slothful, captained the ten *askaris*, the soldiers, who were the pick of the caravan and whose duties were to act as night guards, policemen, hunters and general assistants to the headmen. Finally came the rank and file – an indescribable rabble of 113 porters. Thomson knew he had taken a gamble recruiting them in the way he did, and they exasperated him beyond belief. 'The heat told with greatest effect after their life of laziness and debauchery on the coast.' They threw down their loads and lay in the path groaning, pretending they were dying. They constantly demanded water and, when no one was looking, attempted to run away, for their sole intention was to get their hands on three months' advance wages and abscond before reaching the point of no return. Precautions were taken to prevent this happening – including instructions to his sentries to shoot deserters on sight. Even so, two managed to escape on the second night out and many more would have followed suit had Thomson not deliberately spread fictitious stories about Maasai warriors to their rear. Since they had already passed through an area strewn with skulls – the scene of a pitched battle between the Maasai and the Wanyika – the rumour had a ring of truth to it.

Their route took them in a north-westerly direction through Duruma country, 'a perfect marvel of vegetable monstrosities', to Taru where deep rain-water pools were invariably found in natural rock cavities on the two hilltops. 'We for the first time in four days enjoyed the glorious luxury of a wash in good water. So far we had only met water that had been characterized by an amount of "body" and "bouquet" that required all the pangs of thirst to make us drink it.' Thenceforth they were travelling in the waterless *nyika* country now known as the Taru Desert.

The dense jungle, the grassy glades, the open forest disappear, and their place is taken by what may be called a skeleton forest. Weird and ghastly is the aspect of the greyish-coloured trees and bushes; for they are almost destitute of tender, waving branch or quivering leaf. No pliant twig or graceful foliage responds to the pleasing influence of the passing breeze. Stern and unbending, they present rigid arms or formidable thorns, as if bidding defiance to drought or storm. To heighten the sombre effect of the scene, dead trees are observable in every direction raising their shattered forms among the living, unable to hold their own in the struggle for existence.

The porters toiled hour after hour through this uninhabited Hades, panting and perspiring under the fierce rays of the tropical sun. The red lateritic soil became so hot at midday that their bare feet developed blisters; overhanging branches forced them to stoop low under their heavy head loads, and 'wait-a-bit' thorn – the aptly named *Acacia mellifera* bush with a double barb – tore their flimsy *kanzus* and gave them nasty scratches, from which blood oozed and trickled down their legs until it blended with the runnels of their perspiration. For all the obvious reasons, everyone was desperately eager to reach Ndara Hill, now Sagalla Hill, some eighty miles north-west of Rabai, where the tangled thorn scrub gave way to extensive plantations tilled by the congenial Wataita people. But even those, like Thomson, who have cursed this abominable country, have also found it at least fleetingly beautiful when the foliage begins to show fresh green shoots at the start of the long rains.

'We moved up to camp amidst the firing of guns and the wondering cries of the native damsels and married women . . . [who] ran alongside with curious stares and excited laughter, their pendant breasts flapping against their bosoms like half-empty, loosely attached leather bottles.' Thomson ordered camp to be pitched at the base of the hill beside a cool stream 'which splashed and tumbled down the rugged face of Ndara and invited us by its merry music to the luxury of a bath. Unfortunately, we had to restrain our ardent desire to strip at once, not on account of the feelings of the Wataita, but in consequence of our own which had not yet become quite hardened to the idea of appearing in *puris naturalibis*'! He was unimpressed by the Wataita men he saw, who were short in stature and very skinny. 'Their dress is a scanty cloth indifferently wound about their loins or hung from one shoulder to flutter in the breeze. A few ornaments of brass, small native-made chains, and beads are noticeable around the neck and arms. Their weapons are a knife, a long spatulate-shaped sword and a bow and arrow.' On the other hand, the girls won his grudging admiration, being well-proportioned (we would say shapely), with a ready smile and coyish look. He was struck by their love for beads. They adorned themselves with several hundred strings weighing anything up to thirty pounds, which were worn as massive collars round the neck, draped over the shoulders, bound round the waist and threaded through ringlets hanging from a circular patch of hair on the occiput of an otherwise cleanly shaven head. Their costume was a small square piece of hide about the size of a ladies' pocket handkerchief which was also decorated with brightly coloured beads. It was suspended from a cord belt, like an apron, in front of their bodies in contrast to a beaded tassel-tail which fell over their buttocks.

Early contact with missionaries and travellers induced the Wataita to give up their traditional styles of dress and forsake ancestor worship, which formed part of their rich cultural heritage, towards the end of the last century. In days of old, when a married man with children died he was buried in a sitting position to facilitate the removal of his skull after decomposition of the corpse had taken place about one year later. After exhumation, the skull was taken secretly to an ancestral shrine, deep in the forest, where it was placed beside those of its ancestors in a cave or rock crevice. The spirits of the dead were believed to live on for ever, bringing trouble and distress to future generations unless periodic sacrifices and offerings were made to propitiate them.

Thomson left Martin in charge of the caravan for the time that it took him to climb Sagalla Hill and see something of the surrounding countryside before taking bearings for his next march. The whole of the upper part of the hill was densely populated and *shambas*, or smallholdings, of cassava, sweet potatoes, sugar-cane and bananas covered the ground like a patchwork quilt. This form of peasant agriculture survives today all over the country and helps to feed a rapidly growing population. As time goes by, the parcels of land are becoming smaller and more fragmented, hence reducing the farmers' capacity to grow cash crops.

Thomson paid a courtesy call on the Reverend J. Alfred Wray at the Anglican mission station which had been founded earlier that year, and rejoined Martin a day later, to catch his Wataita porters kicking up a diabolical row over the quality of cloth they had been given in payment for carrying rice from the coast. For a few minutes the scene was ugly; the slightest accident, such as the firing of a gun, would have started a fight. Thomson moved quickly and positioned himself, unarmed, between the two equally excited parties. Then, by mutually making concessions, the problem was smoothed over.

Hongo, a crafty system of extorting blackmail in a most infuriating manner, had to be paid to village chiefs and elders as a prerequisite for allowing the expedition safe passage to the southern flanks of the Taita Hills. Thomson spent a day climbing one of the hills upon which grew 'a glorious profusion of

tree ferns, brackens, club mosses, orchids, heaths and other plants of a temperate aspect'. Then, narrowly averting bloodshed with the Wataita who had brazenly stolen two guns from the middle of his camp in broad daylight, he strode out through game-rich country to complete the first leg of his journey.

Sixteen days after leaving the coast, the expedition reached Taveta. '[From] the burning heat and barren wastes of the *nyika* to the leafy labyrinths and bosky bowers of the little African Arcadia of Taveta ... it was as if we had passed from a purgatory to a paradise.' Taveta was a densely forested area with exotic vegetation roughly one mile wide and seven miles long, lying just north of Lake Jipe on what is now the Kenya/Tanzania border. Palms, flowering shrubs and irrigated plantations owed their existence to the rich alluvial soils washed down from the slopes of Kilimanjaro and to the perennial Lumi River. Taveta had always been a place of great importance to traders from the coast, situated as it was on the very threshold of Maasai country yet offering perfect security. There was an abundance of food grown by the 'honest, hospitable and peace-loving' Taveta people, who were closely related to the Wataita and Chagga. Fish, fowl, eggs, mutton or goat, tomatoes, sweet potatoes, yams, manioc or cassava, green maize, sugar-cane, golden bananas and vegetables of all kinds were plentiful in season. Thomson found 'grateful shelter and cool water in the shady depths of one of the most charming forest tracts in the whole of East Africa'. Modern Taveta has changed beyond all recognition. Sadly, the relentless pressure of economic development has all but destroyed the unique indigenous forest which so enthralled the pioneer travellers. One hundred years on, it has been replaced by extensive banana plantations which supply truckloads of green, yellow and red bananas to Mombasa and Nairobi every day of the week.

Thomson delayed his departure for Maasailand at the instigation of the small colony of Swahili traders who made Taveta their headquarters. They told him bluntly that his bales of calico would be rejected by the ultra-conservative pastoralists unless the material was cut into six-foot lengths, trimmed with a strip of crimson cloth and frayed to the edges to form a fringe; so his men had to set to and stitch 300 *naiberes*, or capes, in this way. Then his twenty-nine sacks of coloured beads had to be strung into standard twenty-two-inch lengths, which would have been an impossible undertaking on the march. In all 60,000 strings were laboriously threaded on to the extraordinarily strong fibres of doum palm leaves, *Hyphaene coriacea*. This palm is common around Taveta and was of great benefit to the community. Its leaves were favoured for thatching houses and weaving food baskets; slivers from the outside of its fruit are edible; a strong toddy can be brewed from its sap, and its seeds are a source of vegetable ivory from which coat buttons were once made. Despite close supervision, dire threats and a liberal use of the cane, almost 10 per cent of his entire stocks of beads were stolen by the light-fingered porters during threading. Thomson regretted the necessity for beating wrongdoers 'but bitter experience has taught me that corporal punishment cannot on any account be dispensed with, if the traveller intends to be master of his caravan'.

During discussions with another group of traders who had just returned from Maasailand with the loss of 100 men through disease, Thomson confirmed his earlier misgivings that his caravan was far too small to penetrate a hostile region in reasonable safety. The traders never dreamed of entering

Maasai country with less than 300 men and always took more if circumstances permitted. As there were no recognized footpaths or permanent watering places in the district, they cautioned him of the folly of relying on just one guide, however honest and trustworthy he might be. Anyhow, the Maasai were renowned for being great talkers as well as fighters, and a lone interpreter could not possibly be expected to cope with the protracted negotiations which would be needed to secure passage rights through their land. The financial constraints imposed on Thomson by the Royal Geographical Society prevented further large-scale recruitment but he did engage one more guide and interpreter. Saidi had fallen on bad times but Thomson recognized his experience. He had been caravan leader some twenty years earlier to an unsuccessful expedition into Maasailand organized by Baron von der Decken, a Hanoverian naturalist and traveller, who was murdered by Somalis along the Juba River in 1865.

Refreshed by a pleasant two-week interlude, the expedition got under way again, with his men looking longingly towards the coast and Thomson, with equal eagerness, towards the setting sun and the unknown. He had been warned to steer well clear of Mandara, the senior chief of the Chagga people whose territory extended over much of the southern slopes of Kilimanjaro, on account of his reputation for greed and treachery. When the chief sent him a present of a cow and a goat with a personal messenger who implored him to visit, Thomson ignored the invitation. However, he was flummoxed when reports reached him of 2,000 Maasai warriors on the warpath to their front. To retreat would mean his men would desert him; to advance would be to fight against warriors with heated blood and to have his caravan routed. He chose the most sensible plan open to him by quickly changing course and taking shelter with Mandara. Only much later did he find out that the information was false; Muhinna, so it seems, had concocted the story with an eye to driving him into the hands of the capricious chief and robbing him.

Thomson left all his porters under Martin's command in a fortified camp close to Moshi and set out for Mandara's village accompanied by the unreliable Muhinna and Brahim, the one African in whom he placed implicit trust. The village occupied the top of a narrow ridge formed by a deep valley on either side. Skilfully constructed channels drew water from the upper reaches of the clear mountain stream and provided the area with permanent irrigation.

Mandara's residence consisted of a number of round huts in which more than fifty wives were housed. His own private abode was rectangular in shape and built after the style of coastal houses; the walls were plastered with a mixture of dung and clay and the roof was of grass thatch. It was here that he received his honoured guests and stowed away his valuables. Thomson found an imposing, powerfully built man of unmistakable intelligence. 'He had an eye like an eagle's but only one – the other had lost its light for ever.' Mandara was surrounded by:

a group of fine-looking, aristocratic Wa-chagga ... enveloped in voluminous lengths of cotton dyed in ochre ... I explained where I had come from and where I was going; I stated that, having been compelled to leave the trade-route owing to the Maasai, I proposed to camp at the boundary of his domains, and that, having heard so much about his great achievements as a warrior, of his princely character, and his delight in receiving strangers from the coast, I could not possibly pass so near him without giving myself the pleasure of coming to see him!

In the midst of this eloquent harangue, I was rather taken aback by seeing his eye become suddenly fixed on my foot. Then his mouth took a well-known shape, and I was startled to hear a familiar sound generally employed by vulgar little boys to express unbounded astonishment and incredulity. In short, Mandara emitted a long-drawn whistle. Thinking he had discovered a snake in unpleasant proximity to my foot, I suddenly drew it back, and began also staring at the same place. Seeing nothing, I looked up. Then we both laughed – why, I don't know – and a period was put to my speech by a series of questions about my boots which had drawn forth the expression of astonishment. Whistling in that manner was his customary expressive manner of showing wonder or admiration. Our interview, which turned out pleasant, was accompanied by continual ejections of saliva, squirted with great skill from between his teeth, and by a continual quaffing of beer.

Mandara turned out to be the perfect host for three nights; nothing was too much trouble for him. Not only was he hospitable and generous, providing his guest with eggs, goats, bananas and fresh milk, but he laid on guides to the foothills of Kilimanjaro. At 9,000 feet, Thomson made a small plant

collection, including gladiolus and species allied to the buttercup and dock families. The explorer was so delighted that, in return, he invited Mandara to visit his camp, where he showed off his armoury and demonstrated his scientific instruments. A galvanic battery – a voltaic cell that converted chemical energy into an electrical current – 'threw him into fits of astonishment till his eagle eye gleamed with covetousness and he spat and whistled himself dry, requiring incessant libations of *pombe* [local beer] to sustain him'. Mandara took great delight in ordering his sub-chiefs and warriors to submit to the electrical current and gloated over their evident, though suppressed, terror of the strange tingling sensation which, but for their self-control in the presence of their chief, would have had them writhing in agony on the ground. In showing Mandara all his possessions 'with a thoughtlessness for which there could be no excuse', Thompson soon realized he had aroused the cupidity of the chief. To satisfy it, he quickly put aside a snider rifle, a revolver, four flasks of gunpowder, one length of *merikani*, one blue cloth and several other brightly coloured materials. 'Are these the presents for my *askaris?*' Mandara enquired scornfully. 'Or are you offering me a Zanzibar-made gun only fit for a porter?' With unmistakable aplomb, he deemed the presents insulting. What he wanted were European articles befitting his greatness! Thomson was left speechless as Mandara stormed out of camp in high dudgeon muttering thinly veiled threats of preventing further progress. The potential seriousness of the situation forced the young explorer to return to the chief's village the following morning and make a peace offering of his own double-barrelled shotgun (a sad loss, as he had carried it on his two previous expeditions), a steel box, a suit of thick tweed and a pair of good-quality shoes. They were accepted with alacrity. Mandara had won the day, but Thomson just wished that he could have seen the old rascal hobbling about in his shoes!

Thomson moved on to Kibongoto, south-west of Kilimanjaro, and found to his profound dismay that Fischer had taken the route to the north which he himself had planned to follow. This was of little consequence, however, compared with the other news. Apparently, Fischer's porters had fought the Maasai only a few days before Thomson's arrival, resulting in bloodshed on both sides. The prospects for advancing were gloomy. 'How can I continue with under 150 men when Fischer has been driven to use firearms with a caravan more than twice my strength?' he lamented. He was kept in suspense for three days, awaiting word from the Maasai. In the afternoon of the fourth day:

from the labyrinths of the surrounding forest a fine musical chant was raised. The word was passed round that the Maasai had come. Seizing our guns in one hand, and a tuft of grass in the other, in token that we were prepared to fight, but meant peace, we proceeded outside to hear our fate. Passing through the forest, we soon set our eyes upon the dreaded warriors that had so long been the subject of my waking dreams, and I could not but involuntarily exclaim 'what splendid fellows!' as I surveyed a band of the most peculiar race of men to be found in all Africa.

After a most ceremonious greeting performed with much gravity and aristocratic dignity, their great shovel-headed spears were stuck in the ground, their bullock's hide shields rested against them on their sides, and then the oil- and clay-bedaubed warriors assumed a sitting posture, with their knees drawn up to their chins, and their small neat kidskin mantles enveloping them. We on our part took position opposite them, holding our guns in our hands. I, of course, as became my dignity, occupied a camp stool.

After a few words among themselves in a low tone, a spokesman arose, leisurely took a spear in his left hand to lean upon, and then with his knobkerry as an orator's baton, he proceeded to deliver his message with all the ease of a professional speaker. With profound astonishment I watched this son of the desert, as he stood before me, speaking with a natural fluency and grace, a certain sense of the gravity and importance of his position, and a dignity beyond all praise.

The Maasai spokesman sketched the story of Fischer's arrival and of the fight which had ensued, laying great emphasis on the fact that a woman had been killed. This was an unheard-of event in the annals of their quarrels with Swahili traders. The warriors had long debated whether they should oppose Thomson's passage through their land, but in the end their unanimous decision – and by tradition all major decisions had to be unanimous – was to give his party a cautious welcome. Thomson was heartened by this excellent news and adjourned to his quarters, closely followed by the *il-murran*, the warriors, twirling their heavy spears with a flick of the wrist as they loped after him. They showed an intelligent interest in the expedition's stores and cast a calculating eye over the trade goods on which they could confidently expect to lay their hands in a day or so. Their aloof, rather arrogant, behaviour struck Thomson as unique because 'they indulged in none of the obtrusive, vulgar inquisitiveness or aggressive impertinence which make the traveller's life a burden to him among other native tribes'.

On 3rd May Thomson took the important step of crossing the threshold of the dangerous region. Leaving the forest near Kibongoto, his caravan emerged on to a vast treeless plain where he marvelled at the immense herds of game. These animals had been hunted so rarely that they had not yet come to regard human beings as enemies. Buffalo, wildebeest, zebra, hartebeest and impala just stood their ground and stared, within easy gunshot range, as his men moved in single file towards the snow-fed Enkare Nairobi, the cold-water river, through rank grass dampened by an early morning dew. In the distance, he could make out a Maasai *manyatta*, a homestead, set proudly on a ridge to command an uninterrupted view of the surrounding countryside. White wood-smoke hung lazily above the huts, which were reminiscent of giant loaves of brown bread partially concealed in luxuriant pastures. The structures were squat and windowless with individual entrances and contiguous end walls; these formed a circle some 100 yards in diameter, save for three or four narrow pathways which were blocked with acacia branches and always well guarded against surprise attack. Cattle, sheep and goats were herded into the open space in the centre of the *manyatta* at night for, in those days, there was no encircling *zariba*, or thorn fence, as has become the modern practice.

Thomson was jubilant. The reception he and his men had been given seemed too good to be true – as subsequent events proved it to be. The caravan deliberately halted a discreet distance from the *manyattas*, yet his porters did not get the chance to construct a stout perimeter fence of acacia scrub before men and women from the whole neighbourhood flocked into camp, turning the place into a shambles. Orders were quickly given for tents to be pitched and for stores and trade goods to be hidden away from their covetous designs – but to little effect. 'Party after party, each from its own

district, arrived and received tribute and my spirits sank as I saw load after load disappear. How could we ever hope to travel many days further if such was to be our fate?' Little did he realize at the time that this was robbery without violence – another premeditated attempt by Muhinna to prevent the expedition from travelling any further. By late afternoon the largesse had been concluded and Thomson was forced to parade before the assembled company despite a recurrent attack of fever. He was pummelled and pinched, his hair was pulled, his boots were examined with intense curiosity – they were thought to be hoofs – but the final indignity came when a warrior tried to turn up his trouser leg to see what was hidden beneath. It became all too apparent that his first impressions of the noble race had been hopelessly over-optimistic; he had been carried away by the excitement of the occasion.

He was thunderstruck the following day by the unexpected news that the Maasai were planning to revenge the Fischer affray even though 'blood money' had been paid promptly by the German-led expedition. Thomson strongly suspected Muhinna and Saidi of double-dealing, but there was nothing he could do to turn the tables in his favour. They had warned him that warriors would attack them on the morrow and he could not simply ignore the threat of bloodshed. Heartbreaking though it was, he resolved to strike camp that night and retreat. In the safety of Taveta he would be able to lick his wounds and carefully plan his next move.

The night set in gloomy and dark. A black pall of clouds overspread the heavens. Some rain sputtered and with intense satisfaction we saw a storm brewing. Two hours after sunset, the word was given to pack up. Not a sound broke the stillness as each man buckled his belt, caught up his gun, and shouldered his load by the light of the numerous camp fires. Then, when all was ready, more wood was thrown on the fires, and we glided out into the blackness of night. . .

One thing I saw clearly, that it would never do to sit down and mope over my misfortunes. Prompt action was required. More goods must be got, and a few more men; Muhinna, who, I was convinced, had acted traitorously, must be taken to the coast, and, if a substitute could be got, left there. At first I thought of sending Martin to do this work, as I was afraid of the consequences of leaving my now demoralized men in his charge; but on second thoughts, I concluded that I would be able to do the work quicker and more satisfactorily, while I was convinced that inaction at the present low ebb of my affairs would kill me.

When the porters learned of Thomson's plans they threatened to desert, so quick action had to be taken to restore discipline. Personal weapons were placed under lock and key to prevent mutiny, and the ringleaders were punished to bring the rest of his men back to their senses. Within forty-eight hours the situation had returned to normal and he was able to leave.

Thomson's bitter disappointment at being turned back by the Maasai in dubious circumstances provoked him into making a 200-mile forced march to Mombasa with ten hand-picked followers in just six days. He took a masochistic pride in outdistancing his men and boasted that no African could ever beat him, either for a short, quick spurt, or a long, steady trial of endurance. In three days his party covered the first ninety-five miles to Sagalla Hill, where he found time to pay the Reverend Wray a quick visit 'in his mountain sinecure, looking healthy, and evidently, not becoming thin over his missionary labours'. The frustrated explorer must be forgiven for making these rather cynical remarks. Alfred Wray spent a total of thirty years among the Taita and most certainly did suffer distress. Soon after he first arrived at Sagalla the rains failed and questions began to circulate. 'Is it the presence of the white man that is keeping back the rain? Why has he come here anyway? He has not given us presents. He does not buy our ivory or slaves and he refuses to pay our children for being taught how to read and write.' It was evident to the locals that they were not reaping any benefit from the missionary's presence and it took him years of painstaking work to overcome their apathy. When he took his new bride to Sagalla the locals seemed concerned about her failure to conform in appearance to the standards of their women. A few days after her arrival three or four men came to their house and asked to speak to Wray alone. Safely out of his wife's sight and hearing, they produced from their loin-cloths a razor made from a piece of hoop-iron sharpened on a stone, a pair of tweezers and a file. These were intended respectively for shaving his wife's head, pulling out her eyebrows and eyelashes, and sharpening her teeth to a fine point, according to the Taita fashion of the day!

Thomson left Sagalla Hill in the early morning and rested at Maungu for half an hour to breakfast on broiled fowl. The locals had assured his men that water would be found between Maungu and Taru, so they foolishly decided not to waste time climbing the hill to fill their empty water bottles. Since all the seasonal water holes and pans they passed were bone dry, they had no alternative but to walk through the night in the hope of finding water at Taru.

Through the deep darkness we pressed on silently, feeling our way by means of the rut worn by the feet of yearly caravans, rather than by anything we could see. Overhanging branches struck our faces, and thorns scratched the outstretched hands held out to protect them, but stoically we suppressed all expressions of pain, only warning those behind to be on the look-out. About midnight the gathering clouds which now overcast the sky began to drizzle out a dripping rain, which mightily refreshed us, and shortly after, a great sighing and moaning from the distance told us that a storm of some kind might be expected. Gradually it advanced, the drizzle gave place to big drops, which raised a noisy pattering on the trees, and we hailed with delight a drenching torrent of rain. Putting my handkerchief over my head, it was speedily soaked, and then I sucked it with intense enjoyment.

After a sustained burst of speed, Thomson reached Taru at three o'clock in the morning with tender feet and legs withering with pain, to find plenty of rainwater in the *ungurungas* or rock pools.

I staggered forward for a short distance and literally flopped down in a pool of water; there I drank till I reached the bursting-point, then seeing the futility of trying to get any shelter in the dense darkness, or of raising a fire in the drenching rain, I threw myself down on the bare rocks, heedless alike of the elements and the imminent risks from wild beasts, and was only aroused from a deep sleep by one or two of the men falling over me, as they groped their way to the water.

This was precisely the kind of dramatic endurance test in which Thomson revelled. He and his men had marched fifty miles in twenty-two hours to perform 'a pedestrian feat which probably has never been equalled in the annals of African travelling'. Although he was mistaken in his belief that they had covered a distance of seventy miles, it was, perforce, a remarkable exploit.

Thomson could find no replacement for Muhinna at Mombasa and again had the greatest difficulty in recruiting more porters; of those he did take on, almost 10 per cent defected before he regained Taru. However, he was able to replenish his depleted stocks of trade goods with the valuable assistance of Colonel Miles in Zanzibar. He also took the opportunity to augment his inventory of *sengenge*, coils of iron wire – a more favoured item of barter in Maasailand than he had been led to believe. His experiences on the return journey followed similar exacerbating frustrations to those of his first march, so he was thankful to rejoin the main body of his men at Taveta on 2nd July 1883 with an expedition mascot trotting close at heel. Toby, a small terrier half-breed, had been presented to him by the missionaries in Mombasa and had already proved his worth by alerting his master to the dangers of prowling lions.

In his leader's absence Martin had performed magnificently. By keeping the men busy building a semi-permanent camp away from the traders' lines, he had improved morale beyond all recognition. 'From a tall pole waved the English flag, flaunting its colours proudly in mid-air. I could hardly believe my eyes when told that this magical transformation was Martin's work, and that these were our quarters.' Famine had caused food prices to treble and Martin had been compelled to visit Mandara against his better judgment, but he had no cause for worry. He was received with lavish hospitality. While bullocks were killed and his men feasted, loads of food were prepared at nominal prices. Mandara continued to supply food for the entire caravan all the time Thomson was away and quite won over the reticent Martin to his side. Even Thomson was moved to show his appreciation. He presented Mandara with his galvanic battery, on which the chief had set his heart, for he was smart enough to realize that the possession of it would enhance his reputation as a great *mganga* or medicine man. Mandara had confided in Martin the extent of Muhinna's treachery, thus underscoring the explorer's worst suspicions. Muhinna made one last attempt to foment trouble but, by then, Thomson had the measure of his man and was not taken in by his duplicity.

A large caravan from Pangani headed by Juma Kimameta, a notable personality from the coast, had reached Taveta a few days earlier and was recruiting, preparatory to starting out for Maasai country. Thomson rejoiced in the news 'for by this time I was only too glad to stoop to the idea of joining a trading caravan, as our enterprise had become pretty much a forlorn hope'. Kimameta was a one-eyed, heavily poxed little man of above-average character and intelligence, and a deal was quickly struck to allow Thomson and his men to join the caravan on the same footing as other traders, in return for an unspecified reward at the end of the journey if all went well. The rest of the traders were also persuaded to admit the embarrassing presence of a white man into their ranks, even the most prejudiced among them declaring in the end that he would carry the explorer on his shoulders if ever the need arose! All this upset Muhinna's machinations and he did his best to dissuade Thomson from throwing his lot in with the Swahili traders by warning him of their imaginery, but plausible, ill-intentions towards him. Thomson, however, had already made up his mind to side with the merchants, for he recognized in their plan an opportunity to travel round the east side of Mount

Juma Kimameta

Kilimanjaro to Amboseli, Ol-doinyo Orok, Ngong and Naivasha. It was a route which had long been closed, due to skirmishes with the Loikotitok Kisongo and Matapato sections of the Maasai during which several large caravans had been almost annihilated. In this way, Thomson would be able to explore uncharted country far removed from the path that Fischer had trodden.

CHAPTER 8

Trouble and triumph

Usicheze na simba ukamtia mkono kinywani
When you play with a lion do not put your hand in its mouth
Swahili proverb

THOMSON LEFT TAVETA again almost three months to the day after his humiliating retreat from Kibongoto. Despite the extra hands he had recruited in Mombasa, his own party was still only 140 strong. There had been an appalling succession of men – fifty-eight to be exact – who had deserted, died or been returned to the coast as useless. At the very last moment, all eight young men whom he had enlisted at the Rabai mission absconded with their rifles. This left him with barely sufficient porters to shoulder his chattels and stock-in-trade, which included forty-four loads of iron, brass and copper wire, twenty-two of beads, eleven of stores, eight each of cloth and ammunition and about twenty of miscellaneous camp equipment. Extreme care had to be taken to prevent more defections as the caravans snaked their way slowly north in single file along the banks of the Lumi River to the picturesque crater lake of Chala, the most perfectly preserved of all the parasitic cones of Kilimanjaro and undoubtedly its last manifestation of volcanic activity. When the violent erruption took place many centuries ago, the *manyatta* that stood on the site was said by the Maasai to have been blown sky-high, with only the ghosts of the departed bringing the tragedy to light. The Maasai still claim that the lowing of cattle, the bleating of sheep and other village noises can occasionally be heard from the depths of the forest-fringed lake.

When the traders reached Rombo they chose to rest for several days, much to Thomson's ill-concealed irritation. Ostensibly, the reason for the halt was to enable the caravans to buy in more food, but it was really grounded in the fact that it was the Moslem holy month of Ramadan and the traders had no inclination to exert themselves on empty stomachs. Indeed there was nowhere better to fast and pray than in the idyllic surrounds of Rombo. The traders' decision heralded the beginning of a frustrating three weeks in which Thomson began to realize fully that his movements were inexorably tied up with the whims of a bunch of unpredictable merchants. By linking up with them, he was no longer master of his own destiny, until his own strong will and forceful personality prevailed. Rather than loiter in camp all day, he tried his hand at big game hunting in a district where the rhinoceros was numerous. In the cool of the early morning he stalked and shot his first victim in a manner about which few hunters would have wished to boast. But the excitement of the charge and a near brush with death tempted Thomson to strike a triumphant pose with one foot on its two-ton hulk, before sauntering back to camp to bask in a little reflected glory while the exaggerated accounts of his prowess spread like wild-fire through the traders' lines.

Several days of haphazard hunting succeeded one another until the traders unexpectedly announced their intention to move on again. Thomson's joy was short-lived; the move was merely a change of camp-sites with the traders seizing on a trivial pretext to make another prolonged halt. This time he made his indignation plainly felt in a manner which would have had them quaking

in their shoes – had they worn any! But his *bombastes furioso* manner had no noticeable effect. It took another nine days of soul-destroying boredom, relieved now and then by hunting, for the new moon to be sighted signalling the end of Ramadan. Thomson was as enthusiastic as the devout Moslems but for entirely dissimilar reasons; to him, the faint silvery bow, still bathed in the rays of the setting sun, ushered in a new era of hope and an end to the long delays which had sapped his vitality. 'To mark the occasion I had to give a present to each of my men, and then, arrayed in a new tweed suit, I took up my post near my tent and held a levee, considerably diminishing my small stock of comforts in trying to sustain my dignity as the most important man in the caravan.'

On 11th August 1883, the caravans made a fresh start for the countryside which the travellers from Europe had despaired of ever penetrating. On reaching the forest edge beyond the headwaters of the Kimangelia River, another halt was called while the traders indulged in a bizarre mumbo-jumbo to propitiate their gods. At length everyone was ready and set off in dense fog with the intrepid explorer in command of the vanguard. Good progress was made, to Thomson's obvious satisfaction, through Loitokitok and the rolling plains beyond. The Maasai were conspicuous by their absence but rhinos were everywhere, snorting, charging and putting the fear of God into the heavily laden porters. At times the men began to waver, the less brave spirits taking to their heels, while the *komas* or sacred magic staves and flags which led every trading caravan were unfurled and brandished to exorcise the demon and put it to flight. Like a red rag to a bull, these great cumbersome creatures of an antediluvian age often charged, heads down and tails twisted into a piglike curl, towards the bearers of the trusted charms. Only rarely did Thomson have to turn them with his gun. He had come to fancy himself in the role of hunter, with seven long-horned specimens already to his credit. His tactics were to approach his quarry until it was only twenty to thirty yards away and then open fire with his non-repeating Express rifle – a risky business which did not leave him much room for error. He continued to shoot daily for the pot and, as a change of diet, ate ostrich eggs 'which, when beaten up into an omelette, are barely distinguishable from ordinary eggs ... While to some extent I enjoyed the excitement and adventure arising from hunting, the whole tenor of my thoughts revolted from the idea of shooting game from mere love of sport. I can conscientiously say that except in the case of buffaloes, rhinoceroses and elephants, I never shot a head of game for anything but the prosaic requirements of the pot.'

When the travellers encountered the Maasai near Amboseli, Thomson admired the cool, fearless manner in which the elders came into camp 'with all the dignity of lords of the creation'. Even though their own people had murdered traders and broken a few heads from time to time, the greybeards had the temerity to suggest that no merchant would ever dare to retaliate for fear of the consequences. They touched lightly on the causes of the route having been closed for so long, as if it were a trifling affair, and the excesses of their warriors were quickly brushed aside. 'Boys will be boys and their wild oats must be sown' was their defence. Now they were glad to see the traders back again, as they were running short of iron wire, beads and jewellery chains for their young women. Fortunately for Thomson, the warriors were away rustling cattle in Ukambani, which made for an easy passage across the savannah and acacia woodlands to Ol-doinyo Orok, the black mountain, overlooking modern Namanga on the Kenya/Tanzania border. From Thomson's description, the flora of Amboseli has changed little in the last 100 years – that is, if we disregard the degradation caused by mass tourism.

There is not a blade of grass to relieve the barren aspect of the damp muddy sand, which, impregnated with various salts, is unfavourable to the growth of any

vegetation. Here and there, however, in the horizon are to be detected a few sheets of water, surrounded by rings of green grass, and a few straggling trees or scrubby bushes. Other green patches of tall waving sedges and papyrus mark the position of various marshes . . . Besides these, there extend considerable tracts covered with pure white crust of natron or saltpetre, formed by the efflorescence of the salts left by the dried-up marshes of the wet season. These areas appear to the eye as sheets of pure white snow or lakes of charmingly clear water. At other times, struck by the rays of the sun, they shine with the dazzling splendour of burnished silver. A weird haze envelops the land with an influence shadowy and ghostly, while the mirage adds to the strange effects, till indeed everything seems unreal and deceptive. The exceptional nature of the sight is emphasized by the stupendous mass of Kilimanjaro, the pyramidal form of Meru, the double peak of Ndapduk and the dark height of Doinyo Orok . . . In spite of the desolate and barren aspect of the country, game is to be seen in marvellous abundance.

Wild animals can still be seen in large numbers against the scenic backdrop of Mount Kilimanjaro, making the area one of the most popular game parks to be found in the entire country. The elephant population has increased since Thomson's day but several other species, in particular the rhinoceros, have diminished.

Thomson called the place 'Njiri' and made no mention of Amboseli in his diaries, so a brief word of explanation will not be out of place. The Maasai, with their love of descriptive place names, have three different names for the area. The best-known is Amboseli, which is a derivative of the Maasai word 'Empusel' meaning 'white soil' – a feature of the friable soil which is encrusted with natron or saltpetre in areas adjacent to the swamps. Then there is the Maasai word 'Ngiro' (not 'Njiri' as Thomson had written), which means 'brown' and aptly describes the large expanse of brown soil, or less occasionally brown water, of the seasonal lake to the west of Amboseli. It is shown on our modern maps as 'Lake Amboseli' whereas it should be 'Enkare Ngiro', the brown lake. Lastly there is the word 'Ol Tukai', the Maasai name for wild date palms, *Phoenix reclinata*, which characterize the belt of vegetation surrounding the swamps. The self-service *bandas* or cottages are thus named. A small nucleus of them was built around 1950, then quickly extended to accommodate the stars of the film *Where No Vultures Fly*.

The caravans had now entered the most dangerous stage of their journey through Maasailand. Strong perimeter fences had to be built at every halt, orders were issued for men not to go outside camp singly or unarmed, and guards were doubled. The columns got under way again after a brief interlude at Ol-doinyo Orok, where Thomson amused himself hunting and the traders vied with one another to buy donkeys, cattle and ivory. The base of Ol-doinyo Orok was teeming with wild animals and as an indication of the extraordinary numbers and variety in the district at the time, Thomson shot four rhinos, one giraffe, four zebras and four antelopes in under six hours – quite a bag if it was just for the pot! These days only a few small herds of buffalo and the occasional eland survive on the mountain top. As the vanguard emerged from the thick acacia forest on the east side of the mountain, it soon became evident that the surrounding countryside supported a large population. The explorer was singularly unimpressed by the armed warrior groups from the Matapato section of the Maasai which

A Maasai woman

showed up in force to impede their progress. Many of them had casts in their
eyes and others were weaklings, although their looks were belied by their
bellicose nature. The once-haughty merchants submitted meekly to numerous insults and indignities at the hands of men, women and children alike.
Thomson was obliged to put away his camera and hide his theodolite because
these strange mechanical instruments were looked upon with hostile alarm.
Nor did he as an individual escape their special attention, in spite of an
ingenious plot that he and Kimameta had hatched to give everyone a measure
of protection. This involved posing as an important *laibon (ol-oiboni)*, a
clairvoyant, ritual expert and medicine man, who was blessed with
supernatural powers. He had to hoax the warriors into believing that he was
greater than Mbatian, the most respected and revered *laibon* the Maasai have
ever had.

Mbatian controlled his people by personal influence augmented by an
uncanny knack of accurately foretelling the future by casting magical stones
on to a sacred cowhide, examining animal entrails, interpreting dreams and
prophesying under the influence of alcohol. He directed the warriors as to
how and when they should fight, in return for which he received first choice
of the stock they rustled. Like all good leaders and politicians he was a past
master in the art of double-talk. One of his first tasks after assuming
command of his people was to unite the pure pastoral sections of the Maasai
against their contemptible, semi-agricultural Iloikop cousins (a derogatory
name literally meaning 'the dead ones') – namely the Uasin-Gishu, or people
of the dappled cattle, and the Laikipiak, the greedy ones. Before he died in
1890, he was credited with predicting the rinderpest and smallpox epidemics
which swept the country two or three years later, decimating livestock and
seriously depopulating the country; the arrival of people as white as cattle
egrets from the direction of the sea; and the coming of an iron snake that
would belch forth fire – a startling vision of railway engines which did not
appear in the country until the building of the Kenya–Uganda railway, the
'Lunatic Line', five years after Mbatian's death.

Thomson did, of course, have a head start over Mbatian. After all, who
among the warriors could have imagined that somebody with a skin as white
as his and with teeth that popped in and out of his mouth at will – he had two
false ones – was just another ordinary human being! Then there was his
inexhaustible supply of Eno's fruit salts, a laxative invented for sailors in the
1850s by Mr J.C. Eno, a Newcastle chemist, and still widely sold throughout
the world. Fresh water which mysteriously frothed and bubbled – and had
interesting involuntary side-effects when drunk – never failed to impress his
audience. On one occasion Thomson's ingenuity was extended to the full
when a wealthy old man and his pretty young wife came to him secretly for
help in having a little white boy of their own. They were prepared to bestow
bullocks and donkeys on him if he would consent to give them the
appropriate medicines, and to curse him if he refused. They stubbornly
rejected his pleas that their request was beyond his superhuman powers so,
just to get rid of them, he brewed a good strong draught of Mr Eno's crystals
as a specific warranted not to fail. 'They drank the effervescing liquid with
eager expectation, yet in fear and trembling. They still seemed, however, to
have some lingering doubts whether the coveted result was a certainty.
Unfortunately, I had not one of Eno's pamphlets about me at that time, or
doubtless I should have proved to their entire satisfaction that it had never

been known to fail in producing even more astonishing effects.' After spitting on them vigorously, Thomson blandly gave the wife a parting present of a nice string of beads in trust for the white baby when it was born!

Spitting in those days was an expression of goodwill and best wishes, similar to today's kiss. The more Thomson's fame as a *laibon* spread, the more blessings he had to perform. 'The Maasai flocked to me as pious Catholics would do to springs of healing virtue and with the occasional draughts of water I was equal to the demand. The more copiously I spat on them, the greater was their delight.' Thomson did admit, however, that there were occasions when he had to chew on bullets and stones to stimulate his salivary glands.

Safari routine followed much the same pattern day after day and required everyone to rise as the first glimmer of daylight appeared in the east. After a quick wash in cold water, Thomson and Martin settled down to breakfast in the open, while the *askaris* pulled down their tents and packed up the camp equipment. As the crimson flush of dawn turned to gold, the signal was given for the porters to shoulder their loads. Thomson positioned himself at the head of the advance guard and Martin took up his post at the rear of the column, whereupon orders were issued to break camp. Within minutes it was deserted and the smouldering fires died out as the rising sun flamed over the rim of the world. In the cool, invigorating morning air they walked briskly, but two hours after leaving camp, a short halt would be called to let the long file of men close up, for around that time the warriors would come out of their *manyattas* to shouts of 'Lo Shore! Friend! Give me a string of beads!' As the hours passed and the sun became hotter, the pace slackened until the weak and lazy began to lag behind and rest. At about midday the place selected for camping was reached and a mad scramble took place for the shade of the trees. Muhinna seemed intuitively to know the best and most comfortable corners and had a knack of always being there first. The moment everyone was in camp, the goods of each trader were stacked and covered with skins to hide them from prying eyes. Guards were then appointed, guns placed at the ready and, without more ado, the men set to work under Martin's supervision cutting down acacia trees to form a strong perimeter fence. Meantime Thomson kept a watchful eye on their huge pile of stores, refreshing himself with a cup of coffee, generally in the company of Kimameta who had a habit of always turning up at the appropriate moment. Work would proceed smoothly until the *il-murran* appeared on the scene to demand tribute; from then on, the camp would be in turmoil for the rest of the day.

Flies and dust were the distinguishing features of the country beyond Ilbisil, now a small trading centre situated on the main highway from Nairobi to Tanzania. 'The Maasai were in extraordinary numbers and proportionately insolent and troublesome; while astonishing myriads of flies, with characteristics comparable to those of the tribe they prey on, made life a burden.' Anyone who visits a traditional *manyatta* today will still be tormented by the swarms of flies. Young children suffer enormously and trachoma, a contagious eye disease spread by flies, leads to a high incidence of blindness.

Thomson was immensely relieved to reach Ngong after three weeks' continual harassment at the hands of belligerent warriors.

A grand expanse of undulating country lay before us, the hollows knee deep in rich succulent pasture in which peeped forth familiarly the homelike clover. The ridges were covered with trees of moderate size, and markedly temperate in their aspect, though splendid Cape calodendrons [Cape chestnut trees] formed an unwonted spectacle with their glorious canopy of flowers. The interspaces of the woodland were filled with a dense mass of beautiful and fragrant flowering shrubs in great variety. These open spaces were the haunts of large herds of buffalo, and the feeding ground of numerous elephants and rhinoceroses while in the grassy reaches could be seen vast numbers of elands, hartebeestes, zebras and ostriches.

Thomson described Ngong as 'a glorious bubbling fountain of clear, cold water which formed a charming pond in which ducks swam and water-lilies reclined in vernal beauty'. He was doubtlessly gilding the lily slightly; the Maasai were much more down to earth and nicknamed it 'Enkongu Enchorru Emuny', the spring of the rhinoceroses' water hole, by virtue of its importance as a wallow in times gone by. Ngong is now a satellite town of Kenya's capital city, Nairobi, where uncontrolled urban development has led to an unattractive jumble of modern houses mushrooming across the plains. Nairobi simply did not exist in Thomson's day. The place was an unspoilt corner of Maasailand where the 'Enkare Nairobi', the cold water river, spilled its cool mountain waters on to the Athi plains. The plains were endless, as they were empty of human habitation, which makes the contrast with today an astonishing one. Hardly 100 years have elapsed since a collection of corrugated iron shacks marked the beginning of a railhead terminal. The bustling city of one million people with its high-rise skyline is now one of the most modern and impressive in Africa. The knuckle-shaped hills known today as the 'Ngong Hills' have several Maasai names. One of them is 'Ol-doinyo Lamuyoo', the hills of soldier ants – the aggressive little insects known as *siafu* which march and forage in long columns, especially during the rainy season. When the army spreads out like a vast carpet and moves in its tens of thousands, the grass turns black and the traveller must take great care to avoid being nipped in the most unsuspecting and embarrassing places.

Thomson and his companions had now reached the south-west frontier of Kikuyuland, where the Bantu-speaking forest dwellers bartered with their Maa-speaking neighbours. Though the two sides were in constant conflict, their womenfolk were never molested; they continued to intermingle and trade even when the warriors were in deadly combat. Another decade was to pass before *Pax Britannica* brought an uneasy peace to this troubled area. Neither the merchants nor the Maasai had anything complimentary to say about the Kikuyu, so Thomson's first published account of them was far from flattering.

They have the reputation of being the most troublesome and intractable in this region. No caravan has yet been able to penetrate into the heart of the country, so dense are the forests and so murderous and thievish are its inhabitants. They are anxious for coast ornaments and cloth, and yet defeat their own desires by their utter inability to resist stealing, or the fun of planting a poisoned arrow in the traders . . . The young men and women affect the Maasai dress with modification . . . they carry a small spear and shield, the knobkerry, the simi [a double-edged sword knife] *and a bow and arrow. The Maasai have made repeated attempts to penetrate into the country, but they have found that the Wakikuyu were more than a match for them in their dense forests.*

Thomson had heard one side of the story only. Had he heard the other, he would have realized that their reputation was not so richly deserved. When Kimameta and the traders had last visisted Ngong, they had taken advantage of the villagers who came to sell their produce at the forest edge and captured them. Some were redeemed by their relatives; the remainder were taken to the coast and sold into slavery. The traders followed this incident by attacking several villages, killing a number of people and kidnapping others. If Juma Kimameta and his friends suffered later at the hands of the Kikuyu, it was a just reward for their misdemeanours.

It stood to reason that the traders deemed the ordinary protection of a thorn fence inadequate at Ngong, where poisoned arrows could have been loosed off so easily into camp at dead of night. The porters took two days to surround the five-acre site with a palisade of stout tree-trunks and a deep outer trench. Many of them were already experiencing the unpleasant symptoms of dysentery, having been fed on a purely meat diet without salt for nearly a month. Since the Maasai look on agriculture as a menial occupation and to this day seldom till the soil, fresh vegetables had to be bought from the Kikuyu, who were understandably distrustful of leaving their forest enclaves because of the enmity of the traders and the large numbers of Maasai ever-present around the camp. The only way markets could be established was to penetrate the forest and approach them direct. Thomson undertook this somewhat dangerous enterprise and set foot in one of the most lovely woodland scenes he had ever seen.

A two-hour march brought his well-armed party face to face with the Kikuyu for the first time. After a tense wait, some women appeared, their shaven heads bent low under the weight of laden baskets which were slung from forehead straps across their backs. Years of toil had left a perceptible groove across their brows. A flourishing market, the first of many, was soon set up, where sweet potatoes, yams, cassava, sugar-cane, maize and millet were sold very cheaply. However, the time taken to buy sufficient rations for the journey ahead took days longer than Thomson had anticipated; so he explored the forest and hunted elephants, at the same time chancing upon the most graceful of all Kenya's monkeys, the black and white *Colobus occidentalis*. Both animals have long since vanished from the precincts of Nairobi.

The explorer had been thwarted by delays perpetrated by the Moslem merchants at the start of his journey through Maasailand; now his departure from Ngong caused similar frustrations. A *sadaka* or Moslem feast-cum-prayer-meeting was held to determine the most propitious time and day for travelling. It was obviously imperative that an early start be made in order to leave ample time to select a secure camp-site near water; but Kimameta's search into the decrees of fate made it clear that no one could leave Ngong till four hours after sunrise, on pain of bringing down the wrath of the unseen powers. No Pangani or Mombasa caravan dared to disregard the outcome of this pious act; so the heavily laden caravans did not resume their march for Lake Naivasha until ten o'clock the following morning. Thomson and his men set out with twenty-eight days' dry rations and livestock to last seven days, whereas the traders had loaded almost three months' reserves on to the pack-animals they had acquired for carrying ivory back to the coast. They followed winding forest trails in a north-westerly direction, where the intransigent Kikuyu hovered like birds of prey ready to pounce on stray oxen.

A Kikuyu woman carrying firewood by means of a forehead strap

Thomson, his eye on the dramatic, went so far as to suggest that they were on the lookout for an opportunity to dye their spears in blood. The dismal late start resulted in an equally late halt around sunset at a picturesque pool set deep in the forest. Normal security precautions were totally disregarded due to the lateness of the hour and a terrific thunderstorm, accompanied by torrential rain and hail, which passed overhead at dusk. While the porters foolhardily dried themselves in front of roaring log fires, the Kikuyu attacked, sending a shower of poisoned arrows into the poorly protected camp. A quick volley from hastily loaded guns scattered the raiders but, in the confusion that followed, all the cattle would have been stolen had not Thomson, Makatubu and Brahim taken swift action to head them off. Several bullocks were taken in subsequent raids during the night and two porters were posted missing, presumed speared or taken prisoner. Casualties from poisoned arrows would have been serious, had most of the men not bought hides from the Massai at Ngong, which were transformed to great effect into protective shields.

As dawn broke on a cool, colourless day, the furious traders organized prompt retaliatory measures against their unprovoked attackers. A large group of villagers was soon taken captive to the deafening sound of high-pitched war-cries, which reverberated through the bleak forest. Thomson sensed that a bloody massacre was imminent and intervened most effectively to prevent an escalation of the dangerous conflict. When the well-bunched caravans got under way again, they were harried mercilessly. However, a little sabre-rattling kept the hostile marauders at bay until they thinned out, leaving the travellers in peace to descend to the floor of the Great Rift Valley on a well-worn cattle trail which sloped diagonally down the precipitous face of the escarpment. Later this became a motorable dirt track, until Italian prisoners of war constructed a new paved road in the 1940s; the little chapel they built still stands at the foot of the escarpment to this day. Thomson had already shown his delight in the forest at seeing huge coniferous trees – junipers and podocarpus – and magnificent Cape chestnut trees covered with a mass of cyclamen-pink panicles. Now, 2,000 feet below him, lay the unmeasured vastness of the Rift Valley, extending to distant purple horizons where his knowledgeable eye immediately identified two extinct volcanic craters. The most southerly and larger of the two craters, Suswa or Ol-doinyo Nanyokie, the red mountain, appeared as a huge crater with one side blown away, in the centre of which had risen a secondary cone. The mountain to the north, Ol-doinyo Loonongot (nowadays spelt Longonot) – the mountain which is bisected by many deep gullies – gave the appearance of a broad truncated cone and was so very suggestive of a fine crater that he resolved to climb it if the opportunity arose.

The late afternoon sun cast long shadows across the darkening plains as the main body of porters reached the bottom of the escarpment and took a well-earned rest. It had been a hard day, with everyone utterly exhausted from carrying back-breaking loads without food and water to sustain them. They were taken completely by surprise when lions attacked a string of laden donkeys and threw them into disarray. Several donkeys were killed outright by the lions; others, mistaken for the predators in the heat of the moment, were shot dead. Porters ran for their lives, cattle panicked out of control and those donkeys which had escaped injury shed their loads and disappeared at breakneck speed. Traders, everyone for himself, deserted their men and fled, while Thomson and Martin coolly and calmly shepherded their own porters to safety. They reached camp beside the warm waters of the Ewuaso Kedong two hours after sunset, but the traders took another three days to round up the stray livestock and pacify their badly shaken men. Miraculously no one was killed or wounded in the fracas and there were no Kikuyu or Maasai close at hand to plunder what would have been a glorious haul.

Twelve years later the Kedong Valley was the scene of a massacre without parallel in the history of early British rule in East Africa. In November 1895, a large caravan consisting of some 1,000 Swahili and Kikuyu porters camped beside the Ewuaso Kedong on its way back from stockpiling food at the government station at Eldama Ravine. The Swahili headman in charge of the party unwisely ordered two young girls to be abducted from a nearby *manyatta* for his evening's entertainment. The village elders resisted this outrage most vigorously and succeeded in getting the girls handed back, unmolested, before nightfall. However, the infatuated headman refused to give in. Shortly before the caravan resumed its journey the following morning, he again ordered armed men to grab hold of the damsels; in the struggle, a shot was fired which accidently killed a cow. This incident gave the warriors a perfect excuse to reap their revenge. Within minutes they ferociously attacked the caravan and in the ensuing hand-to-hand battle impaled over 550 porters on their spears.

News of the bloody massacre reached the ears of an English trader, Andrew Dick, who was travelling in the neighbourhood at the time; he promptly attacked the Maasai and seized a number of their cattle. After blazing away at the warriors in a prolonged engagement, his ammunition ran out and, as he tried to extricate himself from the scene, he too was speared – the first European to be killed since the establishment of British rule seven years earlier. It was a quixotic venture which met with little sympathy in official circles, for Dick had been warned more than once to refrain from taking the law into his own hands.

Thomson chose to climb Mount Longonot as the column wended its way slowly towards Lake Naivasha. In a surprisingly difficult excursion for what is now a day's outing from Nairobi, he stumbled, panted and perspired through a minefield of leg-breaking lava boulders and a wilderness of 'wait-a-bit' thorn trees to reach the bottom of the steep-sided cone. Then a determined spurt, at times scrambling on hands and knees, brought him to the crater rim where:

the scene that lay before me fairly overwhelmed me with wonder. I found myself on the sharp rim of an enormous pit, as far as I could judge, from 1,500 to 2,000 feet in depth. It was not, however, an inverted cone or volcano, as rivers frequently are, but a great circular cavity with perfectly perpendicular walls ... So sharp was the edge of this marvellous crater that I literally sat astride it, with one leg dangling over the abyss internally and the other down the side of the mountain. The bottom of the pit seemed to be quite even and level, covered with acacia trees, the tops of which, at that great depth, had much the general aspect of a grass plain.

From this high vantage point Thomson had an uninterrupted view of the shimmering waters of Lake Naivasha, behind which rose, to a height of more than 9,000 feet, the dark sombre range of the Mau. Few lakes can have a more striking setting.

'Enaiposha', the large expanse of water which heaves to and fro, 'was a moving mass of ducks, ibises, pelicans and other aquatic birds'. Even now, it is one of Africa's foremost ornithological treasures, where more than 400 different species of land and water birds make their homes. A century ago hippos were exceptionally numerous but the only indigenous fish was a species of small carp. Today, the waters abound with tilapia and black bass which provide good sport for weekend fishermen living fifty miles away in the capital city. Another recent introduction, this time in the 1960s, is the Louisiana red swamp crayfish, *Procambarus clarkii*, which has multiplied so rapidly that commercial exploitation has become viable. To some extent, mystery still surrounds this lake, since no one has yet offered an incontrovertible explanation as to why its waters should be fresh – unlike the other closed basin lakes immediately to the north and to the south of it, which are alkaline and saline. Professor J. W. Gregory – famous for his analogy of the Great Rift Valley – surmised that subterranean outlets through deep lava faults accounted for the phenomenon, which may also explain the numerous steam jets close by.

Gustav Fischer reached Naivasha almost three months before his arch-rival, but fell foul of the Maasai at the entrance to Hell's Gate where a remarkable volcanic plug has been named Fischer's tower. Had he not been forced back here, the course of history in East Africa would have turned out very differently. Though illness was said to have been the main cause, Thomson could scarcely conceal his delight:

that fact [illness] *certainly is not to be wondered at when we understand the atrocious life one is compelled to lead among the Maasai savages. They ordered us about as if we were so many slaves. I had daily to be on exhibition and perform for their delectation. 'Take off your boots'; 'show your toes'; 'let us see your white skin'; 'Bless me, what queer hair'; 'Good Gracious! What funny clothes' ... greeted me as they turned me about, felt my hair with their filthy paws while 'Shore! Give me a string of beads' was dinned into my ear with maddening persistence.*

A newly ordained African chaplain, a freed slave who had been baptized William Jones, accompanied Bishop James Hannington to Uganda two years later and his account of the Maasai in their camp at Naivasha reinforces – through African eyes – what Thomson wrote.

Nobody dared to tell a Maasai to move. My own tent was guarded at both entrances, but they peeped under the flaps, and pulled out whatever they could lay hold of. Everywhere they were pilfering. Whenever the men tried to resist them they pointed their spears at them. All got nervous; all were hungry, but none dared to sit down and eat. Our visitors began to tear open the loads and turn over the boxes, while the guards were shamefully handled. I could not sit for a minute; my heart would not let me rest. Every moment I anticipated an attack. Our men were all on tenter-hooks of apprehension. The Bishop himself was puzzled and confused. His tent was filled. The chair, the cot, the wash-tub, bags, biscuit-boxes – all held Maasai. One could not go through. The cloth of the tent was spoiled by the red earth and oil with which their bodies were daubed, and everything was more or less smeared with it . . . The iron pegs of the Bishop's tent were being pulled up and stolen. A Maasai seated himself behind Pinto the cook and coolly stole a table-knife. He was running off when I saw him and gave chase, and with difficulty got it back . . . One of our men got his head cut open with a spear thrust; another had his clothes taken . . . We all looked toward the sun and longed that it should go down . . . Hungry and thirsty the Bishop and I sat down to our evening meal. The place at length seemed clear. But no, our friends came in to see us eat. They touched and befouled everything eatable with their filthy fingers. We were at our wit's end.

Thompson sited his camp in the shade of yellow-barked fever trees, *Acacia xanthaphloea*, on the eastern side of the lake close to what is now the main Nakuru highway. 'Not a moment was lost in stacking the loads, and setting to work fence building, for we had now arrived at one of the most precarious parts of the entire route. Everyone worked with a nervous energy that left nothing to be desired, and long before the warriors had gathered in any numbers, we were safely surrounded by an impenetrable barrier.' They were obliged to remain there for nearly five days while hordes of *il-murran* descended like locusts to collect their peace offerings. Resplendent in a thick coating of red ochre, they carried long spears which flashed in the sun and shields painted in the heraldic devices of the section to which they belonged. Each group performed a series of military-style manoeuvres, ending up with a dance in which they took turns to leap high in the air, before getting down to the serious business of extorting as large a gift as possible from the brow-beaten travellers. Enormous quantities of trade goods were dispensed to appease their lordships without whose cooperation further progress was out of the question. Arrogant and overbearing as they were, Thomson still had a sneaking admiration for their self-possessed, aristocratic style. The obligatory break in the journey allowed him time to befriend the local maidens, who 'would have been without fault if they had only discarded clay and grease and used Pears' soap'. He also chatted to several elders from a nearby *manyatta* who delighted him by showing a frankness and absence of suspicion which he had found nowhere else in East Africa. They displayed a comprehensive knowledge of the geography of a vast region and imparted this most valuable information to him without reserve. From them Thomson learned that the mountain to the north-west of Lake Naivasha, which forms a spur to the Mau escarpment, was called Eburru – more correctly Ol-doinyo Opuru, the steam or smoke mountain. Never one to waste time, he made up his mind to see for himself whether its description was justified and the reasons why. He prevailed on a Maasai to guide him there and set off early one morning, with a party of eight, across grassy plains teeming with large herds of zebras totally oblivious to the dangers represented by man.

He rounded the northern shoulder of Eburru, past outcrops of pure black obsidian, and reached the volcanic area at 7,000 feet. Here, clouds of vapour billowed skywards from the bowels of the earth, as though hissing from the safety valve of a steam engine, and gave the mountain its characteristic name. This caused Thomson's superstitious men to placate the troubled spirits of the earth by throwing handfuls of grass into a vent from which jets of steam puffed out at regular intervals, accompanied by gurgling and rumbling

noises. The friable bedrock surrounding these jets had decomposed into a crimson-red clay which was said by his Maasai guide to contain medicinal properties. While his men daubed themselves all over, Thomson spotted his forehead Hindu-style and took a closer look. He was right to conclude that the phenomenon was of recent volcanic origin. Indeed, several of the most vigorous jets may one day be capped to supplement the geothermal power being generated at Olkaria on the opposite side of the lake. The present level of generation represents about 15 per cent of Kenya's electricity requirements and can probably be sustained for up to thirty years.

As storm clouds massed over the Mau, the explorer turned for home to complete the round trip of not less than thirty miles in just eleven hours – another astonishing feat of endurance, considering the rough conditions in which it was accomplished.

CHAPTER 9

Lakes and mountains

Mla cha uchungu na tamu hakosi
He who eats bitter things gets sweet things too
Swahili proverb

THOMSON HAD NOT FORGOTTEN the promises he had made to the Royal Geographical Society, upon which his own future depended, so he mooted a scheme at Naivasha to pay a flying visit to Mount Kenya with a small band of men, while Martin took the main body to Baringo to await his arrival. Kimameta had already decided to go straight to Baringo, which past experience had taught him was the most lucrative source of ivory in the land. The merchants were flabbergasted at the young explorer's idea. 'How do you think you can penetrate a district with a mere handful of men when Fischer failed with a whole army?' they asked incredulously. As for Muhinna and Saidi, 'On their knees they implored me, with abject tears, to give up the project, which, to their cowardly imagination, seemed a march to certain death.' A stubborn man by nature, their pleas made Thomson more determined than ever to succeed. Besides, he had gained confidence in his ability to get through by masquerading as a *laibon*, when more men and greater firepower would almost certainly have evoked stiffer opposition. Above Lake Elementeita – Olmuteita, the round lake with no obvious inlets or outlets – he selected thirty of his most trusted followers and, to his amazement, some of the braver spirits among the traders declared their intention to accompany him. It was not so much the increase in manpower which pleased him, but the fact that they knew the route well and he would no longer have to depend solely on his own guides, in whom he wisely vested no trust.

On 6th October 1883, Thomson enjoyed a 'hasty' breakfast of zebra steak and millet porridge washed down with honey-sweetened tea before parting company with Martin and Kimameta. As the main body continued its journey north through thick grey-green leleshwa scrub, *Tarchonanthus camphoratus*, Thomson and his men climbed laboriously out of the Rift Valley over a series of rocky fault lines where orange-red aloes added a splash of colour to otherwise forbidding precipices. At about midday they escaped from the shattered sides of the escarpment on to a plateau 8,000 feet above sea-level where Thomson saw cedar trees, *Juniperus procera*, and olive trees, *Olea africana*, growing in the markedly temperate climate. The Laikipia plateau, the enormous upland steppe about the size of Wales which extends east of the Rift Valley to the foothills of Mount Kenya, owes its name to the Laikipiak section of the Iloikop, who were extremely aggressive and regularly stole cattle from their Maasai cousins. Thomson saw evidence of conflict near Gilgil but moved on lest he become embroiled. When one Maasai section challenged another to fight, it was customary to give advance warning of its intentions and the proposed site of battle. Having established their *manyattas* two or three miles apart, the warriors, in the full panoply of war, closed on each other in long serried ranks. As they came within spear-throwing range, the defenders each dropped to one knee to form a solid phalanx behind the protection of their huge buffalo-hide shields while the challengers, still

line-abreast, continued to advance with measured gait. At the very moment they broke formation in a frenzied rush to engage their foes, the magnificent kudu war-horns were sounded and blood-curdling battle cries filled the air. Egged on by the girlfriends and sweethearts of the young braves, fierce fighting developed into a series of man-to-man duels using spears, long knives and vicious knobkerries. The well-defined ground rules of combat forbade the use of underhand tricks, such as stabbing a man from behind; moreover, no one was tempted to show cowardice in the face of defeat for fear of ridicule or disgrace. Dog-fights often continued for days on end until one of the sections, seriously weakened through death and injury, acknowledged defeat and handed over its prized herds of cattle to the victors.

After a long period of internecine battles in the 1880s, the Laikipiak were decimated to such an extent that they ceased to maintain their separate identity. When Thomson journeyed through their country, however, they were by no means a spent force. He had expected to complete the detour in eight days, but it was beset with dangers and took him a good three weeks. The warriors viewed the white *laibon* with grave suspicion despite his wizardry. 'I was actually pulled about as if I was a toy to be played with. They grasped my arm, pulled my hair and took off my hat. If I went into my tent, they would squeeze themselves after me until everything was filthy. They gloried in frightening my men by making a show of stabbing them, and roars of laughter greeted their piteous terror. Cooking food, under the circumstances, was out of the question and I had to be content to sit and munch some boiled Indian corn.'

Cattle were dying in their hundreds and the dreadful stench emanating from heaps of putrefying carcasses made life in the *manyattas* almost unbearable. From Thomson's description of the symptoms, it was an outbreak of either rinderpest or *actinomycosis* – a fungal disease – which was known to have spread south from Ethiopia at about that time. The Laikipiak reasoned, with some justification, that if Thomson really was the powerful medicine man he had made himself out to be, he could surely stop the plague and cure their cattle; until he had done so, there was no way they would allow him to leave. It was an awkward situation requiring Thomson's considerable powers of persuasion to convince them that his cures would only start to take effect ten days after he had left the district. At last, they began to believe in his elaborate collection of promises and, since they could extort nothing more from him, they let him go.

His route now lay over a hilly region where the tall straight trunks of the cedar trees, with their upper branches bearded fantastically with pale green lichens, produced a ghostly effect in the early-morning mist. It looked less like Africa than anything else he had seen. Camping at an altitude of just under 9,000 feet, he awoke one day to find the rich pastures outside his tent covered with an unmistakable frost and his men huddled round a log fire cursing the bitter cold in no uncertain terms. In the nearby marshes he noticed for the first time red hot pokers which, though similar to those of European gardens, were of a species unknown to science and were named after him, *Kniphofia thomsonii*. Thomson could see a fine mountain range to his east which was about fifty miles long and rose to an altitude of more than 13,000 feet. Since there appeared to be no general name for the range, only for the individual peaks, he called it the 'Aberdare Range' in honour of the president of the society which had despatched him to these lands. The Aberdares, recently re-christened the Nyandarua Mountains, are now a feature of Kenya's mountain national parks, in which are to be found the world-famous Treetops Hotel and The Ark. Here, in armchair comfort, visitors can view wild animals coming to floodlit water-holes and salt-licks at night.

As Thomson rounded the western flank of the mountain range, he caught his first glimpse of Mount Kenya, 'a gleaming snow-white peak with sparkling facets which scintillated with the superb beauty of a colossal diamond . . . While I stood and gazed a moisture-laden breeze touched the peak, wove a fleecy mantle and gradually enshrouded the heaven-like spectacle.' He had seen a vision which added fresh impetus to his dangerous journey.

Every group of Laikipiak the caravan came across was as troublesome as the first. They were torn between the belief that the strange white man was the perpetrator of the disease systematically destroying their herds and the possessor of the medicines which could cure them. They refused point-blank to sell him healthy cattle with which he could have rationed his half-starved porters and, just to be thoroughly awkward, forbade him to shoot 'their' wild animals. Thomson was desperate enough to risk a showdown as he crossed the equator within sight of modern Nyahururu. Two zebras were dispatched in quick succession and Brahim was on them in a flash, plunging his knife deep into their throats and hacking off a huge chunk of meat which he promptly ate raw. There was no time to cut up the carcasses into manageable portions before warriors appeared at the double over the horizon, as if from nowhere, their huge shovel-headed spears glinting ominously in the sunlight. Thomson beat a hasty retreat towards his men as the warriors shouted for the column to stop. They insolently demanded an explanation for this outrage –

and if the white *laibon* wanted a fight, they were ready! At once Thomson put on his most ' 'umble' Uriah Heep manner' and apologized for transgressing their custom, but he had shot the animals, so he told them, solely for the purpose of making medicine from their entrails! The warriors were placated by a little largesse from his dwindling stock of trade goods and allowed his party to proceed. To his great relief, he had survived another day.

Early travellers had a wonderful predilection for mispronouncing and misspelling local names and Thomson was no exception. He somehow contrived to twist the onomatopoeic Maasai word 'naiurru-ur', the water-falls, into 'Ururu', from which Nyahururu subsequently gained its name. Characteristically, he took it upon himself to explore the falls and became so enthralled at the sight of the river thundering several hundred feet down a rocky gorge that he bestowed on them his own name. In those days, Nyahururu was an uninhabited no-man's-land between two warring Maasai clans and it was not until the early 1920s that the first permanent building was erected, to shelter members of the Narok Angling Club who ventured there to fish for trout. The place is now a bustling district headquarters in the middle of a predominantly Kikuyu farming area, with a tourist hotel which boasts a viewpoint of Thomson's Falls at the bottom of its gardens.

Thomson and his henchmen rested undisturbed for two days before starting out in the direction of Mount Kenya. When they reached the Suguroi River, warriors accosted them once more. 'They were more insolent than any I had yet met, dispensing even with the polite salutations of their tribe. As they followed us up with extortionate demands, uttered in the most peremptory manner, I was surprised to see that they were all apparently short of breath and seemed, indeed, to breathe with difficulty.' The explorer had disturbed the *il-murran* eating meat in a forest retreat prior to setting off on a cattle-rustling raid into Pokot country. They customarily gorged themselves on a diet of blood, milk and meat for between two and four weeks to build up their stamina. Meat was either spit-roasted or stewed in a potent broth that was prepared by boiling a number of different roots for an hour or so to extract their medicinal properties. The Maasai use several species of trees and shrubs for this purpose and by drinking the decoction regularly over a period of weeks, it acts as a drug and affects the body's nervous system to a point when fits may occur similar to those suffered by epileptics. The warriors become fearless, belligerent and insensible to suffering. This was the disagreeable condition in which Thomson found them. 'They played with us as a cat does with a mouse and the ending would without a doubt have been the same, but for a certain hazy respect and fear they had of me as a phenomenon, the power of which it was not safe to rouse. I had to sit continually on exhibition ready to take their filthy paws, pull out my teeth for their admiration and spit upon them to show that I did not mean any harm.'

Thomson was obliged to prepare a variety of medicines in his role as *ol-oiboni o-ibor*, the great white *laibon*, during an enforced four days' halt. Lckibes, the local *laibon*, demanded medicines to make him all-powerful and the young married women sought Thomson's assistance to improve their fertility. He simply photographed the warriors as a ruse to make them invincible – the only opportunity he had of doing so throughout his travels, for the appearance of his photographic apparatus antagonized his subjects, who normally fled. Anyway, the sensitive plates were affected by heat and most of them were rendered useless by the time he arrived home.

His cure for their dying cattle was a more elaborate affair. He set up his sextant, put on a pair of kid gloves and ceremoniously brewed up Eno's fruit salts to an incantation along the lines of the well-known children's ditty 'Ten green bottles hanging on the wall' while Brahim fired a one-gun salute. It was a deft performance which enabled him to move quickly on to the Ewuaso Ngiro, the brown river, situated some twelve miles short of modern Nanyuki, where:

as pious Moslems watch with strained eyes the appearance of the new moon . . . so we now waited for the uplifting of the fleecy veil, to render due homage to the heaven piercing Kenya . . . Suddenly there was a break in the clouds far up in the sky, and the next moment a dazzling white pinnacle caught the last rays of the sun, and shone with beauty, marvellous, spirit-like, and divine, cut off, as it apparently was, by immeasurable distance from all connection with the gross earth . . . Presently as the garish light of day melted into the soft hues . . . the 'heaven-kissing' mountain became gradually disrobed, and then in all its severe outlines and chaste beauty it stood forth from top to bottom, entrancing, awe-inspiring – meet reward for days of maddening worry and nights of sleepless anxiety.

Although Thomson overestimated its height by 1,342 feet, he rightly presumed its volcanic origin and, from a distance of thirty miles, gave a surprisingly accurate description of its formation and environs. The peak was so steep in places that he could see bare rocks showing black through its snowy mantle, an appearance which had prompted the Maasai to call it Ol-doinyo Keri, the speckled mountain. The peak rises to a height of 17,058 feet and is the hard plug which formed in the vent of the crater as it cooled. The loose ashes and soft rock of the crater walls have been washed away over five million years, leaving a fitting pinnacle to its massive base. Had the walls been of granite, Mount Kenya would stand, cone-shaped like Kibo of Mount Kilimanjaro, between 23,000 and 25,000 feet high.

Thomson would dearly have loved to explore the mountain at close range but realized that his *laibon* act was wearing dangerously thin. He had already performed the near impossible and had no wish to push his luck too far. Anyhow, his trade goods had run out, Eno's fruit salts and a couple of false teeth were no longer novelties and the cattle were continuing to die. Moreover, his tormentors were becoming more brazen in their demands, one of which required him to remove his nose and replace it at will! When he received word that his camp would be attacked, he decided to forgo the unsurpassed opportunity he had of being the first person to attain the snowline. In the early hours of 29th October, his porters shouldered their loads and slipped quietly out of camp, safe in the knowledge that there was an escape route to the north which bypassed the provocative Laikipiak. The traders opted to stay behind and go into hiding in the secret forest retreats of their Wandorobo friends in order to buy ivory.

Everyone was in high spirits after such an agonizing time among the Maasai and their obnoxious cousins. Game was plentiful and small gin-clear streams meandered through the countryside; Thomson's men worried little that, with only a compass to guide them, no one knew the precise direction of Lake Baringo. Passing the Ewuaso Narok, the black river – so named because the waters coursed their way over black volcanic boulders and rocks – they entered dense forest with thick undergrowth close to modern Rumuruti. 'We had to get along by means of buffalo tracks, in constant fear of stumbling on the dangerous brutes themselves. Sometimes we had literally to crawl below the bushes, and we were soon in a most filthy condition with dirt and wet.' They took two full days in drizzling rain to reach the Laikipia escarpment and behold 'the mysterious Lake Baringo, gleaming apparently at our feet, though several thousand feet below'.

Some geographers had compared the lake to Lake Victoria in size, although others had doubted its very existence. Livingstone, in what was thought to be one of his most serious geographical blunders at the time, reasoned that all fresh-water lakes had to have outlets, and tacked it on to Victoria. Then it was moved around the map a little, at one time being shown as the source of the Nile before being separated from Victoria by a thin watery line. After all this conjecture and controversy, Thomson was delighted that another riddle had at last been solved. He had seen many sights in his time but none to equal the sheer beauty of the majestic panorama before him. Surrounded by rugged mountains rising to a height of 8,000 feet, Lake Baringo was 'a dazzling expanse of water, glittering like a mirror in the fierce rays of the tropical sun. Almost at its centre rises a picturesque island, surrounded by four smaller islets – a group of nature's emeralds in a dazzling setting of burnished silver . . . A remarkable assemblage of straight lines, wall-like extensions and angular outlines produces an impressive and quite unique landscape.' Thomson estimated that it would take him two hours to reach its shores from where he stood, but distances in Africa are notoriously deceptive. It actually took him eighteen hours and his porters two and a half days to hack their way through a barricade of thorn scrub and emerge, footsore and weary, on to the grazing grounds of the Njemps. Martin was greatly relieved to have his leader back. Thomson was doubly pleased to relax peacefully in a camp chair at last and reflect on the events of past weeks. Moreover, fish, millet and melons were 'glorious fare after the old shoe-leather-like beef of the buffalo and the more juicy than savoury messes of diseased cattle'. Today Lake Baringo is reached on a fine tarmac road and, with a choice of two luxury hotels, the visitor can enjoy the beauty without the discomfort of yesteryear.

The Njemps, who inhabit the lake area, are really the Il Chamus but are still known by the inaccurate name that Thomson called them. Of Nilo-Cushitic stock, they are close relatives of the Maasai but have never had any of their aggressive traits. Their forefathers devised a wonderfully efficient system of irrigating the rich loam at the southern end of the lake by artificial canals and a modern irrigation scheme has followed this pattern. Their fishing craft, *lkadich*, were equally ingenious and can be seen on Lake Baringo to this day. Fast and unsinkable, they are a unique type of raft made from poles of the ambatch tree, *Aeschynomena elaphroxylon*, which grows in the waters of the lake and, when dried, is as light in weight as balsa wood. Sections of ambatch are carefully shaped and, until the recent introduction of nylon cord, were tied firmly together with rope made from fibres of the indigenous sansevieria. The bow of the boat is tapered and drawn upwards to form a peak, while the stern is left open. When the outer shell is complete, a flat decking of ambatch is inserted into it for greater buoyancy.

Thomson and the explorers who followed after him found the Njemps to be a friendly and singularly honest people. They formed a small close-knit community with two main villages where the houses were built with their floors below ground-level. They had never set eyes on a white man before, yet

they completely accepted the strangers into their confidence. 'To me, one of the most remarkable features in the character of the young women and girls was their absolute unconsciousness of fear . . . They scrupled not to sit down on my knee, and with feminine blandishments which I could not resist, compelled me to go through my fashionable and highly original entertainment of drawing my own teeth.' He found time in between resting and entertaining his enchanting guests to supplement his men's rations by shooting oryx beisa, lesser kudu and waterbuck in the vicinity of their camp. To him and other weary travellers, Baringo was a Shangri-La after the trials and tribulations of Maasailand. If there was one single drawback to the place, it was the hordes of tenacious rats. They devoured his books, nibbled at his nose and toes as he slept at night and even sank their teeth into his bullets.

After a week's rest Thomson put in hand preparations for the final stages of his journey to the Victoria Nyanza. All the while his merchant friends beseeched him to abandon them and this time lent force to their argument by recounting how hundreds of men had been lost to the caravans that had preceded him. One will simply never know if they were trying to prevent his progress for their own selfish ends, or whether a few of them had genuinely come unstuck due to their involvement in slaving. Thomson recognized that this would in all probability be the most uncertain part of his entire undertaking, since he had no one to guide him. Inevitably, his path would be strewn with thorns but he was ready to take the risk if it meant succeeding where others had failed. With Maasailand conquered, his porters had complete faith in his ability to attain his cherished goal. Almost to a man, they volunteered to accompany him, though Muhinna feigned illness and was left behind in charge of the sick. The change in morale and discipline of Thomson's followers was little short of miraculous. From an undisciplined rabble barely eight months before, he and Martin had transformed them into a spirited and trustworthy body of men.

CHAPTER 10

The Victoria Nyanza

Siku njema huonekana asubuhi
A good day becomes evident in the morning
Swahili proverb

THOMSON HAD BEEN AGGRAVATED on two previous occasions by the traders' insistence on coinciding their departure with the decrees of fate, yet he involved himself in the very same mumbo-jumbo before leaving Baringo, on the pretext that 'when in Rome do as the Romans do'. A magic bullet was cast and shaped in an oblong form encapsulating a verse of the Koran. At precisely 1 p.m. Thomson fired it off facing due south, its destination the hearts of all who meant harm to him. There were no startling reports of a bloody trail, so he concluded that he had no enemies! An hour later Martin placed a specially prepared piece of steel wrapped in a red cloth into a blazing fire while he prayed aloud for a safe and successful journey. Thomson then put out the fire with water, as an expression of his desire to see all those who meant harm to the expedition extinguished like the flames. His men roared with laughter at the farce, because they were of a more irreverent nature than the superstitious traders who had moved ahead of them to scour the countryside for ivory. That being so, it is difficult to understand why the Europeans bothered with the charade. A goat was sacrificed and eaten at the conclusion of the ritual and the Master of Ceremonies ruled that 11 a.m. on Friday 16th November 1883 was the day and hour decreed by the Almighty to start out on the last leg of their journey.

On the appointed day Thomson bade farewell to the Njemps and set off at the head of his expedition on a switchback path which took them over angular boulders and through a tangle of thorns to the top of the rugged Tugen Hills. Their arrival was speedily announced by the shy inhabitants shouting the news from hilltop to hilltop across the deep gorges.

Living in isolated houses perched on the sides of the mountains [they] have no other means of communicating news but that of shouting. It is truly marvellous with what apparent ease they seemed to be able to project their voices immense distances. I have seen a man speaking across a deep valley to another who could barely be distinguished and yet not raising his voice more than if he was speaking to one a few yards off. The reply of the other could be heard with remarkable distinctness.

The district appeared to support a fairly large population of Tugen people who dressed in similar style to the Maasai; every man carried a distinctive spear with a narrow ribbed blade and a bow with a quiver of poisoned arrows. Their land was prepared for cultivation by slashing and burning the thick undergrowth, laboriously repeating the process each year on new ground. Eleusine and sorghum – two types of millet – were their main food crops with surplus produce being sold to caravans which staged at Lake Baringo, a full day's march away. Thomson crossed over the 8,000-foot range and was filled with awe at the sight of the Elgeyo escarpment, a frowning wall of rock and forest on the far side of the twelve-mile-wide Kerio Valley (Thomson's Wei-Wei Valley). A permanent river flows down the centre of the valley and,

in the rainy season, empties its turbid waters into Lake Turkana. The porters forded this river close to the Chebaloch gorge, over which the road from Kabarnet to Tambach now passes. When the river was in spate, the crossing had to be negotiated by means of a crude log bridge over the narrow gorge itself. Here the floodwaters have carved a dramatic perpendicular-sided channel out of solid metamorphic rock some twenty feet wide and fifty feet deep. There is an oft-repeated Kalenjin legend which relates how cattle rustlers returning to the Elgeyo escarpment after raiding deep into Maasai country stampeded their stolen stock downhill at this point and, by holding on to the tails of the oxen, leapt over the gorge to safety on the far side.

Thomson took two days to climb the steep escarpment whose sharp ridges reminded him of the flutings of a column, only more picturesque and irregular. Once his men had cleared the last precipice, the full strength of a gale-force wind slapped them in their faces and forced them to crawl forward on hands and knees a short distance for fear of being blown back over the edge. Half an hour later they broke cover from a narrow belt of giant cedar trees festooned with mosses and orchids on to the wide open spaces of the Uasin Gishu plateau. Towering above the surrounding countryside, some sixty miles to the north-west, stood Mount Elgon – 'a magnificent mountain ... famed for its caves and which I had been led to believe was an insignificant hill' Thomson's information had come from Stanley who, seeing it from a distance of 100 miles in 1875, had underestimated its height by over 7,000 feet. The summit of 14,178 feet is still below the height required in the tropics for permanent snow and glaciers, although transient snowfields do sometimes occur with patches that never completely melt. Stanley had called the huge, gently sloping extinct volcano 'Masaaba', a name widely used by the peoples of Western Kenya and Uganda. However, Thomson preferred the name 'Elgon', which he contrived from the Il Kony, or Sebei, people who lived then, as now, on its lower slopes.

On his first full day's march west from Elgeyo country, Thomson came across a curious circular wall of earth and stones with random openings which had a surprising resemblance to a Roman encampment. His Wandorobo guide dismissed the construction as the site of an old Maasai *manyatta* whereas it was in fact an ancient 'Sirikwa hole'. The Sirikwa people, of Hamitic origin, preceded the arrival of the Kalenjin and Maasai in Uasin Gishu and Trans Nzoia districts by a long and undefined period. They were said to have been large stock owners but, at the same time, they are credited with founding an extensive network of irrigation furrows on the slopes of the Cherangani Hills. Their dwellings were built partially underground and consisted of a living room large enough for an extended family adjoined to a cattle shed. They first dug a sizeable hole and surrounded it with roughly dressed stone bonded with mud. Then crossbeams were laid on the walls, covered with branches and layers of grass before being caked all over with a mixture of earth and cow dung to form a flat top. Frequent removal of dung over a period of years usually resulted in the cattle shed being somewhat deeper than the living quarters. The Sirikwa were not a dominant race and by the early part of the nineteenth century the Kalenjin and Maasai invaders had begun to evict them by force from their traditional lands. Some people speculate that they simply disappeared, being either killed or absorbed into the families of their conquerors. However, there appear to be such strong similarities of ethnic origin, language and house construction between the little-known Sirikwa and the Wa-Mbulu, who live north-west of Lake Manyara in northern Tanzania, that a southerly migration of the former over 150 years ago cannot be ruled out. Indeed, Nandi legend supports this hypothesis.

Thomson had been warned to avoid the heavily forested, mountainous and wet country of the belligerent Nandi, who were notorious for their fierce attacks on strangers and caravans which attempted to scale the great massif of the Mau. They showed themselves at different times very inimical to the white man and obstructed the building of the Uganda railway twenty years later, regarding the rails and telegraph wires as an inexhaustible supply of good-quality steel and copper with which to fashion their weapons and ornaments. 'One can imagine,' wrote Sir Charles Eliot, 'what thefts would be committed on a European railway if the telegraph wires were pearl necklaces and the rails first-rate sporting guns!' The Nandi were the first people to rebel against early British rule and were not finally pacified until their chief *laibon*, a man called Koitalel, was shot dead in a questionable encounter with a British Army officer in 1905. Thomson sensibly heeded the caution he had been given by rounding the northern spur of the Nandi escarpment and descending to the fertile plains below. Progress was slow and tiring since his men had to force a passage through thick clumps of elephant grass ten to fifteen feet high. They reached the village of Kabaras on 28th November – 'picturesquely situated on the face of a boulder-clad hill, and surrounded by smiling fields'.

The expedition had now set foot in Buluyia, whose people are a Bantu race consisting of seventeen sub-tribes living within the borders of present-day Kenya and a further four sub-tribes in Uganda. They all speak a common

language of Bantu origin though dialects vary to some extent. They suffer from one of the highest birth rates in the world which has put tremendous pressure on their bountiful land. Thomson called them the Wa-Kavirondo, instead of the Baluyia, which was possibly a corruption of the Swahili name for them – 'Wakwafi rondo'. The traders had portrayed them in a very unflattering light, so the explorer was agreeably surprised to find a warm welcome extended to him once, he supposed, the villagers had overcome their abject horror at seeing a white man, 'the newest human prodigy', for the first time. It was much more likely that his sudden appearance at the village provoked panic, as he would have been mistaken for an Arab slaver. Kabaras village was protected by a thick wall of compacted mud and a deep outer trench. He was taken aback to find himself surrounded by a 'bevy of undraped damsels whose clothes and ornaments consisted of a string of beads' and men who dressed up in anything but clothes. Only the married women wore garments – a four-inch square leather apron in front of their bodies with a long corded tassel hanging over their buttocks. When he had stopped staring bashfully into space – remember, it was the prudish Victorian era – and grew accustomed to their natural beauty, while reflecting on the ills of an over-civilized society, he began to feel at home. 'We were now in the midst of abundance. The hardships and horrors of our late fare were forgotten as we picked the bones of fat Kavirondo fowls with accompaniments of groundnuts, sweet potatoes and maize.' However, he was not quite so keen on the milk he was offered. The custom of the day, so his diaries incorrectly inform us, was to dilute it with cow's urine in vessels plastered with dung!

The Baluyia adopted the novel approach of positioning beehives in the conical roofs of their thatched houses. 'Though the house is frequently filled with smoke, and the honey acquires a black colour and most disagreeable taste, it does not drive the busy insects away.' Every household had a fine array of clay pots ranging in size from a few inches to three feet and, in some of the huts, he noticed grotesque horned and feathered head-dresses which were worn by men in battle or on ceremonial occasions. The maidens, spurred on by lavish gifts of beads, put on an impressive display of dancing for their visitors in the cool of the evening.

With demure aspect, bashful and doubtless blushing ... with hands laid close to each other in front of the waist, they advanced to the singing and clapping of the crowd. Next ... there was a jerk of the shoulders as if a dynamite pill had burst beneath the shoulder blade. This was repeated with growing rapidity culminating in a grand 'break-down', and shoulders and arms seemed as if they would fly off, so marvellous was the celerity with which they moved the muscles of the upper part of the body.

Thomson had witnessed the shoulder dance, the most exciting of all Baluyia dances.

Since it was essential that news of his peaceful motives and open-handed generosity preceded him, Thomson and his men spent an extra day at Kabaras before resuming their journey west to Kwa-Sundu, the principal village of the district. They passed through a fertile region watered by a perfect network of small streams. Large granite outcrops and termite mounds, each mound a city of millions of bustling, soft-bodied, industrious little inhabitants, dotted the countryside at regular intervals.

The mounds near Kwa-Sunda are flat and grey but, earlier in his travels, Thomson had observed numerous red ones with tall earth flues like monolithic towers reaching skywards. In the rains, when the soil is soft and moist, an echelon of males and females becomes sexually mature. They burst forth from their underground fortresses in the failing evening light for a short

flight of nuptial fantasy before fluttering back to earth like falling snowflakes. The few that escape the waiting predators then shed their wings and start their life-cycle over again. They are commonly called flying ants though they are not really ants at all; a delicacy of many tribes, they can be eaten either raw or fried in their own fat. The Baluyia have developed a clever deception to induce the ants to fly by pouring drops of water down the flues, all the while beating an irregular pat-patter with sticks on the top of the mound to simulate rain.

Thomson was impressed by the surprising number of seemingly prosperous villages in the neighbourhood. Almost every foot of ground was under cultivation and several impromptu markets were set up where the travellers bought honey, milk, eggs, chickens, beans and maize. Four men's food in flour cost one string of beads and eight men's rations of sweet potatoes the same; a sheep sold for fifteen strings whereas the more preferable and valuable goat fetched twenty strings.

Kwa-Sundu occupies the summit of a ridge overlooking a splendid river named the Nzoia . . . The present chief is a mild and pleasant young man, and we were soon on the best of terms with each other . . . he enjoyed enormously examining my photographs [and] *became so enthusiastic over the charms of one young lady, who was represented as posing aesthetically over a sunflower, that he gave me a large order for a bevy after that pattern at two tusks of ivory a head. I said I would see what I could do for him!*

The young chief was called Mumia and he turned out to be a staunch supporter of the early British administration. His village grew into a permanent station for the Imperial British East Africa Company in the 1890s and became known as Mumia's – only later to change its name again from the possessive to Mumias. Mumia prospered with the advent of a regular trade link to Uganda and by the time he died in 1949 at the ripe old age of about ninety, he had married 300 wives and sired hundreds of children – ample proof of his early interest in the opposite sex!

Thomson carried with him maps which had been carefully drawn from information collected by early explorers to the lake region, including Burton, Speke and Stanley. After chatting to Mumia, he concluded that their data was inaccurate. He had expected Kwa-Sundu to lie four or five miles to the north of Lake Victoria, whereas its true position was thirty-five miles to the east of the nearest inlet which now marks the boundary between Kenya and Uganda. Much of the expanse of water shown on his maps was, in fact, Buluyia and Luo country. He also had to correct Stanley's mistake of making Ugowe Bay a broad gulf to the north-east of the lake, instead of an insignificant indentation of the shoreline to the north of the much larger Kavirondo Gulf, beside which modern Kisumu was built.

Thomson was restless with the lake as yet unseen and made up his mind to start out immediately on the last leg of his dangerous journey. He selected fifty of his best porters for the trip but left Makatubu in charge of the rear party. They forded the 100-yard wide Nzoia River where its muddy waters rushed over shallow rock rapids and followed a westerly bearing along the line of the river towards the lake. Much of the open ground over which he walked has now been developed into sugar-cane plantations, making Kenya self-sufficient in sugar and a potential exporter in years to come. The local populace was rather less friendly to travellers than the people Thomson had met a few days earlier, and it is quite possible that the column was again mistaken for a slaving party. A number of slavers had been known to operate with impunity in the district, including one particularly unsavoury character called Sudi the slaver. The activities of people like Sudi kept the region in a chronic state of tribal war, as chief fought against chief to get captives to sell for firearms and trade goods. The slavers entered Buluyia from Uganda round the north end of Lake Victoria or sometimes paddled their canoes across the north-east corner to Bunyala and Samia. Here they captured unwary people and ferried them back by boat to Busoga. As often as not, the Arab slavers stayed behind in Buganda and relied on local Basoga strongmen to do their dirty work for them.

War-cries had been sounded frequently at the sight of the travellers and Thomson had to use all his powers of persuasion – and a little force – to maintain his forward momentum. He had a narrow escape when the sons of a village chief tried to prevent him from taking away a bullock which their father had given him in exchange for brass wire. When another present was demanded, Thomson testily called for his wire back and told them in no uncertain terms what they could do with the bullock. The chief then

interceded and begged the explorer to accept the gift but his sons were not so easily satisfied. A row ensued and a noisy crowd gathered round to hustle Thomson. In a fit of anger, he knocked the principal agitator to the ground and, folding his arms with extraordinary nonchalance, laughed derisively as the young brave pranced around him like a dangerous madman. Brahim stood guard with his leader's Express rifle raised menacingly, until the old man succeeded in removing the ringleaders from the scene. 'The moment was critical,' Thomson confessed later, 'for in spite of my heroic attitude I was anything but comfortable inwardly.'

Thomson realized that he was among a people who spoke a language akin to those of the middle and upper Nile when he reached the half-way mark to the lake. Thus, he differentiated between the Bantu-speaking Baluyia and the northernmost settlements of Luo, a Nilotic or riverine people whose ethnic relation stretches all the way from Khartoum in the Sudan southwards to Victoria – embracing Nuer, Shilluk, Dinka, Acholi, Lango, all part of the great people who have been migrating up the Nile for several hundred years. Tall and graceful, the women with a wonderful carriage to their bodies gained from their habit of carrying water pots on their heads, the Luo and the Turkana are the only people in Kenya who do not carry out an initiation ceremony based on a circumcision rite. The men could also be distinguished from the Baluyia by their habit of removing the six lower incisors, and the older women were the first the explorer had seen smoking pipes whose bowls were beautifully made of burnished clay. Unselfconscious in their nakedness, Thomson remarked that 'they eloquently illustrate the fact, which some people cannot understand, that morality has nothing to do with clothes'. In fact, the Luo had a very strict moral code – much more so then than nowadays, when they are considered to be the sartorial dandies of Kenya, spending lavishly on fashionable Western-style clothes.

When the locals deliberately threw themselves in his path and tried to murder the two guides Mumia had provided, Thomson began to lose his normally calm composure. He managed to get through the worst, however, without serious incident, thanks to Martin's sterling support from his usual and all-important position at the rear of the column. They camped at Mudembi (Thomson's 'Seremba'), a village of iron founders, on their third night out from Kwa-Sundu, where they witnessed craftsmen smelting ore in open charcoal-fired furnaces whose heat was enhanced by means of a double bellows operated with astonishing dexterity by a standing man. The bellows were made from a hollowed log, loosely fastened to which were a goatskin bag and two long light sticks, each stick being worked with a piston action to pump air into the furnace. It took a whole day to produce an ingot of iron weighing fifteen to twenty pounds which was speedily fashioned into spears, hoes and personal ornaments of excellent quality and sheen. The smiths would not allow Thomson to proceed any further. Why was he rushing so obsessively towards the lake? What did he want there? Perhaps he would invoke witchcraft to stop its waters – whatever that might have meant. The caravan would have to be quarantined and submit itself to a period of 'observation' to see what symptoms were likely to develop. Thomson was furious! The lake was so close, yet still seemed just beyond his reach. He went to the nearby Nzoia River to vent his anger and promptly shot three hippos, which straight away put the villagers in a better humour. Now, only the chief and his cronies opposed his passage in the hope of extorting a few more presents from him. Thomson was in no mood to be stopped again at the eleventh hour. He boldly broke down the guarded entrance to the village and, after a fierce tussle for possession of the loads, marched triumphantly towards his goal.

On 11th December 1883, the redoubtable explorer reached the end of his pilgrimage:

a glistening bay of the great lake surrounded by low shores and shut in to the south by several islands, the whole softly veiled and rendered weirdly indistinct by a dense haze. The view, with arid-looking euphorbia-clad* slopes shading gently down to the muddy beach, could not be called picturesque, though it was certainly pleasing. This scene was in striking contrast to all the views of African lakes it had yet been my privilege to see. In all previous cases I had looked down from heights of not less than 7,000 feet into yawning abysses some thousands of feet below; but here I stood on an insignificant hill and saw it shade gently into a great sheet of water.

We had no patience, however, to stand and take in all the details of the scene, we were too eager to be on the actual shores. An hour's feverish tramp, almost breaking into a run, served to bring us to the edge of Lake Victoria Nyanza, and soon we were joyously drinking deep draughts of its waters, while the men ran in

knee-deep, firing their guns and splashing about like madmen, apparently more delighted at the sight of the lake than I was – though doubtless the adage held good here, as in so many cases, that still waters run deep.

It is generally acknowledged that Thomson touched the lake at, or very close to, present-day Port Victoria. He shook hands all round and, with tears welling up in his eyes, delivered a short speech 'on heroic lines' to the assembled company. The excitement over, he turned his back on Africa's largest lake and headed for Samia's, the village of the second most important chief of the district, where he rested up for two days. He and Martin were in high spirits and cast away their natural reserve to demonstrate the dances of Scotland and Malta to the girls of the village. A jovial and friendly evening was had by all until Thomson discovered that his entire canteen of cutlery had been stolen from the cook's hut. Conjuring up a picture of eating from wooden platters using chopsticks or his fingers for the rest of their journey, he realized prompt action was essential to avoid that unpleasant possibility. Shouting 'Bunduki! Bunduki! Guns! Guns!' at the top of his voice, he quickly mobilized his porters to secure all the entrances to the village.

The scene that now took place was indescribable as the entire population rushed from their huts with the idea that the town was captured, and that they would all be killed. The men shouted and the women screamed and yelled. They went utterly out of their senses, and rushed about like madmen from gate to gate, only to find on their approach stern-visaged men with guns levelled at them. Then, more at that

★*Euphorbia candelabrum* – a giant succulent tree bearing a mass of candelabra-like branches and named accordingly.

The snow-clad peaks of Kibo *(right)* and Mawenzi seen from Amboseli.

(Left) A Maasai warrior in full battle array. His head-dress is edged with ostrich feathers, his shield is made from a buffalo hide and his anklet from the skin of a colobus monkey.

(Right) A Maasai warrior, *ol-murrani*, smeared with ochre and grease. The warrior's hair is plaited and is rarely cut.

(Below) Maasai warriors dancing during the *Eunoto* ceremony, when they hand over their duties to a younger generation and become elders.

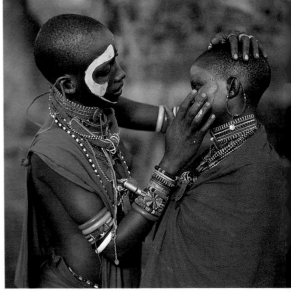

(Above) Ole Senteu Simel. Until his death in 1986 he was the senior Maasai *laibon*, grandson of the famous Mbatian.

(Above) Maasai girls decorating each other with ochre and chalk.

(Right) A Maasai warrior wearing a lion-mane head-dress. He had killed the lion with his spear as a sign of bravery.

(Opposite) During the *Eunoto* ceremony warriors daub themselves with chalk and have their heads shaved by their mothers.

(Opposite) Thomson's Falls, the spectacular cascade at Nyahururu named after the Scottish explorer.

(Left) Njemps in their traditional canoes, *lkadich*, constructed from poles of the ambatch tree, on Lake Baringo.

(Left) A Nandi woman drinking *busaa*, a drink made from fermented maize, through a hollow stem.

(Overleaf) A Luo man in typical regalia. Hippo teeth adorn the head-dress; from his necklace hang warthog tusks.

moment from three to four hundred men in the village, but so utterly were they paralysed by our prompt and audacious action that they knew not what to do. I found myself in the midst of a large crowd, and I knew what to do. Pointing to my men carrying brands, I announced my ultimatum: 'Restore my stolen property, or I burn down the town!' I was the more remorseless in my demand as I had every reason to believe that almost the whole town was implicated in the affair; indeed on the previous day the chief, Massala himself, had been specially anxious to have some of the very articles now stolen.

Thomson had the village at his mercy and his bluff paid off. The canteen was restored to him without any ill-feeling or loss of goodwill.

He gave serious thought to pressing on to the source of the White Nile, which he estimated, incorrectly, was only forty-five miles away. However, he was suffering from a severe bout of fever, his trade goods were getting inconveniently low and he had learned from Mumia that the people beyond Kavirondo were at war with the dreaded *Kabaka* Mutesa, the ruler of Buganda. Even if these were not justifiable reasons for turning back, then he had two questions of a more personal nature to ask himself. Was there any point in risking his life to travel to a place which had already been explored by Speke, Grant and Stanley? And would he discover anything of scientific or geographic interest in the low shores and sedge-lined waters of the lake? To both questions the answer was 'No'. 'As I had thus considerable uncertainty in front of me, I came to the conclusion that in this case discretion was the better part of valour. To gain a little by going further I might run an imminent risk of losing all. Here then, I resolved to make my turning-point. My hopes and footsteps henceforth must be homeward.' His decision proved to be intuitively wise.

The Baganda had always looked upon an approach to their country from the north and north-east with extreme suspicion and dislike. Had Thomson tried to force an entry, he would almost certainly have been killed. The tyrannical Mutesa died less than a year after the explorer visited the lake and his young son, Mwanga, acceded to the throne. Mwanga was a feeble-minded monster of eighteen who indulged himself in every possible vanity and vice, killing his subjects with no more care than if he was sweeping toy soldiers off a battle-board.

The murder of Bishop James Hannington, the first bishop of East Equatorial Africa, on 29th October 1885 heralded an unprecedented reign of terror in Buganda which reached a climax seven months later. It has been described as a story of appalling brutality, savagery and debauchery on the part of *Kabaka* Mwanga; at the same time, one of unbelievable courage and love of God on the part of the persecuted Christians. The first Catholic to die was Joseph Mukasa Balikuddembe, who had rebuked Mwanga for his complicity in the bishop's death. His position as a trusted personal servant of the *kabaka* did not save him from public execution. The day after he died, the *kabaka* issued a decree: 'All those who profess the Christian faith will face summary execution.' Thirty brave young men promptly and publicly confessed their faith. They included Mwanga's personal bodyguard, his pages and his servants. Mwanga, bereft of all reason, ordered them to be put in chains and burnt on a blazing pyre atop Mamungongo Hill. Some were hacked to death on the way there; others were speared and had their heads chopped off; Athanas Bazzekuketta was slowly dismembered, then his arteries were tied up to ensure an agonizing death; Mark Mawaggali was caught instructing Christians in a house at Mityana and was tied to a tree before savage, man-eating dogs were set upon him; and on Ascension day 1886 Charles Lwanga, the resolute Christian leader from the *kabaka*'s household, had his legs burnt off, leaving the rest of his body intact. He was subsequently burnt alive with the other Christian martyrs, their voices raised in praise of Jesus. In all, twenty-two Catholics and fifteen Protestants were murdered by the *kabaka*'s henchmen in conditions of abject cruelty. This terrible episode in Uganda's history will never be forgotten, for the Catholic martyrs were canonized in 1964 by Pope Paul VI at a moving ceremony at St Peter's Basilica in Rome. One could almost be excused for thinking that the infamous dictator, Idi Amin, was a reincarnation of *Kabaka* Mwanga.

Thomson and his stalwart men carefully avoided the iron smelters and smiths and hurried back to Kwa-Sundu on a more northerly path, where deserted villages manifested the cruel hand of Mutesa's imperial policies. The explorer's fever had become worse, almost to the stage of delirium, but he struggled on manfully in the belief that stiff exercise would be his best cure. After a six-hour march, he collapsed like a machine wound up to do a certain job and no more. The following day's march was equally trying for the number of marshy streams they had to cross. 'The village at which we rested was distinguished by two features – its excessive neatness and cleanliness, and its possession of an undraped young lady, certainly not less than seven feet in height. One of my men who stands six feet three was quite dwarfed by comparison with her. She was unmarried, which would seem to indicate that even in Kavirondo they can have too much of a good thing.'

They arrived back at Kwa-Sundu three days after leaving Samia's to find Makatubu and the rear party in good spirits. Though still suffering from fever, Thomson set himself the task of determining the exact position of Mumia's village by a series of astronomical observations which required him to be up at all hours of the night. While he was busy with this work the chief continually pestered him for medicines to bring rain. 'On his becoming importunate, I told him to be quiet. Did he not see that every night I was inquiring with my instruments into the secrets of the sky? Let him just wait and he would see the result! Curiously enough, in the evening after my oracular announcement there was a sharp thunderstorm and a heavy rainfall, which hardly required any self-satisfied comments on my part to secure for me immense prestige and applause.'

CHAPTER 11

Life in the balance

Mchovya asali hachovyi mara moja
He who dips his finger into honey does not dip it only once
Swahili proverb

THE TIME HAD COME for the Victoria Nyanza and Mount Kenya expedition to set out on its return journey to the coast. On Christmas eve 1883, Thomson and his heavily laden porters forded the Nzoia River for the last time and struck north to explore the caves and cave-dwellers of Mount Elgon before retracing their steps to Lake Baringo. 'Christmas day was not marked by any feast or revelling among good things. And yet I was supremely happy, for I was brimful of the thought that an arduous piece of work was completed and that I was homeward-bound.' A day later they were concealed in the forested foothills of the mountain without a guide to show them the way. They saw no signs of habitation and were at a loss to know what to do. After firing three guns – the customary signal of a caravan – and getting no response, Thomson sent off Makatubu and some men to reconnoitre. They returned with information that smoke could be seen issuing from several caves round a shoulder of the mountain. Next morning Thomson went to investigate the accuracy of this report and found that the caves were inhabited by a people who 'had all the appearance of the natives of Kamasia [a misnomer; they are the Tugen] and Elgeyo, and I believe their language to be very similar, probably a dialect slightly removed'.

These were the Il Kony or Sebei people who built their houses into the sides of the caves and whose cattle and granaries were well-protected by high palisades. They never lived in these houses permanently, though, rather looking upon the place as a refuge in times of conflict. Despite categorical assurances from the Sebei elders that the caves were a natural phenomenon – 'How could we have possibly dug them with our puny tools?' they exclaimed – Thomson preferred to believe that they were the work of a powerful ancient civilization, possibly Egyptian, which excavated them in search of precious stones and metals. How wrong he was! It is a geological fact that the huge caves were formed by the erosion of volcanic material by underwater streams, some of which have surfaced and conceal the entrances with delicate opal-tinted veils of cascading water. They are now home to millions of bats, while elephants often visit at night to dig out the salt with their tusks. The explorer could have disproved his own theory on closer examination of one of the largest mountains of volcanic origin in the world, but he chose to hurry away to the east.

On the last day of 1883 Thomson was determined to shoot something, however tough its meat, to celebrate the New Year in true Scottish style. He kept ahead of the column for three hours through scraggy forest which clothed a rich, rolling country, until he was rewarded at last by the sight of two buffaloes grazing in long grass a short distance away. A heart-shot at fifty yards failed to find its mark so, crawling closer with his Express rifle at the ready, he fired again at his chosen target, first through the shoulder and then through the head, whereupon a big bull staggered a few yards and collapsed, as Thomson thought, to die. He ignored a warning from Brahim that it might not be dead and, tucking his rifle nonchalantly under his arm with the jaunty air of a conqueror, walked forward to secure his prize. At six yards' range, the buffalo turned its head, let out a ferocious, blood-curdling grunt and got to its feet bent on revenge. Thomson was completely taken by surprise and had no time to fire; instinctively he turned and took to his heels but, in his weakened state, was not quite fast enough. The beast upped him from the rear and tossed him skywards.

For a time it seemed as if I had reached the limits of my earthly existence as well as that of the year … My next recollection was finding myself lying dazed and bruised, with some hazy notion that I had better take care! With this indefinite sense of something unusual I slowly and painfully raised my head, and lo! there was the brutal avenger standing three yards off, watching his victim, but apparently disdaining to hoist an inert foe. I found that I was lying with my head towards the buffalo. Strangely enough even then, I had not the slightest sensation of dread; only the electric thought flashed through my brain, 'If he comes for me again I am a dead man.' It almost seemed as if my thought roused the buffalo to action. Seeing signs of life in my hitherto inanimate body, he blew a terrible blast through his nostrils, and prepared to finish me off. Stunned and bruised as I was, I could make no fight for life. I simply dropped my head down among the grass in the vague hope that it might escape being pounded into jelly. Just at that moment a rifle-shot rang through the forest, which caused me to raise my head once more …

Brahim had fortunately remained close at hand and gave the bull the *coup de grâce* before it charged again. Although Thomson had lost a lot of blood from a six-inch gash in his thigh, he was lucky that his injuries did not seriously incapacitate him. 'I now learned that I had gone up in the most beautiful style, my hat going off in one direction and my rifle in another as if I was showering favours on an admiring crowd below … The curious thing is that I have no recollection of anything after feeling myself touched on the thigh by the buffalo's horns … [which] proved to be both massive and beautiful, the curves being exquisitely graceful.' Cheerfully but painfully he drank to the New Year in buffalo broth, reflecting that he would have an exciting story to relate to the family gathering in Scotland the following year. 'New Year's day found me little better than an animated log … I had to submit to the humiliation of being carried – the first time that I had ever sunk so low … the carriers dubbed me "our dollars" and continually incited each other with delightfully expressive freedom to "Hurry up with our dollars!" ' Thomson had no illusions about this nickname. At least once before, the death of a European traveller had resulted in the porters' entire loss of their wages, honourably and arduously earned. With his customary thoroughness, Thomson had taken care to make proper provision in Zanzibar to safeguard his men from this eventuality.

His original plan had been to cross over the 11,000-foot Cherangani Hills to determine their exact height and to get an unrestricted view of the country to the north; as a stretcher case, this route was now out of the question. He had to content himself with a detour round the western foothills and a hair-raising descent of the Elgeyo escarpment near Tot. The road down the escarpment is arguably the most scenic, if not one of the most tortuous, in Kenya today. It is often included in the route of the world-famous Safari Rally. Driving down it in a vehicle is one thing, but riding along the precipitous footpath on the back of a donkey is quite another. It must have been an excrutiating experience for Thomson, balanced precariously on 'Nil desperandum'. He reached Lake Baringo in five days, where he convalesced for a fortnight before pronouncing himself fit. Separate groups of Pokot and Samburu tribesmen visited the Njemps during this period and their knowledge of the region helped Thomson to piece together a little of the geography beyond Baringo. He learned that the Laikipia escarpment extended north-east to Mount Nyiru which formed the eastern side of 'Lake Samburu', a great salt-water lake from twenty to thirty miles broad and of inestimable length. It was said to have enormous white fish in its waters as well as hippos and crocodiles lining its shores. 'Clearly there is a region of great interest and importance here, the exploration of which will be a rich reward to the adventuresome traveller; and I can only say I shall envy the man who is first in the field.' Later Count Teleki was to verify the surprising accuracy of this report.

Thomson's contact with the Pokot – he called them the Suk – was the first published account of a people who were hitherto unknown to the New World.

They were strong-boned, ugly-looking fellows … [who] went absolutely naked …
A piece of flat brass hung from the lower lip of each and must have been both
painful and awkward to the wearer. The most remarkable feature of the Wa-Suk,
however, was the manner in which they dressed their hair … into the shape of a
bag, pointed somewhat at the bottom, having a piece of horn curling round and
upwards as a termination. By some glutinous preparation the hair is worked into a
solid mass, resembling in texture a cross-cut of unpolished ebony wood. The
entrance of this remarkable bag was from beneath, the hand requiring to be passed
backwards over the shoulder. In this, they placed all their small articles, beads, etc.

Kimameta had promised to return from his hunting expedition in Turkanaland by the end of January, but his non-appearance gave Thomson the excuse he had been looking for to stay put a while longer. In the back of his mind he knew that he should not delay unduly because food supplies were insufficient for a prolonged halt. However, his personal ambition was to shoot a trophy elephant and there was nowhere better to do this than in the uninhabited country north of the lake, which was known to be a pachyderms' paradise. In the course of ten days he bagged six zebras, four rhinos, four buffaloes, three elephants, one giraffe and one small gazelle. The lovely rich rufous-brown gazelle, with a distinct blackish lateral stripe, white belly and a black tail which is constantly in motion, was new to science. It is unquestionably one of the most strikingly beautiful antelopes of the East African plains and was named Thomson's gazelle, *Gazella thomsoni*, after the great explorer. Curiously, Thomson dismissed this exciting find with a few cursory remarks, and instead filled the pages of his journal with exaggerated and over-dramatized tales of elephant-shooting, since he knew that yarns of big game hunting would increase the sales of his books.

Getting with some trepidation on to one knee, I waited till the great hulk swung round . . . The next moment I fired with my 8-bore, causing it to grunt out as the ball went crashing into its body . . . just to miss the heart. As the elephant went off at a quick trot, I gave it the contents of the second barrel . . . then I seized the Express, both barrels of which I fired. On the fourth shot we were fearfully taken aback by the elephant trumpeting out, hauling round and coming down at full speed straight for us. Giving myself up as a lost man I had, however, sufficient presence of mind to fall down behind a slight tussock of grass . . . We were clearly in for a life-and-death fight, in which the odds were vastly against us. We knew that our

balls would have no chance of dropping the elephant . . . [but] we must still fight for life! The space between us was lessening with horrible rapidity. My eyes were almost blinded by the profuse perspiration . . . 'shall I fire, or shall I wait?' Nearer and nearer it came! Fifty yards – thirty yards – twenty – and still it held a straight line, pledged to our destruction! My men implored me to fire . . . My gun was at my shoulder, and my eye glanced along the barrel. The elephant had reached within ten yards. I must fire. But just as I was on the point of pressing the trigger, the elephant swerved a little to one side. Thank God! It had not seen us, and we were saved!

And so it goes on! That tusker, incidentally, was one of the many that got away.

It was a foregone conclusion that Thomson's extended hunting safari would put his men at unnecessary risk. The rains had come and gone and, in the height of the dry season, grain supplies from the Njemps and their Kalenjin neighbours had run out. In his absence, Martin had imposed strict food rationing, but there was no way in which the caravan could reach Ngong without shooting frequently for the pot. This proved a burden for Thomson whose health was now failing. Within days of breaking camp on 24th February 1884, symptoms of dysentery became all too apparent and he suffered great distress. He took note of the hot underground streams that fed a large marsh south of Lake Baringo and saw numerous hot springs which gushed from fault lines above the Enkare Ronkai, the narrow river. It is somewhat surprising nevertheless that he failed to set eyes on Lake Bogoria, since his route took him only a ridge or two away from its dramatic setting. Lake Hannington, as it was formerly known, first came to light when Bishop Hannington camped along its shores on 18th September 1885 during his fateful journey to Uganda. To give Thomson his due, his mind was no longer on exploration. He was unable to eat or sleep, he was too weak to walk and all his strength was needed to stay in the saddle of 'Nil desperandum'. Fortuitously, he still found sufficient reserves of energy to shoot a variety of animals, sometimes from the mounted position and at other times at extreme range.

As the column wended its way slowly across the Ang'ata Nderit, the parched dusty plains beyond Nakuru – Nakurro, the barren grassless place – and rounded the flamingo-fringed shores of Lake Elementeita, it became evident that the outbreak of rinderpest or *actinomycosis* had not been confined to the Laikipia plateau, for cattle carcasses, bleached bones and dried hides were littered everywhere. Thomson began to doubt his own powers of self-preservation with all this death and destruction pervading the air. Having kept going for seven days on a few cups of clear soup 'the one refrain that passed hopefully through my brain was "let us get to Naivasha and milk will put me right" '. He reached Naivasha on 4th March unable to stand or sit, more dead than alive, only to find that milk curdled in his stomach and made him feel very much worse.

The Maasai had no healthy cattle to sell them owing to the deadly disease, so it fell on Martin's shoulders to hunt zebra for the pot and stave off a growing food crisis. They soon realized the hopelessness of staying by the lake without proper rations and two days later resumed their journey to Mianzi-ni, a small trading centre located in thick bamboo forest above Kijabe – Le-nkijape, the cold place – where they hoped to buy food from the

Kikuyu. Two porters had already died of dysentery and several others were destined to suffer the same fate unless their diet changed quickly. The Maasai would never permit burial of the dead, for corpses were believed to poison the soil, and Thomson could not bear the thought of his bones being picked over by ghoulish hyenas, which are tolerated by the pastoralists because they are the traditional undertakers of their dead relations. For this and other reasons he never lost hope. The lamp of life flickered a little, then became more steady. After being carried for three long marches in a hammock rigged on poles, he felt well enough to be propped up and enthuse over the spectacular view from the top ledge of the Rift Valley escarpment.

We were looking across a great plain, slightly undulating and perfectly treeless, bounded on the east by the magnificent mass of the Aberdare Range, with Doinyo Kinangop rising picturesquely from the mass. Through a slight gap the snowy peak of Kenya glittered in crystal purity. To the south-east lay the wooded highlands of Kikuyu, with forests of bamboo in the foreground. To the south-west we saw the yawning pit of Doinyo Longonot and the romantic expanse of Naivasha. To the south the desolate plains of Dogilani, and to the east [he meant west] *the massive escarpment of the Mau.*

Mianzi-ni is a Swahili place name meaning 'the place in the bamboo' and properly described the site where a regular market was established for traders' caravans travelling the Naivasha route. It was located on the common border of the Maasai and Kikuyu peoples, a short distance from the highest point on the main Nairobi to Nakuru highway (part of the new trans-Africa highway), near Kamae forest station. When construction work on the Uganda railway reached the floor of the Rift Valley at the turn of the century, the market became unprofitable and closed down. The Kikuyu called it 'Magumu', the place which you travel very far to reach, for they deliberately left a broad belt of virgin forest round their fertile lands to keep Maasai raiding parties out.

At an altitude of over 8,000 feet, the bitter easterly winds chilled Thomson to the marrow. 'It felt worse than the east of Scotland in early spring.' Daily thunderstorms added to his misery, for the damp permeated his clothes and bedding. He was taken from his tent and put into an imperfectly thatched grass hut just as a terrific hailstorm burst overhead. For an hour lumps of ice the size of small cannonballs pounded down from the skies until the ground lay perfectly white like a winter's scene in Europe. Lying helpless on his camp bed, he was quickly soaked to the skin and suffered a relapse. For six long weeks he lay in darkness hovering between life and death, while his diaries tellingly remained blank. Martin, good soul, tried to prevent the Maasai from tormenting him, by spreading a story to the effect that Thomson was communing with God to find an infallible cure for their dying cattle and under no circumstances could be seen or disturbed. 'I became an object fearful to look upon, with eyes sunk away deep into my skull. A skin bag drawn tightly over a skeleton enclosing a few indispensable organs.' No fires could be lit, there were no candles left in the expedition's stores and it was too cold to leave the door ajar. He slept fitfully, lying awake for long periods listening to the wind howling through the bamboo, and relieved to hear the dawn chorus of forest birds heralding yet another weary day. At one time he lost his powers of speech and honestly thought his days were numbered, but somehow he fought back from the depths of despair. At length it became quite obvious that the wretched climate of Mianzi-ni was inhibiting his recovery; as a result a plan was adopted to leave for Ngong and, from there, to return home with a minimum of delay.

Kimameta had shown up towards the end of April with his caravan laden with ivory from areas that had never before been reached by traders or hunters. He joined forces with Thompson again at Kedong where an ivory cache he had buried on their outward journey was safely unearthed, although a Maasai *manyatta* had been built on top of it in the interval. They regained Ngong two days later, where Kimameta used all his powers of persuasion, spiced with the most lurid tales of massacres and plunder, to prevent Thomson from returning to the coast through Kamba country and the Taita Hills. This was still an uncharted route which, the trader argued, would expose the explorer to unnecessary danger. All the merchants were united in their appeal that he should accompany them to Pangani but he obstinately refused. He was determined to sell his life dearly for, in his poor state of health, he had nothing to lose by taking the most direct route home. Kimameta found Thomson incorrigible and, with surprising generosity, gave him a large gift of beads, cloth and wire. 'A more thoroughly good fellow than Jumbe Kimameta never lived,' Thompson enthused. 'I was assisted by him in every way, and rarely thwarted – a statement that can seldom be made by a European with regard to his connection with a coast trader.' Kimameta was no angel but his unstinting help had been invaluable. Thomson kept his word and left £100 in the hands of Sir John Kirk, the British Consul-General at Zanzibar, with instructions that it should be spent solely to benefit the trader when he got home.

On 7th May the expedition left Ngong for the last time. As the columns crossed the Athi and Kaputei plains – now part of the Nairobi National Park – to Ukambani, Thomson began to feel a little better for the first time in many weeks and even took a pot-shot at a lion. 'The only bar to a rapid recovery from my state of emaciation was the absence of any digestible food.' They moved quickly through the densely inhabited, fertile hill district of Ulu to the marginal rainfall areas south of Kibwezi, where the Wakamba were dying of starvation.

The two white muscat donkeys collapsed and died just short of Ndara, either victims of a tsetse fly bite or poisoned by a noxious weed or shrub in an area devoid of grass and hay. The Wataita were so short of food that the porters had to make do with a few sticks of sugar-cane. Thomson was a little more fortunate. The Anglican missionary at Sagalla took pity on him and generously provided a cupful of rice and a pinch of sea salt. A day later Thomson urged his men forward across the formidable *nyika* at a gruelling pace and in three remarkable marches covered roughly ninety miles to the coast – a notable achievement in stark contrast to the inauspicious start to their journey fourteen months earlier.

No news of the expedition had reached Mombasa or Zanzibar for ten months, so it came as a great surprise and a cause for jubilation when at the end of May or early June 1884 – the exact date is in dispute – Thomson led his men into Rabai to a volley of gunfire and a hero's welcome. He took his first painful steps in over three months to celebrate the occasion. Within days he had sailed for Zanzibar, where good food and a comfortable bed at the British Consul's residence helped him to regain some of his former strength.

Thomson received lavish praise from all quarters on his return to England and Scotland. His exploits elevated him to the foremost rank of distinguished explorers. Newspapers and fellow-travellers alike extolled his virtues; geographers and cartographers rejoiced in his detailed observations and solutions to hitherto unsolved riddles; and scientists delighted in his discoveries, especially his gazelle and a collection of 140 species of flora, of which five were new to the Western world and were named after him. From the Royal Geographical Society he received an honorarium of £360 and, in the summer of 1885, its Gold Founder's Medal, making him the youngest recipient ever of this highest and most coveted award. In his own words, he 'had penetrated through the most dangerous tribes in Africa, traversed a region unequalled in that continent for the interest and variety of its topographical features, and for the unique peculiarities of its inhabitants'. Furthermore, he had accomplished it without bloodshed. His unassuming manner and his ready sense of humour helped him to overcome many difficult moments. His style was one of compromise rather than confrontation, of persuasion rather than persecution; he took pride in proving that a gentle word was more effective than the mighty sword. Whereas some critics thought his journey could have been made easier by firing a few bullets, others paid tribute to his wisdom and patience. His motto had been his guiding principle – 'He who goes gently, goes safely; he who goes safely, goes far'.

If Thomson can be faulted in any way, it is because he failed to realize that the Swahili and Arab traders purposely depicted the Maasai and other inland tribes in a murderous light, in order to defend – as well as extend – the land over which the blood-red flag of the sultan fluttered ominously. At a time when the moral indignation of Christian European nations was forcing an end to the ghastly brutalities and degradation of the slave trade, they took great pains to conceal their nefarious and inhuman activities by spinning an elaborate web of lies and chicanery. Massacres, both real and imagined, heightened the illusion and helped to protect their lucrative sources of ivory – the white, to say nothing of the black – from acquisitive minds. Diplomacy was never their strong point and without the explorer's restraining influence, many lives would have been lost.

The major casualty of this epic journey through Maasailand was Thomson himself. Although his health showed periodic improvement, he never fully recovered from dysentery and the complications which resulted from his prolonged illness. His tremendous energy, however, and his compulsive desire to travel enabled him to journey extensively in Africa for another seven years. In 1885 he sailed up the Niger River on behalf of the National African Company, later the Royal Niger Company; in 1888 he visited Morocco and explored the Atlas Mountains; and in 1890 he was engaged by Cecil Rhodes for the British South Africa Company to negotiate treaties with tribal chiefs in Central East Africa. In all, he visited Africa six times and trekked almost 15,000 miles.

In his latter years Thomson was rarely free of pain. In failing health, he travelled the length and breadth of Europe in search of cures. After lying critically ill with pneumonia for the first two months of 1893, his doctors advised him to recuperate in a hot, dry climate. Cecil Rhodes on hearing of this, generously placed his house at Kimberley at the invalid's disposal. Here, Thomson's health steadily improved. But when he returned home to the

miserable English summer of 1895, his African wounds again overwhelmed
him. This time there was no hope of recovery and he died within weeks of his
return, at the age of thirty-seven, with the spirit of Africa still in his heart.
Even if his great journeys of exploration and discovery have been forgotten in
the mists of time, his name will long be remembered in East Africa for the
beautiful 'Tommie' gazelle which gambols over and graces the vast expanses
of the Maasai plains.

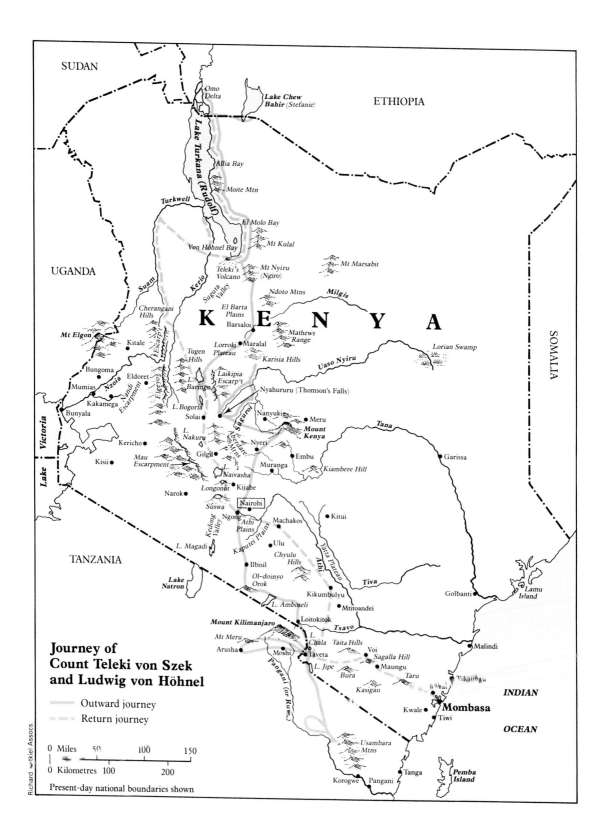

SUDAN

ETHIOPIA

Omo Delta

Lake Chew Bahir *(Stefanie)*

Lake Turkana (Rudolf)

Allia Bay

Turkwell

Moite Mtn

El Molo Bay

Von Höhnel Bay

Mt Kulal

UGANDA

Teleki's Volcano

Mt Nyiru (Ngiro)

Mt Marsabit

Suam

Kerio

Suguta Valley

Ndoto Mtns

Milgis

Cherangani Hills

El Barta Plains

K E N Y A

Barsaloi

Mt Elgon

Kitale

Lorroki Plateau

Mathews Range

Lorian Swamp

Maralal

Tugen Hills

Karisia Hills

Uaso Nyiru

Bungoma

Eldoret

L. Baringo

Laikipia Escarp't

Mumias

Nyahururu (Thomson's Falls)

Kakamega

L. Bogoria

Nanyuki

Meru

Tana

Bunyala

Solai

Nanyuki

Mount Kenya

Kericho

L. Nakuru

Nyeri

Garissa

Kisii

Mau Escarpment

Gilgil

Muranga

Embu

Kiambere Hill

L. Naivasha

Narok

Longonot

Kijabe

Suswa

Nairobi

Ngong

Machakos

Kitui

Kedong Valley

Athi Plains

Ulu

L. Magadi

Kaputei Plains

Chyulu Hills

Athi

TANZANIA

Ilbisil

Ol-doinyo Orok

Yatta Plateau

Tiva

Lake Natron

L. Amboseli

Kikumbulyu

Mtitoandei

Golbanti

Lamu Island

Loitokitok

Tsavo

Mount Kilimanjaro

L. Chala

Mt Meru

Taita Hills

Arusha

Moshi

Taveta

Voi

Sagalla Hill

Malindi

L. Jipe

Maungu

Bura

Taru

INDIAN

Journey of
Count Teleki von Szek
and Ludwig von Höhnel

Kasigau

OCEAN

Outward journey

Return journey

Kwale

Mombasa

Tiwi

0 Miles   50   100   150

0 Kilometres 100   200

Pemba Island

Present-day national boundaries shown

Usambara Mtns

Korogwe

Pangani

Tanga

Pangani (or Ru...)

Richard ...kiel Assocs.

PART III

Count Samuel Teleki von Szek and Lieutenant Ludwig von Höhnel

*The 'discovery' of Lakes Rudolf
and Stefanie*

1886–8

*We gazed in speechless delight, spell-bound by the beauty
of the glittering expanse of a great lake which melted
on the horizon into the blue of the sky.*

VON HÖHNEL

CHAPTER 12

A leisurely start

> *Haraka, haraka, haina baraka*
> Hurry, hurry, has no blessing
> Swahili proverb

JOSEPH THOMSON'S BOOK *Through Masai Land*, published in early 1885, focused considerable attention on the region of tropical Africa that had remained closed longest to European exploration. Wealthy big game hunters rushed to visit areas which offered the best prospects in the world for hunting the rhinoceros, buffalo, elephant and lion; travellers and explorers aspired to be the first to climb snowcapped mountains and to discover mysterious inland lakes; and adventurers dreamt of making themselves fortunes out of ivory, precious stones and untapped mineral resources.

Count Samuel Teleki von Szek, a Hungarian count of the Holy Roman Empire, was enthralled by Thomson's experiences in Africa and immediately planned a hunting trip of his own to the region. Born into a noble family on 1st November 1845, Teleki owned large estates in Transylvania (now part of Romania). He was a *bon vivant* and gourmet whose pride and joy was his stud farm which specialized in breeding 'tough horses with gazelle-like eyes and Arab heads'. Being of independent means, he was in the fortunate position of not having to seek expedition sponsors. It took him a relatively short time, therefore, to organize his journey in 1886 with the blessing of his influential friend Crown Prince Rudolf, son of His Imperial and Apostolic Majesty Franz-Josef I, Emperor of Austria, King of Hungary, etc.

Rudolf personally persuaded Teleki to broaden the scope of his hunting safari in order to explore the unknown lands that Thomson had mentioned north of Lake Baringo. He also introduced him to Lieutenant Ludwig von Höhnel, the navigation officer on His Majesty's yacht SMS *Greif*, with the recommendation that he should accompany Teleki as companion and second-in-command. As von Höhnel succinctly put it: 'thanks, probably, to powerful influence my petition was granted, and the very next day I heard that I was to go'. It turned out to be a remarkably successful partnership that blossomed into lifelong friendship.

Von Höhnel was thirty at the time and spoke fluent Hungarian although he was born in Pressburg – now called Bratislava, in Czechoslovakia. He had graduated from the Marine Academy at Fiume – now Rijeka, the main seaport of Yugoslavia – in 1876 and served on various ships during his early career. Von Höhnel was an accomplished cartographer and was responsible for the maps of the expedition and most of the scientific collections. He also kept the diaries and wrote the published accounts of their travels entitled *Discovery by Count Teleki of Lakes Rudolf and Stefanie*.

Teleki and von Höhnel did very little joint planning for an undertaking of such magnitude. After a few brief interviews, von Höhnel was left on his own in Austria to purchase stores and to handle the expedition's administrative preparations, while Teleki visited France and England to seek advice from people who were experienced in African travel. They planned to meet up again in Zanzibar towards the end of October. Von Höhnel reached the Spice

Island on 31st October 1886 but Teleki was delayed in Europe and did not arrive until a month later.

Teleki had been given much information, some of it conflicting. Sir Richard Burton, the eminent explorer, was one person whose advice was invaluable. He pressed Teleki not to rely solely on local guides and porters but to recruit Somalis as a personal escort in case of trouble. He insisted that they were reliable, loyal and honest and had proved their worth on several occasions in the past. Teleki accepted this recommendation and, on his way to Zanzibar, stopped over at Aden where he signed on eight Somalis headed by Dualla Idris. Dualla was born in Aden and had visited Europe and America as a seaman in his youth. Though only twenty-four years old at this time, he had been one of Stanley's most faithful followers in the Congo for six years. He spoke fluent English, Arabic, Hindustani and Ki-Swahili and proved to be of immense help to Teleki, rising to a position of undisputed authority. The expedition might well have floundered without him. 'Every day we learnt to value Dualla more; he was such a sympathetic fellow, so thoroughly to be relied upon, and although he did not look particularly strong, he had wonderful pluck and powers of endurance.' Teleki was not alone in praising Dualla. Four years later, the Somali became a key man to the success of Captain, later Lord, Lugard's important expedition, which extended the British sphere of influence to Uganda. 'There is probably no living man who has travelled so much in Africa,' wrote the influential Lugard. 'He was the most energetic, valuable native I have ever met, thoroughly trustworthy and very conscientious and willing.' When his leaders fell ill and were carried on litters, Dualla quietly and competently took charge. No African made a greater contribution to the early exploration of East Africa; if anyone deserved a medal, he did.

Early on, Teleki and von Höhnel had agreed to invite James Martin, the Maltese sailor who had distinguished himself on Thomson's journey through Maasailand, to join the expedition. So von Höhnel's first task on arrival in Zanzibar was to call on Martin, whose house was beautifully situated in the country. 'There I found him, and, fortunately, also several faithful comrades of his, such as Mwana Sera, Kacheche and Bedue, all celebrities in their own way, whose names had become familiar to me in various books of travel, so that I was very much interested in making their personal acquaintance . . . Alas! I must confess that the somewhat romantic idea I had conceived in my study of books on Africa received a very severe shock, for they were altogether different from what I had expected.' Von Höhnel was disappointed to learn that Martin was not free to join them, having already been engaged to guide a party of English sportsmen – Robert, later Sir Robert, Harvey; Sir John Willoughby Bart, DSO; and H.C.V. Hunter – to the excellent hunting grounds near Taveta. Looking for a replacement, he was given to understand that Juma Kimameta, the well-known ivory trader who had also gained recognition with Thomson, was in Zanzibar having been summoned by the sultan at the insistence of his creditors to liquidate his long-standing debts. Within a day von Höhnel had tracked him down and arranged a meeting.

'Kimameta seemed very nervous at first, even after the handing round of cigarettes and sherbet, to which I treated the whole party with a view to setting them at their ease. The leader's face was deeply pitted with smallpox and his right eye had been injured by that disease, but the expression of the other was bright, honest and intelligent.' A cordial understanding was soon reached and Kimameta declared himself ready to join the expedition as a freelance. 'As I was favourably impressed by him, I did not hesitate to secure by a considerable present of money his remaining in Zanzibar until the arrival of Count Teleki.'

Both von Höhnel and Teleki were struck by Kimameta's forceful personality; he spoke several languages and was adept at avoiding trouble. They agreed that he should take charge of packing the barter goods and hire the necessary men and donkeys at Pangani, the flourishing coastal town on the African mainland whence most journeys into the interior started; and that he should act as their guide through those regions which he had visited frequently in search of ivory. At his own request, he was neither to administer the caravan nor control the porters. Teleki granted him permission, however, to take his own entourage so that he could trade in ivory when time allowed. They negotiated a contract for 2,000 Maria Theresa dollars, equivalent to about 420 English sovereigns at that time. It proved to be a good deal on both sides.

Fortunately for the newcomers, they also met up with 'The General' - General Mathews, later to become General Sir Lloyd Mathews, KCMG – whose benign character and unostentatious ways concealed his tremendous influence over all sections of the Zanzibari community. He subsequently became the sultan's *wazir*, in effect his prime minister, until he died of malaria and overwork at the age of fifty-one in 1901. He kindly helped Teleki to make a selection of the items demanded by the tribes of the interior, which Kimameta divided up into loads of between seventy-five and eighty pounds, before weighing, numbering and cataloguing them. Then the camp stores, tents, medicines, provisions and wines and spirits had to be repacked, and a large assortment of miscellaneous items properly bundled and entered in the master ledger. These included 'cowries, knives, scissors, looking glasses, picture books, jointed jumping dolls, gilt wire bracelets and rings, daggers, naval and cavalry sabres, with many other miscellaneous trifles which happened to take our fancy or come our way, and which we thought might be useful in our dealings with the black chieftains whose favour and co-operation it was so important for us to secure.'

Teleki had brought an iron boat in six sections and a canvas boat in two parts totalling twenty-two man-loads; he also had plenty of ammunition, rockets and explosives, shovels, axes and saws, strong cables for crossing rivers, rifle grease and copper coins for buying food in the coastal districts. In all, the expedition had a staggering thirty-five tons of stores divided up into more than 470 loads, with insufficient porters to shoulder them. Teleki hired about 200 porters* in Zanzibar with the help of Issa Ben Madi, a captain in the sultan's army and a native of the Comoro Islands, but he found recruitment on the mainland almost impossible. A visit to the *wali*, or governor, of Pangani proved fruitless despite the usual letter of introduction from the sultan, since he was a feeble individual with little influence.

---

*In his diaries, von Höhnel claimed that at Zanzibar in mid-January 1887, Teleki recruited 200 Zanzibaris and 450 porters for the expedition but such a cumbersome force must be open to doubt. There was no mention of massive desertion yet, within two weeks, von Höhnel asserted that their porters were only 283 strong – seventy-two of them having been recruited at Pangani in the meantime. I have taken this to be correct, since it ties in with his subsequent reports. It also explains why Teleki had to procure pack-donkeys to carry their excess loads.

Kimameta had also let him down due to the large number of caravans assembling at the time. There were simply not enough able-bodied men to go round and an incentive of an extra dollar a day failed to produce the expected response. In a week, only seventy-two more men had signed up. Teleki decided to wait no longer, content in the knowledge that Kimameta had bought twenty-five donkeys to alleviate the human shortfall. Anyhow, he was anxious to break camp and move inland for fear of falling prey to an endemic coastal fever.

Two small river dhows sufficed to take the travellers and their new recruits up the winding Pangani River in the afternoon of 28th January 1887.

This was really our first step into the wilderness, and was full of the deepest interest to us on that account; but the exquisite scenery would have charmed us in any case. Wild and varied vegetation clothes the banks instead of the dense impenetrable forests usual in the northern tropics. At first – that is to say, as long as the water was brackish – this vegetation consisted chiefly of mangroves, weird-looking growths, the dark crown of leaves rising from above the bare aerial roots as if from stilts; farther on came sugar plantations, with hedges of banana trees and betel-nut palms, the banks still retaining their primeval appearance. Here and there on the smooth surface of the water appeared the snouts of hippopotami which had come up to breathe with much snorting and puffing. Now and then some old fellows rose right out of the water, plunging back with a tremendous splash, converting the smooth river into a rough sea of waves . . .

Teleki met up with Dualla and the rest of his men at Mawia and quickly got down to the business of re-sorting his carefully prepared loads by putting the non-essential items to one side. Arrangements had been made to ship seventy loads of wire to Mombasa by dhow to await his collection; now other stores had to be left in the care of village elders until Teleki was ready to send for them.

Directly a man had received his load he carried it off to have a distinctive mark made on it, and also to get used to its burden. Many of the porters stuck a forked stick into the load so as to get it more easily on to their shoulders; whilst others, especially the Wanyamwesi, liked to divide each load into two parts, fasten each half at the end of a stout stick, and carry the stick on their shoulders; but of course this could only be done with such things as wire, etc.

The sectionalized iron boat was placed firmly in the pile of essential stores, much to the displeasure of the porters who had been chosen to carry the unwieldy and heavy contraption. 'We had to use a great deal of persuasion and soft-sawder to reconcile men to their burden.' But they could have saved their breath! It took a superhuman effort to hump the 'white elephant' all the way to Taveta where it was unceremoniously dumped, never to set sail on an African lake.

The count spared no expense on a first-rate armoury. For his personal use, he patronized the foremost English gunsmiths, Holland and Holland, indulging in their finest sporting guns and rifles, which never once let him down. These included two double-barrelled 8-bore rifles firing solid bullets of hardened lead, one 577-bore Express rifle for explosive and ordinary bullets, one 10-bore rifle and two 500-bore Express rifles. Teleki had brought for his men 200 rifled muzzle loaders, eighty breach-loading Werndl carbines, twelve Colt repeating rifles complete with bayonets and cartridge pouches, and several revolvers. At the same time his Somali bodyguard and his servants were armed with modern magazine rifles and were coached on how to handle them. Others received some basic instruction which included firing a few shots on a makeshift range.

As the day approached to leave Mawia, final arrangements had to be made for detailing assignments and briefing key personnel. Teleki had recruited nine *askaris* who were given quite separate tasks to those of his Somali bodyguard. They performed general duties and were responsible for loading and escorting the string of pack donkeys, which was a thankless chore. Then there were nine guides to be consulted about the best routes into the interior. They knew of Teleki's plan in outline only. He had told them with masterful understatement that the caravan would journey 'mpaka Baringo na mbele kidogo' – to Lake Baringo and a little way beyond! These guides included two from Thomson's expedition – the elderly Muinyi Sera (Teleki called him Mwana Sera) and Makatubu, the ex-slave from Nyasaland, now Malawi. As it turned out, Dualla and Kimameta between them left the guides little to do, with only Makatubu proving his worth. 'He became one of the most valuable men in our service, for he far excelled every other guide we had. Of exceptional physique, and with unrivalled powers of endurance, he was reliable, energetic, full of resource, excelling all others in obedience, ever ready to work, the first to begin, the last to go to rest.' The remainder of the guides, in Teleki's own words, were not worth a charge of powder! Lastly there were three personal servants and Mhogo, the safari cook, to be given their orders. Mhogo had previously travelled with Speke and Cameron into the interior of East Africa.

[He] *was not what you would call a first rate caterer for the table, but from long experience he was quite unrivalled in knowing how to manage in the wilds; he always carried his own cooking apparatus, one of the heaviest of all the loads; so that, take him all round, he was a great acquisition.*

Early in the morning of February 4th we were roused for the first time by the noisy preparations of a caravan about to start. We soon discovered that we had been roused too late, for the greater number of the men were already some hundred paces from camp, only waiting for the tents to be struck and the signal to be given to be off. They did not have to wait for us long. Very soon sounded a shrill, discordant blast from the barghum, *or trumpet of kudu antelope horn; Count Teleki placed himself at the head of the force which, as it swayed from side to side, with much*

shouting and gesticulating, looked more like the coils of a long serpent than anything else.

Leaving the mosquito-infested coastal belt with its myriad of fireflies, the column wended its way inland past doum palms festooned with yellow-brown leopard orchids, *Ansellia africana*, and umbrella-shaped acacia trees placed by benevolent nature as welcome shelter to weary travellers from the tropical sun. They had scarcely marched for an hour when trouble started. The leading porters, shirking their heavy loads, demanded to set up camp; meanwhile, von Höhnel and his small rearguard had found out to their cost that Kimameta's donkeys had not been trained to carry baggage. 'When it came to saddling them, they behaved like mad creatures. Their burdens on, they seized the next opportunity to rush off and roll about till they got rid of the obnoxious loads, and we could see them quietly grazing again in the distance, when the whole ceremony had to be gone through once more.' It was a hopeless task, though, and von Höhnel had to give up the unequal struggle. As the unladen donkeys trotted forward to catch up with the column, he toiled in the midday sun to store the goods which had been left lying on the ground. 'I very soon gave up the idea that one can wander about in Africa in a light-hearted, careless way.'

Within days their plight had become serious. At the little village of Lewa – a singularly apt Swahili name meaning 'drunk' – the porters drank themselves into a stupor on potent banana wine and threatened to mutiny. That night fifty men deserted, followed several days later by another thirteen who took

A mutinous scene at Lewa

with them the expedition's precious scientific books and maps – an incalculable loss at such an early stage. No one was apprehended in spite of search parties being dispatched on both occasions. After all, there is a saying that one crow does not peck out the eyes of another. While von Höhnel rushed back to Zanzibar to recruit more porters and to alert the authorities to be on the lookout for the runaways, Teleki, to avoid the possibility of further mass desertion, doggedly continued his journey as far as Korogwe, a trading station of the German East Africa Company on the Pangani River. It was here, three weeks later, that von Höhnel rejoined the expedition with over forty new recruits and seventeen deserters brought back in chains. In the meantime, Teleki's men had had a fight with the local villagers over a young girl whom they had abducted to their camp; it had been an ugly clash resulting in several deaths on both sides. All in all, they had made a thoroughly bad start to their journey but, judging by the troubles of other travellers in similar circumstances, this was not unusual. The further the porters marched into the interior, the more likely their behaviour was to improve – as, indeed, was to happen with Teleki's followers. By the time they reached the idyllic forested enclave of Taveta on 30th April they had settled down under his leadership with reasonable discipline.

Even though the local inhabitants beyond Korogwe were friendly, nature was not so welcoming. On their first night out, *siafu* or soldier ants invaded in their thousands and had to be repelled with hot ashes and glowing embers. In subsequent marches through the humid low-lying country the travellers encountered crocodiles in the rivers, leeches in the streams, scorpions under rocks, fleas in all abandoned camping grounds and disused *manyattas*, and swarms of bees which attacked the column on three occasions, causing pandemonium with some badly swollen faces and hands. As they neared Taveta the vegetation became greener and more luxuriant, the trees higher and closer together and the undergrowth thicker. They had to stoop, twist, creep and crawl in single file through a perfectly preserved primaeval forest until they reached the protected entrance to Taveta village. While the barrier of tree trunks was being removed, excited greetings were followed closely by volleys of gunfire which echoed on every side, startling birds and terrifying monkeys.

Taveta enchanted Teleki and von Höhnel as it had done Thomson four years earlier. Since they planned to make it their base for several weeks, a semi-permanent camp was erected under the supervision of 'architects' Muinyi Sera and Makatubu. The picturesque forest clearing in which they camped was less than 100 yards from the clear waters of the Lumi River. 'It was bounded on three sides by the forest, and on the fourth side by a banana hedge. A few monarchs of the wood, with their mighty crowns of leaves, had been left standing; beneath the grateful shade of one of them our daily market was generally held, and it became to us what the spreading chestnut tree was to the village blacksmith.' A wonderful variety of home-grown produce was offered for sale, including large bunches of bananas – some ripe and golden, others still green for slicing and frying – ground maize flour, skinned and dried cassava, yams, potatoes, tomatoes, sugar-cane and honey. Sometimes a young lad would appear with a hen tucked under his arm, at other times fresh fish would be caught in wicker traps set in the Lumi River or Lake Jipe. The porters received one and a quarter yards of cloth or thirty strings of beads every six days with which to buy rations of their choice but, with food so cheap, they often had 'money' left over to exchange for tobacco or banana wine, which was sold in far from hygenic-looking earthenware vessels.

Teleki and von Höhnel also ate like kings. On a visit to Martin and the English sportsmen, the spread was no less impressive. 'We sat down to a sumptuous repast including fish from the Lumi River, buffaloes' tongues, antelope steaks and a guinea fowl ragout, actually succeeded by a regular English plum-pudding. The best part of the meal, however, was, without doubt, the lively talk we all kept up, our hosts entertaining us with anecdotes of their hunting adventures with the terrible big game of Africa, which seemed the more thrilling when listened to with an accompaniment of the clinking of champagne glasses.' No wonder Taveta had become such a popular resort!

The community at Taveta was patriarchal, with the eldest and most respected men being consulted on every occasion. The friendly people practised circumcision in the same manner and with the same attendant ceremonies as the Maasai and dressed identically. As a rule the young men wore only one garment, made of hairy goatskin or calico dyed a brownish-red colour, which covered the left side of the body and was fastened over the right shoulder. Their hair was twisted and plaited to form a pigtail at the back; the lobes of their ears were artificially elongated and ornamented with trinkets; while their wrists and ankles were smothered with a striking accumulation of bracelets and anklets, mostly made from coils of brass wire or strips of leather decorated with beads. The young girls wore tanned or dressed goatskins trimmed with brightly coloured beads; they were particularly fond of bead necklaces, which seldom comprised less than 100 strings twisted together.

Like their menfolk, they smeared their bodies with a mixture of animal fat and red ochre, giving themselves an indelicate appearance.

While Teleki set his men to work re-stringing beads into regulation 'Maasai' lengths, porters were sent to Pangani and Mombasa to collect the expedition's scattered trade goods. At the same time, Teleki took the opportunity to explore Mounts Kilimanjaro and Meru. Leaving Dualla behind to guard his base camp and stores, he headed first for Marangu, situated on the south-east shoulder of Kilimanjaro, where the young chief Miriali gave him a warm welcome. Although only about twenty-five years old, Miriali announced that he was 100! He wore in the pierced lobe of his right ear a round splinter of wood some four inches long and the thickness of a pencil, while in the unusually distended left lobe was stuck a decorated wooden plug the size of a saucer.

Through a low narrow plank door we came first to a little wood of banana trees, then through a second opening into an avenue of lofty dracaena, *leading to a group of huts surrounded by a strong palisade of sawn planks. Then, without the slightest embarrassment, our host's whole harem – three wives and three slave girls – came out to greet us, one of the former being, as Miriali informed us, a daughter of his notorious neighbour, Mandara, whom, as a matter of policy, he had bought for 300 cows. Miriali had shown better taste in the choice of his slave girls than in that of his wives . . . The wives were all wrapped in long purple mantles, whilst the girls wore the simple but picturesque costume common to all unmarried women of the Kilimanjaro.*

The most beautiful aspect of Miriali's house was its site, for 'like the worthy burghers of old with their town halls, the architects had forgotten the windows, so that it was quite dark inside'. As the chief drank *pombe*, a mildly alcoholic fermentation of millet and bananas, his wives and slave girls squatted at their visitors' feet, gradually sidling up closer and whispering every now and then a soft request for *kilengele* – beads – in their ears. It was an intriguing variation on the same old begging theme, and the story does not relate how successful was this seductive approach!

Since Teleki had planned to explore Mount Meru first, his short stay with Miriali was merely a courtesy call with the added aim of assessing the suitability of using Marangu as a base for climbing Mount Kilimanjaro. Forty-eight hours later he bade Miriali farewell with a promise to return soon, having exchanged a revolver and the usual quantities of cloth, beads, wire and gunpowder for an ox, a fine spear, a *simi* (sword knife) and the skins of three colobus monkeys. Travelling in the height of the rainy season, he found the going uncomfortably wet. Rivers were in flood and his porters had great difficulty carrying their heavy head loads through a glutinous morass of claylike soil. Although Teleki had taken with him an emergency larder of cattle on the hoof, wild animals had to be shot daily for the pot and the numerous rhinos became the main target. He encountered large numbers of Maasai on the plains between the two majestic mountains and in spite of the small size of his party – only sixty-six men in all – Teleki had no occasion to complain of their conduct towards him. Once the customary *hongo* had been handed over, he found travelling in their midst presented no special danger and surmised that Thomson's and Fischer's harassment had arisen from the injustices the Maasai had suffered previously at the hands of unscrupulous

Zanzibaris and traders from the coast, rather than from a particular hostility towards Europeans.

Teleki abandoned his attempt to scale Mount Meru when he reached some unfriendly Wameru settlements on the lower slopes. Anyhow driving rain and low swirling mist in the first week of May would have made further progress towards the 14,979-foot summit insufferable; so he diverted to Arusha to buy more pack-animals. Nothing tried his patience more than bartering. Every transaction was watched by a crowd of spectators drawn together by curiosity or a desire to show off their cleverness. Even if buyer and seller were satisfied, their friends frequently were not. One did not like the colour of the cloth, another thought the price was too low, and so on *ad infinitum*. Even Kimameta became annoyed on this occasion, because four times the price was fixed and four times the owner of the donkeys tried to back out of the bargain. As a result hours were wasted in fruitless haggling. The return journey to Taveta was equally trying. All the rivers were in spate and the unwilling donkeys had to be dragged, tugged or pushed across raging torrents with ropes. Moreover, the rains had brought on a plague of tsetse flies, which inconvenienced the travellers and killed their Muscat riding donkeys before the column regained Taveta.

Teleki realized the futility of an attempt on Kibo until the heavy rains abated, so it was another month before he returned to Marangu.

We started on 9th June with sixty-two porters. The beautiful blue sky was perfectly cloudless, and Kibo, the goal of our wandering, stood out clear and distinct before us ... Miriali received us as before in a flowing red toga. His sharp eyes at once spied the eighteen shot repeater Count Teleki had promised him, and they sparkled with delight as he led us to our old meadow, where two fine cows, his present in token of welcome, were already tethered. Miriali asked at once for the weapon; the other fine things we had brought for him could wait.

The chief showed little enthusiasm for Teleki's rather unusual gifts, which included a grand gilded dragoon's helmet, a magnificent sabre and picture books for his wives and slave girls. However, this affected neither his lavish hospitality nor the military tattoo-cum-war-dance that he laid on specially for them because he was determined to score off his powerful father-in-law, who had always been accustomed to having his own way in deciding how visitors to Chaggaland would be entertained. There was method in Miriali's madness, of course, for this also meant that he had first pick of all their valuables. Half-way through the spectacle Miriali left to don his gala costume, the pride of which was a general's red coat complete with gold braid. How it had found its way from America to Marangu was anyone's guess. High-ranking officers from the New World would have been astonished to see their uniform embellished with skins of the black and white colobus monkey and a broad band of vulture's feathers.

When spies told Mandara what was going on behind his back, he sent irate messages to his son-in-law chiding him for becoming the Europeans' donkey driver, since the young chief had minded a few pack-animals as a favour to Teleki. He also accused Miriali of dishonestly accepting presents which, he asserted, Sultan Seyyid Barghash had sent expressly for him. 'Since Europeans are as fond of fat oxen as hyenas,' Mandara wrote disparagingly, 'it comes as no surprise that you have succeeded in enticing them away from me.' Miriali took these insults in his stride but his audacity eventually landed him in trouble. Mandara attacked and laid waste to his country in 1889, and some fifteen years later the colonial administration of what was by then German East Africa banished him from the Kilimanjaro region for a time.

While the chiefs worked themselves up over their guests, Teleki and von Höhnel quietly prepared for their mountain venture by hiring the same four experienced guides whom Harry Johnston, later Sir Harry Johnston, had employed three years earlier. Understandably, they followed in Johnston's footsteps to the saddle which connects the peaks of Kibo and Mawenzi. Climbing beyond Marangu, they passed tree heaths, conifers, everlasting flowers, irises, amaryllises and a number of giant groundsels, every arm of which bore splendid upright panicles of yellow-orange flowers three to four feet long. These striking treelike shrubs were first collected by Johnston and were named *Senecio johnstonii* after him.

[On 19th June] *we started with fifteen Swahili carrying our instruments, two little mountain tents, rugs and provisions. The fog came on again and again, but was always dispersed by the sun. At nine o'clock we had reached an altitude of 10,897 feet, and our men already showed signs of fatigue, though none of the loads exceeded 44 lbs in weight; so we halted for a short rest ... At a quarter to twelve we were at the source of the stream on our left, at a height of 13,230 feet. The water murmured underneath a springy bed of turf several inches thick, and so close and firm that we could stand upon it. Here lived many water rats and we could see them happily swimming about, but we could not catch any. There was a good deal of ice about this spring too, although the temperature of the water was +7° Centigrade. The path now led rapidly to the saddle by way of a low wall of rock, and, arrived there, we bore more to the left so as to approach Kibo more closely. Although we were now marching over level ground, we were obliged to halt at two o'clock on account of our black companions, who already showed signs of exhaustion. We made them just put up our two little tents and collect some brushwood; then we sent them back to the lower camp, with orders to return here at the same time the next day.*

This was their highest camp on Kilimanjaro and an intensely cold one, with the temperature dropping to minus eleven degrees Centigrade. They ate a

hearty evening meal of preserved ham, cocoa and ships' biscuits washed
down by a draught of red wine, before foul weather drove them into their
tents for the night. 'We had thick woollen underclothes and heavy overcoats
on, with warm wraps to supplement them, but for all that we were kept awake
all night by the bitter cold.' Rising well before daybreak, they warmed
themselves over a roaring fire and melted the frozen water in their flasks to
make cocoa. Then, as dawn broke, they set off briskly in the direction of
Kibo, past lava fields and over ridges which had weathered into countless
boulders; the incline was gentle but the going was slow. At 16,240 feet, von
Höhnel was the first to give in. 'Fully satisfied with all I had achieved, I
yielded to my irresistible desire for sleep . . . I was awoken from a short deep
slumber by a strong wind and the dazzling rays of the midday sun.'

'The Count climbed on without the slightest difficulty for an hour, when he began to feel a certain straining of the membrane of the tympanum of the ear, accompanied by a rushing noise to his head but he pressed on all the same.' As he crossed a small depression filled with lava debris to reach the snowline, he felt his lips bleeding. He also became dreadfully sleepy and, realizing that it would be dangerous to submit to this overpowering temptation in freezing snow, decided to turn for home. He had suffered from fatigue and symptoms of altitude sickness, having reached a height of 17,387 feet, less than 2,000 feet short of the summit. He and von Höhnel now hurried back to their tents where they ate a quick snack of biscuits and wine. They returned to base camp with their porters that evening and reached Marangu the following day. Although their guides had demanded, and had been given, many yards of cloth in advance with which to protect themselves from the cold, they never took it with them up the mountain. 'In the garb of Adam in paradise they of course suffered frightfully.' Nor had they taken any food except a bottle of milk, so they were both hungry and half-frozen by the time they got home.

The explorers made final arrangements at Taveta to move north into Maasailand. All the trade goods had been collected from the coast but the expedition was still very short of manpower; seven men had defected with their personal weapons, two had died, one guide had been escorted back to Zanzibar in chains for disobeying orders and eight porters were too ill to undertake the journey. With only 265 able-bodied men at his disposal, Teleki tried to overcome the shortfall by turning the young oxen from his beef herd into pack-animals; 'but all our efforts to train them to carry loads by putting empty saddles on their backs were fruitless, for they simply exhausted themselves in the struggle to get rid of the unusual incubus'. Even the chance purchase of eight strong donkeys from a homeward-bound trading caravan did not save his poor porters from being burdened with massive head loads.

After ten weeks' silence the kudu horn trumpet called the men to muster once more. Extra precautions were taken to prevent last-minute desertions as Teleki and von Höhnel set out in the pioneering footsteps of Joseph Thomson through Loitokitok, Amboseli, Ol-doinyo Orok and Ilbisil to Ngong. Their journey turned out to be somewhat less hazardous than the one endured by Thomson. At Amboseli, for instance, an ox was killed in honour of Kimameta, and in return for buffalo hides which Teleki gave the Maasai – they were much prized for making shields – the il-murran guided him to their best hunting grounds and bravely despatched several wounded animals with their spears. Married men supervised cattle and donkey sales, women brought ox-hides, strips of partially tanned leather and firewood to barter for beads, and children helped by fetching water. The main drawback to the place were the swarms of vexatious flies which were attracted to grease-smeared bodies and tormented the travellers as much as the insatiable curiosity of the people. 'Whenever we sat down to a meal we might be sure of a circle of natives at least three deep, to stare at us, for, as in European menageries, "feeding time" is the most attractive moment of the day. All our food and everything we used, knives, spoons, forks, must be examined.'

Von Höhnel's accounts of the Maasai were rather less exaggerated than those of his predecessors and give us an interesting comparison with a way of life that has changed little in 100 years. 'The Maasai are pre-eminently a pastoral people; as a rule confining their wanderings in search of fresh pastures for their cattle to their own districts,' he wrote.

They cling devotedly to their own customs, and have maintained the purity of their race, allowing no inter-marrying with other tribes ... They are slender and tall, above the medium height, but they are not particularly muscular. They have clear chocolate-brown complexions, pointed prominent chins, noses narrower than those of [other Africans], thin lips and oval-shaped eyes with an upward slant ... Their limbs are beautifully formed and developed, their feet and hands remarkably small. The expression of some of the younger men is almost feminine in its gentleness, and regular features are more common amongst males than the females ... Some of the quite young unmarried girls are, however, charming enough but they soon degenerate into poor wrinkled, shrivelled-looking creatures, whilst the men retain to old age their noble aristocratic appearance ...

Boys between twelve and fourteen years old undergo the rite of circumcision, after which they go with their fellow-sufferers to the woods for two to three weeks, where they shoot little birds with bows and arrows ... When a barnoti *[ol-barnoti – an initiate recovering from circumcision] is fifteen or sixteen years old, he becomes a* moran *[ol-murrani] or warrior ... He receives from his father a spear with a blade nearly three feet long, a large elliptical shield of buffalo hide with the heraldic device of the district on the outside in white, red, or black, a long straight sword, and a club made of heavy wood as hard as iron, or of rhinoceros horn. Firearms have not yet been introduced to Maasailand, and it is only rarely that bows and arrows are used instead of spears ... Thus equipped, the young* moran *goes to the warrior* kraal *[homestead or* manyatta] *of his district, where amongst his comrades and the* ditto *or unmarried sweethearts he leads for a time a life of free love. Although this is the custom of his country, he has to beware of certain consequences which may ensue. Now that he has come to man's estate the* moran *is bold, conceited, easily excited and fond of thieving. His greatest desire is to dip his spear in blood, if it be only in that of some stray, half-starved porter, whilst his chief duty is to protect his district, and on this account the warrior* kraals *are situated near the most exposed portions of each division of Maasailand ...*

There is really more pretension and impudence behind the self-consciousness of the moran *than real courage, and they owe much of the dread in which they are held to their effective get-up. The short mantle of brown haired kidskin, which he generally wears fastened on the right shoulder, is twisted into a girdle and transferred to his waist. He leaves some of the gala ornaments at home, substituting for them an iron bell worn above the knee. His head and shoulders and also his spear are profusely smeared with red grease, which makes him look as if he were dripping with blood. Below the knee he fastens a strip of colobus skin, which, with the long white hair still on it, stands away from his legs in front. Round his neck is tied the* naibere *... a long piece of white cotton with a stripe of coloured [cloth] sewn in the middle. This flows straight down his back, and is supplemented by a deep collar or cape of black vultures' feathers, whilst his face is framed in an extra-ordinary head-dress of ostrich feathers stuck in a band of leather. Thus adorned he dashes on with diabolical cries, his shield in his left hand and in the right his uplifted spear. Such an apparition strikes terror into the hearts of the natives, and at its approach they flee without coming to blows at all.*

At Ol-doinyo Orok, the large black mountain overlooking modern Namanga, the much-feared warriors of the Matapato section were no less friendly than their kinsfolk at Amboseli.

The moran *and their inseparable* dittos *or sweethearts stood about our tents at a respectful distance, made no attempt to beg, and gave us no trouble at all. They watched us at our work of taking astronomical observations, writing up our journals, and so on, and when they got tired of that they went outside the camp and amused themselves with singing and dancing . . .* [they] *here allowed me to photograph them without taking any notice of what I was doing.*

This account is in stark contrast to the belligerent behaviour from which Thomson had apparently suffered only four years earlier. It is just possible that he was partly to blame for his own plight by failing to appreciate the absolute power of the *laibons*. It is also possible that he may unwittingly have joined forces with a bunch of traders whose past conduct had left the Maasai with old scores to settle, for Swahili-led caravans never hesitated to rob and rape when they thought themselves invincible. As a result, Thompson could have been a victim of guilt by association, made worse by the principle that gentleness and courtesy were taken as signs of weakness by the haughty sons of the steppe. Anyhow, he was the first European to set foot in Maasailand and it was invariably easier to follow another's footsteps, if the one who paved the way trod gently. Teleki must have derived considerable benefit from his predecessor's humane approach although he, too, was a shrewd leader. Moreover, he had mustered a larger, better-armed body of men, ably controlled by a posse of Somalis which took firm command whenever the need arose; this was something the coastal people never seemed willing to do or capable of achieving.

Admittedly, the traders had little alternative but to ingratiate themselves with the Maasai, in the hope of being told the whereabouts of the nomadic Wandorobo people. The Wandorobo lived under Maasai protection in forests adjoining their rolling grassland plateaux, and controlled many of the most lucrative sources of ivory within easy access of the coast. 'Maasai' ivory was highly prized, though the Maasai themselves never killed elephants. Wandorobo hunters were the experts in this field, using arrows and short stabbing spears with detachable heads whose tips were dipped in a deadly, fast-acting vegetable poison. The most widely used poison in Kenya is made from *Acocanthera schimperi*, an unmistakable tree which averages twenty to thirty feet in height with the circumference of the bole ranging from a few inches to two feet. Its fragrant flowers are tubular in shape and white in colour, sometimes flushed with pink. It grows throughout the drier districts of Kenya and can be found in Kajiado district between Ilbisil and the rear of the Ngong Hills. Although manufacturing techniques vary, young trees are normally favoured to produce the most effective poison. The wood, bark and roots of the tree are boiled with a minimal covering of water for at least seven hours, until a sticky black mass with a consistency of tar is produced. The arrow-heads are dipped in this and, when dry, are covered with a sheath to protect them from the elements. In this way, the potency of the poison is retained for a long time though it will eventually decline with age. When introduced into the bloodstream through a wound, fresh poison may kill a man within half an hour and an elephant in less than a day by halting the muscular action of the heart in systolic.

'The neighbourhood of Ol-doinyo Orok is a regular zoological garden. The steep slopes, especially near the base of the mountain, are clothed with luxuriant vegetation, chiefly acacias, the nickname of *orok*, or black,

originating in the dark colour of the foliage ... the bush-grown steppe beyond the mountain was tenanted by numerous rhinoceroses, giraffes, zebras, wild boars [warthogs], gnus, gazelles, ostriches, bustards, guinea-fowls and partridges.' As it was Maasai custom to eat neither the flesh of wild animals nor of domestic fowl, their grazing areas abounded in game. Today, it is no coincidence that East Africa's finest game parks are to be found in Maasailand. Their very existence would be in doubt except for a rare tolerance the Maasai have towards our heritage which man has so ruthlessly destroyed elsewhere. Teleki saw warriors hunting the lion, buffalo and ostrich, but these were speared only occasionally for making head-dresses and shields. Otherwise, the land was an unspoiled paradise – until the first gun-toting hunters appeared on the scene.

Von Höhnel brought down four rhinos, but his first encounter with elephants was not so successful. In the failing evening light, he stalked a small herd to within twenty-three paces and took careful aim at a large bull. As he fired, missing a heart-shot, the barrels of the heavy 8-bore rifle jerked up and the sharp-edged comb of the left hammer split his nostrils wide open and cut the bridge of his nose. This quickly put an end to any thoughts he may have had of following the spoor. On his return to camp, Teleki acted as doctor and hastened to get out all his surgical instruments, carbolic and sublimate liniments and piles of bandages with which, by the light of a hurricane lamp, he treated his blood-stained colleague. Although the wound was not particularly painful, it took a good six weeks to heal.

Mohammedans will not eat unhallowed meat. They insist on a ritual cutting of the throat when the animal is still alive, with its head pointing towards Mecca. Since the majority of Teleki's porters were followers of the Prophet, there was a mad rush every time a shot was fired. In the nineteen days it took them to walk from Ol-doinyo Orok to Ngong everybody was kept busy hacking and tearing at the carcasses of slain animals in a free-for-all for the meat. The hunters wounded an elephant and a lion but bagged fourteen rhinos, eight zebras, four giraffes, six impalas, five gnus or wildebeests and several other species of plains' game. With a good many oxen bought *en route* to supplement these rations, there was a surfeit to eat. Only milk was difficult to procure, a bowl costing almost as much as an ox. 'The Maasai, in fact, hold milk in very high esteem, and think it desecration to boil it. They believe, too, that any adulteration of the milk leads to the sterility of the cow which yielded it.' These old-fashioned views no longer hold true, but the principal diet of the Maasai is still milk and blood, the latter being richer in protein than either milk or meat. Blood is drawn from the jugular of their cattle using a special arrow with a small metal tip. About one litre may be bled from an animal at a time and is usually drunk warm by the men although it is invariably diluted with milk for the women and children. The wound is sealed with mud and the animal will not normally be bled again for two months. Some people may feel squeamish about drinking ox blood but they should remember that it was advocated as a cure for tuberculosis in Europe 100 years ago. Patients afflicted with this disease regularly attended slaughterhouses to drink prescribed draughts of warm blood.

CHAPTER 13

A new route to Lake Baringo

Msasi haogopi miiba
A hunter is not afraid of thorns
Swahili proverb

'OUR MARCH THROUGH MAASAILAND was over and we stood upon the threshold of Kikuyuland, on the eve of a time full of trial and adventure . . . Our camping place at Ngongo Bagas [Ngong] was in a very pretty neighbourhood, on the edge of a thick wood behind which dwelt the dreaded people of Kikuyu, whilst on the south stretched vast pastures tenanted by the great herds of cattle belonging to the Maasai.'

Ngong had lost none of its importance as a staging post strategically located mid-way between Taveta and Lake Baringo, where trading caravans stocked up with provisions and livestock on the hoof before moving north. The Kikuyu were always delighted to sell their surplus farm produce but never dared to venture beyond the boundaries of their forested homelands for fear of attack by the Maasai. Instead, they established their markets near the forest edge in an atmosphere of antipathy and mutual distrust. The slightest misunderstanding, however unintentional, resulted in food sellers fleeing, thus bringing the day's proceedings to an abrupt end. The market would resume the following day until interrupted once more by a careless move on the part of either the buyer or the seller. Timid porters required nerves of steel to remain calm and collected amid hordes of gesticulating warriors with swords flashing on every side. Teleki's men could be forgiven for imagining that they were being lured into a vulnerable position by these fickle tribesmen whence they would find it impossible to extricate themselves alive.

Teleki was open-minded about his route beyond Ngong. He preferred to travel through Kikuyu country to Mount Kenya, but Kimameta remonstrated against the idea for he dreaded mixing with a people who were anathema to him. He predicted that even if the tribesmen living along the border allowed them to gain entry, those in the districts beyond would exact revenge for the excesses of previous Arab and Swahili-led caravans, not least his own. Eventually, two factors decided Teleki to attempt a route to which other European travellers had given a wide berth. For a start, timely showers of rain, the first for many weeks, had boosted his popularity in the eyes of the Kikuyu, because it was generally believed that he was responsible for them. Second, with the help of Dualla and an old Maasai woman called Nakairo, who was held in high regard by the Kikuyu and whose son had been restored to health thanks to Teleki's medicines, special permission was given for the caravan to travel through their country.

Dualla knew well how to inspire confidence by his own assured demeanour, and at the very first interview he got so far as to make blood brotherhood with several Wakikuyu. This ceremony takes place thus. A sheep is killed, the liver only is cooked and eaten by the brothers that are to be. A little hitch occurred, however, one of the natives on this occasion having substituted the liver of a dog for that of a sheep. The horror of Dualla, who is a strict Mahomedan, may be imagined.

Von Höhnel's recollection of the *muma* ceremony must be faulty. It was more usual for blood to be extracted from the arms of both parties to the rites and then mixed. A piece of meat was next dipped into the blood, shared and eaten.

While peace treaties were enacted, Teleki ordered forty axes to be sharpened, weapons to be overhauled and ammunition to be given out. 'These were, of course, only precautionary measures . . . We hoped to achieve our purpose without bloodshed, but we did not mean to trust the natives too much, and were prepared for all contingencies.' Later, he was to realize how well-advised were these precautions.

On 7th September 1887, the expedition left Ngong accompanied by a Kikuyu guide and an escort of warriors. 'The path led us over a hilly district in a northerly direction, chiefly through grass-grown clearings surrounded by thick bush.' As was normal on the first day's march after a break in safari routine, the distance covered was relatively short. But it was an encouraging start. The frontiersmen between Dagoretti and Kikuyu, on the outskirts of modern Nairobi, were unusually friendly – albeit a little shy – and sold Teleki 350 rations for a mere 210 strings of beads.

We could not help thinking the traders who had had such difficulties in these parts had only themselves to blame, probably because in their nervousness they always fired a few shots with a view to overawing the people before breaking up camp. This would, of course, at once suggest hostile intentions on their part. There is no doubt, however, that the Wakikuyu are of a very restless and excitable temperament, easily roused to action, their swords starting readily from their scabbards, as proved by the many scarcely healed wounds and scars on the bodies of all the full-grown men . . . Though seldom above a medium height they are well built, muscular and strong. Their characters vary very much. Their natural complexion is a rather dark brown, but the fat with which they smear themselves makes it look red. Their clothes and ornaments are very like those of the Maasai and the Wakamba . . .

The young men wear their hair arranged in several different styles . . . They are fond of binding quantities of feathers from the breast of the guinea-fowl or the wild dove round their heads, so that they look as if they grew there. Boys and older men have their hair cut short at a certain stage of growth, whilst young girls leave only a circular cap-like patch of hair on the top of their heads. Both sexes remove all the hair from the body.

The men, though the temperature is often low, wear no garments but a piece of goat-skin fastened on the right shoulder, and scarcely covering the upper portion of the body, and a heart-shaped bit of leather hanging down the back from a thin string worn round the neck. When it rains this bit of leather is turned up to protect the head. Very often even the scanty wardrobe is found oppressive, and the young men especially are fond of rolling up the mantle and wearing it as a girdle. . . On the left arm the men wear bracelets of ivory, buffalo horn or wood, and round their bodies row upon row of dark blue beads or leather girdles stitched with beads.

The women wear an apron of tanned and dressed kidskin fastened round the waist, which comes down to the thighs or knees, whilst in cold or rainy weather they supplement it with a second and larger leather garment, falling from the throat to the knees. The Wakikuyu load ears, neck, arms, loins and legs with ornaments, most of them imitations of those worn by the Maasai. The rims of the upper portions of the ears are pierced and the lobes distended.

The women spoilt their looks by wearing large bunches of beads in their ears, some three to four inches thick, making them stick out like the ears of an enraged elephant.

A journey that Teleki had expected to complete in eight days turned out to be a nightmarish trek of six weeks. The Kikuyu were like chameleons. At one moment they were disposed to be friendly, at another they wanted to fight; as one group offered to guide them, another plotted and schemed to prevent their passage; while some people stole their stores, others caught the thieves and gave them a good flogging before returning the goods to their rightful owners. Whether it was aggressive, drunken old men shaking their fists in Teleki's face, or a few arrows let fly at the shout of the oft-repeated long drawn-out war-cry *u-u-u-i*, or jittery porters loosing off bullets at real or imaginary attackers, hardly a day passed without a drama to add to the anxiety and excitement of the moment.

Thousands of Kikuyu followed the expedition through districts which are now known as Kiambu, Murang'a and Nyeri and, all things considered, Teleki controlled his men creditably.

[We] *had to abandon all hope that we should achieve our journey without difficulty for we were little more than prisoners, so surrounded were we with ever-increasing crowds of natives whose hostility to us was unmistakable. We were still, however, determined not to give in, and had we turned back there is no doubt that it would have been the signal for an attack ... We were constantly on foot, going about amongst our people to prevent any careless action of theirs fanning the smouldering fire; but at last, when arrows began to fall thickly, and the warriors on a hill on the north grew more and more insolent and aggressive, we thought it was time to damp their ardour by bringing our own weapons into evidence a little ... [Buffalo-hide shields] were set up at a distance, and, making the natives stand aside, we fired at our targets. The shields, riddled with holes, were then exhibited to the warriors, and they were warned that if we were attacked we should point our guns at them ... When night fell we sent up a rocket every now and then in one direction or another, the unusual apparition serving to keep the natives in awe.*

The deeply fissured hill country which they traversed in pouring rain exposed them to constant danger. As the column struggled forward manfully in single file, each porter keeping as close as possible to the one in front of him, their progress was reduced to a snail's pace – ten steps forward, two minutes' halt and so on, while Teleki cleared a way through belligerent tribesmen, on occasions mollifying them with presents, at other times brushing their spears aside and hoping for the best. There was the usual fuss over paying *hongo* at every river crossing – sixty-two major ones in all – where the Kikuyu had excellent opportunities to press home an attack with their

clubs and short double-bladed *simis* in circumstances that would almost certainly have guaranteed them victory. Many of the rivers and streams had carved out steep, often precipitous, descents down almost knifelike ridges where delays extended into hours. Zigzag paths had to be cut, donkeys unloaded and porters had to guard each other as they forded the swift-flowing mountain waters.

Crowds of natives harassed us, especially in the van and the rear . . . I was always totally ignorant of what was going on with Count Teleki's party, and he was in constant anxiety about me. We were both, however, protected by a few warriors who did their utmost to shield us and drive the natives back . . . Day after day passed with constant alarms of war, but with no actual hostilities. The whole burden of coping with the trying situation fell upon Count Teleki as I was too ill to be able to be of much use to him . . . Our white skins were our best protection . . . and I am pretty certain that we should never have achieved our transit of Kikuyuland if there had not been a European at each end of the caravan.

Nor would they have succeeded without the loyal assistance of their Kikuyu guides and warrior escort, who stood by the travellers even when they were branded as traitors by their own kinsmen. It was the guides who helped to organize *barazas* or meetings with countless chiefs; it was they who cajoled the elders into ceremonies of blood brothership, an almost daily occurrence, with Dualla representing the count; and it was they who added a persuasive voice to the calls for the locals to establish food markets. Among Teleki's men, the unsung heroes were Dualla, Kimameta and Kijanja, a guide who spoke fluent Kikuyu and was an accomplished orator.

Despite Teleki's constant efforts to diffuse a potentially explosive situation and his amazing luck with rain showers falling just when he had promised them, blood was shed on four separate occasions. These incidents were the result of overbearing insolence on the part of a few warriors and the pent-up fury of his porters, who had put up with the trials and tribulations of the harrowing journey sufficiently to last them a lifetime. The most serious conflict started when a young drover was wounded on his way to collect water, though he had done nothing to provoke the attack. Then Dualla was three times assailed by a warrior who dashed towards him with his *simi* drawn. At first Dualla put up with this harassment, but as the man came forward a fourth time and pointed his spear menacingly, while another seized the prayer beads dangling from his hand, Dualla lost his temper and opened fire. This was the signal for a general assault on the pugnacious warriors lasting about an hour. Teleki acquiesced to the action, in which the Somalis took colossal pleasure in burning down several villages and confiscating ninety cows and 1,300 sheep and goats, which kept the caravan in fresh meat until it reached Lake Baringo.

Kimameta did not participate in the skirmish but he was delighted with the results, for his opinion of the Kikuyu was coloured by blatant prejudice. He had reasoned for some weeks that a more aggressive stance throughout their journey would have served everyone better, for only by making the Kikuyu fear for their lives and for the safety of their property would they be persuaded to behave. He would have preferred his leaders to emulate Dr Gustav Fischer who, in 1883, had blazed his way west through Kikuyuland in four days, fighting every inch of the way. Teleki, on the other hand, realized that the country lent itself to ambushes. He was sure that the overwhelming numerical odds in favour of the Kikuyu would have resulted in serious loss of life on both sides in the event of an all-out war.

Teleki saw several areas where the primaeval forest was in the process of being burnt and cleared to make way for settlement.

There is no doubt that the whole of Kikuyuland ... a stretch of land from about eight to eleven miles in breadth between Ngongo Bagas and Kenia ... was once densely wooded, but the industrious natives have cleared away almost every trace of forest from the interior, leaving only a belt as a frontier buttress from one to two hours' march deep ... The Wakikuyu are not only zealous agriculturalists, they also keep bees and breed cattle, sheep, poultry and goats – occasionally castrating the rams – which they are willing to sell, though it is difficult to get them to part with their cattle ... The huts of the Wakikuyu present a very picturesque appearance, and are of the beehive or conical shape, thatched with straw or rushes, above which protrudes the central beam; the roof springs from perpendicular walls with outside supports. The walls are made of interlaced branches, supplemented by well-hewn planks or smeared with clay. Near each hut are two smaller structures of the same kind, in which fruit and vegetables are stored.

Teleki and von Höhnel passed through districts 'so carefully and systematically cultivated that we might have been in Europe'. There were abundant signs of prosperity everywhere and despite their trying journey, with von Höhnel seriously weakened by a sustained attack of dysentery, they formed the opinion that the Kikuyu people were destined to play an important role in the future of East Africa. There could hardly have been a more accurate prediction in those early days of African travel and exploration. The Kikuyu are today among the most intelligent, industrious and progressive of all Kenyans. Led by the late President Jomo Kenyatta, himself a Kikuyu, they were in the forefront of Kenya's independence movements thirty years ago. They form part of the largest ethnic group and farm some of its most fertile land in the temperate highlands around Mount Kenya.

With this second difficult stage of their expedition successfully completed, Teleki lost no time in preparing for an ascent of Mount Kenya, Africa's second highest snowcapped mountain. He set off early on 17th October from a base camp on the Enkare Nairobi, a clear mountain stream which flows down the south-western slopes of Kenya. He took with him two Swahili guides, two Somali bodyguards and forty porters. A flock of twenty-four sheep was driven behind the party to supplement their iron rations. How amazed Teleki would have been to see a modern luxury safari with four-wheel drive vehicles, portable electric generators, refrigerators, and tinned and processed foods!

Von Höhnel remained behind to recuperate and to arrange food supplies for the next leg of their journey to the Laikipia plateau to Lake Baringo. 'The short rainy season was now approaching ... We stuck to our tents, which we preferred to a hut as we suffered so much less from vermin in them. These tents we pitched facing Mount Kenya, so that we might look at it whenever the cloud canopy generally shrouding it from view was lifted.' Rains started at exactly the right moment to impress the local Kikuyu rainmaker of the supernatural powers of the white *laibon*. For that reason von Höhnel had no difficulty in buying large quantities of food.

*Soon after the Count had left, a large party of Wakikuyu came into camp laden
with provisions, and almost immediately heavy rain clouds darkened the sky. The
rain, however, still held back, though a change in the weather was evidently
imminent, and just as the old* laibon *reappeared the next morning at the head of
some three hundred of his people bringing food, the downpour began, which lasted
for a good hour. Grey, and trembling with the cold, but at the same time greatly
delighted, the venerable medicine-man led forward a fat black cow and asked for
Count Teleki. This was just what our people wanted, and Jumbe Kimameta,
Kijanja, Juma Mussa, and everyone else who could speak Kikuyu, cried with one
voice, 'What! You ask for the Count when you are wet to the knees, where should
the white* laibon *be but with* Ngai [God] *on Kilimara* [Kenya]? *Who but he gave
the rain?' and so they went on, the old* laibon *listening delightedly, and promising
as much food as we could eat.*

Von Höhnel bought 3,500 rations that day and within a week sufficient
stocks of beans, maize, millet and other dried foodstuffs had been procured to
last the entire caravan between twenty and twenty-four days. 'The natives
also brought eight grey donkeys for sale, which were as welcome as they were
unexpected, for of the fifty-nine with which we had entered Kikuyuland, only
twenty-three remained, and of the twenty-five we had bought on the coast,
not one had survived.' Donkeys invariably died faster than their loads were
consumed and in consequence were never relied upon to replace porterage.

*The change brought about in our surroundings by the rain was charming. Woods
and fields, which had been so dry and dreary-looking, were bursting everywhere
with fresh life and clothed vivid green. The once barren Ndoro* [their camp on the
banks of the Enkare Nairobi] *was converted for a time into a perfect garden, and*

this sudden awakening of nature was one of the most beautiful things we witnessed in the course of our whole journey.

It was rather different for Teleki. All day, every day, the skies hung low with leaden clouds, making it impossible for his men to see where they were heading. He had to rely solely on rough compass bearings to guide them through the forest where, at an altitude of 10,000 feet, they had to hack a way out of dense bamboo in pouring rain. With characteristic determination, the count succeeded in establishing a camp on the moorlands and prepared for his assault on the peak.

It cleared a little in the afternoon, and I was able to take a few observations to help me in the further climb. I found that the course we had taken had been by no means badly chosen, as we had reached the base of the loftiest peak of the mountain . . . After a night during which the thermometer fell for the first time to 0° Centigrade, a moderately clear morning broke, and I started once more with Makatubu, Mahommed and ten men. As I had no intention of spending the night higher up, we did not have to take tents, covers, etc. We were off at six minutes past four . . . At a height of 13,100 feet we saw the last examples of animal life of any size: a humming-bird [the scarlet-tufted Malachite sunbird, Nectarinia johnstoni], *a pretty thrush-like bird* [the Hill or Mountain Chat, Pinarochroa sordida ernesti], *and a light-brown hairy tailless marmot. We came here, too, upon newly fallen snow which, as it thawed, still further increased the difficulties of climbing.*

At ten o'clock we had reached an altitude of 13,600 feet. My barefooted companions were suffering terribly from the cold, although the thermometer marked + 7° Centigrade, so I decided to climb the rest of the way alone.

According to Teleki's aneroid reading, he climbed to a height of 15,355 feet★ accompanied by Mohammed Sief, one of his Somali bodyguards, who refused to give in. Just as he turned his back on the mountain at three o'clock in the afternoon, mist and low clouds wafted up the valleys and enveloped the upper ridges. Three days later he rejoined von Höhnel on the banks of the Enkare Nairobi.

Mount Kilimanjaro had been climbed, geologically mapped and its flora and fauna described in some detail. However, this was the first time anyone had penetrated the moorlands of Mount Kenya. Teleki's account of his ascent provided the only reliable information since Thomson's day and removed lingering doubts that still existed in some people's minds of the mountain's very existence.

The time had come to move on to Baringo but 'a glance at our staff was enough to convince us that we should have to proceed in detachments, as with all the extra food we had to carry, we could not hope to take all the loads on at once'. To make matters worse, several men had to be detailed as drovers for the balance of the expropriated stock, a herd of forty oxen and a flock of 400 sheep and goats, and to guard the animals with the greatest care to prevent theft on the march. Teleki soon realized that ferrying loads took far too long;

★ In a letter to Crown Prince Rudolf ten days later Teleki claimed to have reached 16,200 feet, which he estimated was still 5,000–6,000 feet below the summit. Since Mount Kenya is only 17,058 feet high, one can safely assume that he was exaggerating.

there was a real danger that their dry rations would be finished well before the expedition reached Baringo, despite the precaution he had taken of buying in six days' reserves.

So we had to resort to our old plan of overloading all the men and animals . . . Our difficulties now were greatly increased by the fact that we had no maps with us. Information obtained is generally untrustworthy, and never to be relied on at all for more than a few days' distance. Out of the hundreds of rumours and contradictory assertions it is all but impossible to get a definite idea of what is really before a caravan, and woe to the expedition the food and water of which is uncertain. Our expedition would without doubt have been ruined a dozen times if we had not made a point of being always prepared for the worst.

They crossed the Laikipia plateau in a north-westerly direction and suffered from none of the problems that had plagued Thomson.

Our march through Kikuyuland had made an immense impression upon the Maasai, who were convinced that we owed our safety entirely to our powerful war medicines. The 300 moran *who were then raiding the Wakikuyu were so sure of this that they came back to our camp again to try and secure some of the wonder-working remedies for themselves . . . To get rid of them the Count gave them a little box of mustard, telling them that to secure its efficacy they must camp for four days on the Ngare Nyuki* [Enkare Nanyokie], *a little stream rising on the north-west slope of Kenya. This condition was probably too hard for them, for, after long consideration, they gave us back the box of mustard, telling us that it would not do to consult two* laibons *at once, as, when the time arrived for the division of the spoil, it would be impossible to say what belonged to each.*

The expedition split up temporarily into three parties at Nyahururu, since Teleki had promised Kimameta a three-week break from travelling. This was to give him time to purchase ivory in the forests surrounding Subugo, an upland area east of Ol Joro Orok – more correctly spelt Ol-chorro Orok, the big black waterhole. While Teleki pushed on to Lake Baringo with the main body of the caravan, von Höhnel and forty men unsuccessfully explored the Uaso Nyiro River – Ewuaso Ngiro, the brown river – in the hope of finding 'Lake Lorian', the mysterious lake that never was. He learned from Wandorobo hunters that it was a swamp into which the Uaso Nyiro emptied its floodwaters in the rainy season; as none of his informants had actually seen it and he could not induce any to act as guides for the estimated twenty-day journey there, confirmation of this accurate report had to wait a few more years. The excursion was not without benefit, however, for von Höhnel was able to map out the topography of a vast expanse of country, ranging from Mount Kenya with its attendant Loldaika Mountains (Ol-doinyo Loltaika, the aptly named 'pigtail' of Mount Kenya) in the south to Ol-doinyo Lenkiyieu (the Mathews Range) and the Karisia Hills in the north.

Meanwhile, Kimameta had made contact with groups of Wandorobo hunters living in the Subugo and Marmanet forests and had bought 1,100 pounds of good-quality ivory from them; several tusks weighed 90–110 pounds each, despite the presence of another trading caravan which had vied with him for the best bargains. As soon as von Höhnel rejoined Kimameta, they moved on quickly since food was scarce. Everyone was in high spirits at the thought of reaching the Njemps' villages at the southern end of Lake Baringo. Loud shouts of joy greeted their first sighting of the lake and Juma Mussa eagerly pointed out the landmarks to his leader. 'Kesho samaki! Kesho ugali! Kesho mboga! Kesho tashiba!' they cried. 'Tomorrow there will be fish, porridge and vegetables so our stomachs will be full.'

Within a day the cruel hand of nature had dashed their dreams of a promised land. An old man whom they met by the wayside gave them the bad news that famine was rife at Baringo. Teleki was forced to hunt on the east side of the lake in order to feed his hungry porters. With no prospect of the next harvest being ready for another six weeks, von Höhnel's men trudged wearily over the dusty plains in the depressing knowledge that further privations and hardships were inevitable. They reached Njemps Ndogo, the southernmost of the two villages, to find an almost deserted camp set among isolated acacia trees and enclosed by a withered, dusty thorn hedge near the

banks of the Ewuaso Nanyoike, the red water river. 'The whole neighbourhood was flat, sandy or loamy, muddy or dusty according to whether it had or had not recently rained. There was no sign of Lake Baringo which lay some five and a half or six and a half miles off on the north . . . This then was the real appearance of the El Dorado to which we had looked so eagerly, hastening on in the hope of finding a second Taveta.'

A day later Teleki returned unexpectedly to camp, in the very best of spirits having shot thirty-eight large animals in the space of fourteen days, which had given his men plenty of fresh and dried meat to eat. He realized, nevertheless, that it would be impossible to venture into the sparsely inhabited and unknown lands to the north of Baringo unless he could lay in large quantities of dried food. He had already sent Makatubu to Elgeyo district, the main granary of the region, but famine was rife there too. The best Makatubu could achieve in three weeks' hard bargaining was to buy sorghum to sustain the caravan for just four days. As a last resort, Teleki despatched the shrewd and resourceful Dualla to Miansini, the little village in the bamboo forests above Kijabe where Thomson had battled to survive. He reasoned that if anybody had surplus food to sell them it would be the Kikuyu. On 17th December Dualla set off with 170 porters, *askaris* and guides and twenty-two pack-donkeys, with instructions to make a forced march to Miansini and buy as much corn as he could possibly carry back. 'Ten days are generally allowed for this distance but to ensure all possible speed, we only gave out five days' rations.' Kimameta took advantage of the occasion to send his own men back to Pangani as feeding them had become too much of a burden to him.

Teleki reckoned that Dualla would be away for four to five weeks, which gave him an opportunity to hunt in the vicinities of Lake Bogoria and Lake Solai. Von Höhnel took advantage of this break in their travels to write up his journals, document his scientific collections and compile short vocabularies of several vernacular languages. He also took bearings and mapped out an extensive area, though he could not always concentrate on his field work.

It was not the scenery itself which astonished me, but the number and variety of the animals giving life to it, for in the flat districts overgrown with steppe grass or gleaming silvery leleshwa bushes stretching away on either side of the river [Ewuaso Nanyoike], roamed such countless herds of animals as I had never dreamt of seeing anywhere. I counted eight separate herds of buffaloes, each containing many hundred, with zebras, rhinoceroses, elands, waterbucks, hartebeests, gazelles, wild boars [warthogs], and ostriches in such numbers that I forgot all about my observations and gave myself up entirely to the delight of watching all these creatures in their life in the open.

The birdlife around the lakes was wonderfully varied and still continues to attract ornithologists from all over the world. Plump guinea fowls, *Numida meleagris*, were an easy target for the sportsmen on the plains but large flocks of destructive quelea birds, *Quelea quelea*, were less readily despatched by the Njemps. Often called the locust bird, these rapacious feeders had to be kept away from ripening corn by young children armed with slings and stones and strategically positioned on platforms built around the edges of the fields. At the slightest lack of vigilance on the part of the guardians, troops of marauding baboons were also poised, forever ready, to rifle the crop.

Teleki hunted every other day for as long as Dualla was away, which disturbed the game less than a daily chase. Buffaloes, being so numerous in the district, were the principal target and the porters ended up by calling them 'ngombe yetu' – our cattle. Sometimes Teleki came across bands of Wandorobo hunters who tracked and brought animals to bay with packs of small, fawn-coloured pye-dogs; in those areas, the game was noticeably shy. All caravans lived off the land like vultures and the huge mounds of fresh meat carried back into camp for drying attracted these sharp-eyed scavengers which circled the skies for hundreds of miles in effortless ease supported by thermals. They were constantly watching and waiting for something to die. A mere speck in the sky to the naked eye, they would spot a kill and drop down to earth, flaps down, skidding to an ungainly halt beside the carcass. Often, they quarrelled among themselves before indulging in a fierce struggle with Marabou storks, *Leptoptilos cruminferus*, and timid jackals for the left-overs. The still night air was filled with the chorus of laughing hyenas coming to polish off whatever delicacies remained and by the following day the carcass

had been picked spotlessly clean – a valuable service by nature's dustmen speeding up the process of decomposition.

Our food had now for a long time consisted almost entirely of meat, and only on special occasions did we get some stiff porridge made of millet, dhurra or eleusine meal. The haunches and shoulders of the sheep and goats were reserved for us with the tongues, steaks, humps and breasts of the oxen, the last named being boiled, whilst the tongues were roasted on a spit for a very long time . . . We craved for fat or grease as do the Eskimos. We could have eaten pounds of it, and we gloated over the thought of the fat humps of the oxen days before we ate them. They were to us the daintiest tit-bits and we would not have exchanged them for all the triumphs of European culinary arts.

Dualla showed up on 22nd January 1888 after an absence of thirty-six days. His men looked completely worn out, some with scarcely enough clothing for decency, others with none at all. They had evidently endured terrible hardship as there was serious famine throughout the land. Upon reaching Miansini, Dualla had found three caravans camped there from which thirty men had already died of starvation. Sensing disaster, he acted contrary to the advice of the traders and disregarded the Wandorobo middlemen who insisted that business negotiations had to be conducted through them. Wisely, he took the initiative and pushed straight into Kikuyu country where direct contact was made with the villagers living in the border areas who had been so friendly the previous year. Tribute was not demanded nor was there any gathering of the clans. Dualla was led from village to village exchanging his trade goods for whatever food could be spared. With infinite tact and patience he managed to buy in 128 loads of grain, which he carefully conserved by keeping his men on half-rations of green bananas, sweet potatoes and yams. Although thirteen loads of grain were used to feed his porters on the return march and another nine loads were stolen when a few men deserted him, Teleki calculated that the remainder would just suffice for their needs as long as none of it was eaten at Baringo in the meanwhile.

Teleki was left to provide for the entire caravan single-handed – an immensely arduous and dangerous undertaking. In less than two weeks he was charged eleven times by wounded buffaloes. As time went by he became graver and more reserved, realizing that his luck would not hold indefinitely. When he eventually got back to the expedition's base camp on the banks of the Ewuaso Nanyoike with a shoulder bruised and sore through shooting constantly for fifty days, he had personally killed ten elephants, sixty-one buffaloes, twenty-one rhinos, nine zebras, six hartebeests, four elands and two waterbucks, from which his men dried almost three tons of biltong. It is difficult for anyone nowadays to understand the slaughter which took place in the name of sport. Nobody at that time ever believed that the numerous wild animals would be threatened with extinction; to them, a few more or less made no difference. A century later, Teleki's rich hunting grounds south of Lake Baringo are a prime example of an overgrazed, badly eroded tract of country almost devoid of game. It is true that Teleki was a sportsman at heart and had good reason on most occasions to hunt for the pot. He was not to know that an insatiable demand for rhino horn – to embellish dagger handles in the Yemen and for use as an aphrodisiac for Eastern gentlemen – would make this prehistoric-looking creature one of the most endangered species in the world today.

We had to carry such quantities of food that we were compelled to leave half our goods behind us ... It was difficult enough to decide what to take and what to leave, but yet more difficult to know which way to go. Days were consumed in talking the matter over with Jumbe Kimameta and the natives, but we would get no certain intelligence whatever. No one really knew whether there were two lakes or one in the north, or even how far off was the nearest lake if two there were. We had answers in plenty to our questions but they were all either vague or manifestly false. The size of the lake, for instance, varied from two months' journey round to one year's. It was, in fact, quite immeasurable.

Teleki knew that it was out of the question to depart straight away, for most of the porters who had accompanied Dualla were too run-down and undernourished to carry heavy loads. Moreover, he could no longer afford to leave able-bodied men behind, since his numbers had been steadily reduced, the most recent casualty being Muinyi Sera who had died of consumption, thus ending a long career as a trustworthy guide. Von Höhnel's health had also deteriorated and more than once he felt his end was near. 'On 24th January, there seemed no hope of my recovery. On the evening of that day I felt a strong desire for sleep, and, thinking my worn-out spirit was about to be loosed from my emaciated body at last, I closed my weary eyes, convinced that I was falling into my last long unconsciousness.' He awoke early the next morning wondering if he was in eternity. For a long time he could not believe that he was still alive until his servant, Chuma, answered his call. Convinced at last, he began to perk up a little. What probably saved his life from the recurring attacks of dysentery was a lucky find of eleven fresh ostrich eggs, which for twenty days gave him a beneficial supplement to his monotonous meat diet.

CHAPTER 14

No fish in troubled waters

Mchama ago hanyeli, huenda akauyu papo
A traveller does not make a mess where he has camped,
as one day he might come back

Swahili proverb

COUNT TELEKI SIFTED CAREFULLY through the vague and often contradictory information he had gleaned about the mysterious lake district. In the end, he was convinced there were two lakes lying in arid country somewhere south of the Ethiopian highlands. He opted to travel up the east side of the nearer and larger of the two lakes, reasoning that it would be prudent to pass through uninhabited country while his men still had food and to return down the west side, which was apparently inhabited by the Turkana people, when in all probability his rations would be exhausted. The stark choices forced him to make for Mount Nyiru – Ol-doinyo Ngiro, the brown mountain – which was said to be about fifteen days' march to their north-east. On 9th February 1888, guides were recruited and camp was struck as the expedition which the porters had nicknamed 'safari ya polepole', the slow safari, got under way amid a blur of choking red dust. Teleki had mustered a force of eight Somali bodyguards, three Swahili servants, six guides, fifteen *askaris* and 197 porters and donkey attendants. His livestock had been trimmed to nineteen donkeys, twenty-one head of cattle and sixty sheep and goats, some of which were very weak and would not have been taken with him in normal circumstances. Nine sick porters had to be left behind but the other stalwarts, though not in the best of health, put on a brave face for their journey into the unknown. Teleki took good care to keep his marches short and paused frequently to hunt. He had stressed to everyone the importance of conserving dry rations, but no sooner had they left Baringo than Dualla caught two porters surreptitiously dipping into their loads of corn. This theft was taken as a sin against the whole caravan and fifty lashes were quickly administered as an example to the others.

They followed a north-easterly course to the Lorroki Plateau, near modern Maralal, with its spectacular views from the eastern wall of the Great Rift Valley looking back through a milky-blue haze towards the glinting waters of Lake Baringo and the Tugen Hills beyond. At an altitude of 8,000 feet, the nights were decidedly chilly and the flora scarcely tropical.

The happy mood in which we wandered amongst the lonely beauty of the primaeval world was, alas! dispelled, when, as we got lower down, we came to traces of the destructive hand of man, a fire, lit by some of the Wandorobo who frequent the Leroghi [sic] chain for hunting expeditions, having evidently raged for weeks, for whole tracts were burnt or burning, trunks and branches were scattered on every side, and the ground was covered with a layer of ashes from which smoke and steam were rising in clouds.

To this day, the fine cedar forests are periodically ravaged by bush fires and there is ample evidence of charred tree stumps to prove the serious damage they cause. Most fires are started by irresponsible honey-hunters, who smoke

out bees from their natural hives without caring for the disastrous consequences of leaving lighted faggots carelessly on the ground. The Wandorobo are expert at lighting fires by rubbing two sticks together, their secret being in the selection of the wood. They use a flat, oblong piece of soft, dry wood and a hard wood stick with a rounded end. The stick is twirled in a uniform motion between outstretched palms in a hole on the soft wood until it produces sawdust. As the heat generated by the friction of the stick ignites the sawdust, tinder-dry grass is dropped over it and, with the help of a little judicious blowing, bursts into flames. Just as other people carry matches, the Wandorobo carry their 'firesticks', which enable them to light a fire with consummate ease in a matter of minutes.

From the northern end of the Lorroki Plateau, Teleki could just make out the obscure outline of Mount Nyiru quivering in the heat. From a distance of fifty-five miles, it rose rather unimpressively above a vast open plain where *luggas*, dry river beds, threaded their way like arteries across the blazing land. A backcloth of fine mountain ranges rose to his east and the one known to the local Samburu people as 'Ol-doinyo Lenkiyieu', he renamed 'The General Mathews Chain' (shortened later to 'Mathews Range') 'in honour of our friend General Lloyd Mathews, who had done so much to help us in Zanzibar, and to whose powerful co-operation we owed the fact that we had been able to make this our first geographical discovery'.

The choice of guides was most important to the success of any expedition. Not only were they responsible for showing travellers the quickest and best paths to follow but, in semi-arid lands, they had to be familiar with all the water points along the chosen route. In those early days of African travel, personal water bottles were almost unheard of and porters often had to march all day without slaking their thirst. Although the older of the two guides whom Teleki had engaged at Baringo professed to have minded sheep on

Mount Nyiru in his youth, in reality he had no idea of the way beyond the Lorroki Plateau. He had intended to take a well-worn path east to Barsaloi where, according to his fanciful imagination, hippos and crocodiles would be found wallowing in the waters of a permanent river. After twelve hours without water in the scorching sun, he admitted that he was hopelessly lost. Teleki then turned forlornly to the younger guide to enquire about water. 'We shall get none today,' was the cheerful reply. It did not seem to worry him in the slightest, although Teleki was extremely concerned for the well-being of his men. He gave orders to pitch camp and for seven search parties, each twenty strong, to fan out in different directions to look for water.

[They] *had orders to fire if they came across water, and in terrible suspense we listened in the darkness for the sound of a shot. But hour after hour passed without hearing the longed-for report, and we began to fear there would be nothing for it but to go back as quickly as possible to our last halting place ... Our delight can therefore be imagined when at about eleven o'clock we heard a dull report somewhere in the distance. We dared not even now be sure, for the shot might have been a signal of distress from someone who had lost his way; but, after half an hour of suspense, some dark figures appeared in the gloom carrying the cooking pots on their heads, a sure sign that some of those pots were not empty ... They had followed the channel of the river, but found it continued sandy and dry. They then fell to digging, and for want of better tools had to use their knives, bowls and hands but these served very well in the loose sand, and at a depth of about five feet their labours were crowned with success. There was not much water oozing through the sand, but what there was was clear and sweet. A few signal shots brought back the other and less fortunate search parties, and then everyone rushed with shovels to the newly found supply, to dig different holes and drink their fill. Each hole, however, contained so little water that it took the whole of the next day to satisfy all the men and cattle.*

The 'river' at Barsaloi was no more than a large seasonal watercourse known as the Milgis *lugga*; it has a wide, sandy bed and is motorable for about seventy miles 'downstream' in dry weather. The crocodiles and hippos which Teleki had expected to see there were a figment of a fertile mind, unless the old guide had confused the Milgis with the permanent waters of the Uaso Nyiro. Both guides were now unanimous in their assertion that no more water would be found until the caravan reached Mount Nyiru. Hardly any men had calabashes for carrying the precious liquid and those who did had no idea of self-restraint; water intended to last two days was drunk in as many hours. So Teleki undertook a formidable march to the mountain which he confidently expected to reach in under twenty-four hours.

After resting up for a day or two, they started out in the early hours of 26th February by the faint light of a crescent moon. They crossed the El Barta plains – the undulating country that links the mountain regions of Samburu district together – and marched, except for a short break of half an hour at sunrise and a three hour rest in the middle of the day, until eight o'clock that night. Everything about the landscape was scorched and shrivelled; the colours burnt and brown as their calabashes. As dust devils whipped up the sandy soil and spun it skywards in vicious thermals, the blistering heat turned the stunted sage and thorn scrub into a mosaic of weird and watery images that danced tantalizingly, then vanished, before their eyes. His porters survived their first thirty-mile march remarkably well, but Teleki had no illusions that the remaining stretch would sort out the men from the boys. They set off again well before daybreak the following morning. With every stride the sun rose higher and higher in a cloudless sky until, at its zenith, it beat down with the intensity of molten brass, turning the land into a fiery furnace. One by one the exhausted men lost hope and collapsed by the wayside. The vanguard took a full seven hours to cover the twenty odd miles to the southern foothills of Mount Nyiru, where camp was established beside a little stream overgrown with bush and containing scarcely any water. 'We had broken through the barrier dividing the inhabited from the uninhabited districts, and in so doing had achieved one of the most difficult of the aims we had in view . . . Our first care was to send some men back with water to their exhausted comrades left by the way, and singly or in couples most of them got into camp in the course of the day, but two had succumbed before help reached them, and two more, though they had revived at first, died in the night.' Later explorers took the precaution of pre-positioning water along the route and had no difficulty in getting to Nyiru. A little more planning on Teleki's part would have saved his men from partaking in a very unfair test of human endurance. Parching thirst was, after all, the most dreaded torture of early travel in Africa.

The expedition stayed put for five days. While the survivors recovered from their fearful ordeal, Teleki and von Höhnel went hunting. The enforced delay resulted in severe rationing of dried foodstuffs. Dualla, whose unenviable task it was to dole them out, cut a piece as broad as a finger off the edge of the measuring bowl which, even before he did that, held only half a ration. Since the district was sparsely populated – Teleki counted no more

than forty men, women and children – he was most fortunate to recruit a young Samburu guide who was hard and spare like the country he came from; his only clothing was his black ebony skin and his only possession a spear. He happened to be visiting relatives on Mount Nyiru at the time, although he hailed from the northern regions of Samburuland. Teleki nicknamed him 'Lembasso' after the Samburu word 'Empasso' meaning a lake. He learned from Lembasso of two routes to the north, the more direct one leading to 'Empaso Narok', the black lake, through uninhabited country in less than a week. The longer route followed a north-easterly direction to Marsabit Mountain, the main centre of the Rendille people, in five to seven days, from where Teleki would have to strike north-west towards 'Empaso Naibor', the white lake, which was reputed to be a very long way off. This time the choice was clear-cut. The expedition would head north for the larger of the lakes, 'Empaso Narok' – seemingly one and the same as the lake the Njemps had called 'Samburu'. 'The thought that in a few days we should reach the mysterious Empasso Narok [sic] filled us with great satisfaction.' Needless to say, it was easier said than done.

They skirted the western foothills of Mount Nyiru where they caught a glimpse of the Suguta Valley 'which gave us the impression of the bed of an old lake'. This was an accurate observation, for the low-lying valley was once part of Lake Turkana in the Upper Pliocene period, which was a time of major faulting and folding. Eventually it was cut off from the lake by a large volcanic barrier and, without a permanent water supply of its own, dried up. Teleki and von Höhnel came up against a desolate and forbidding land, riven by great gorges and yawning chasms, with a wild grandeur of its own. To this day it has retained all the savage splendour of the past. 'The scenery became more and more dreary as we advanced. The barren ground was strewn with gleaming, chiefly red and green, volcanic debris, pumice-stone, huge blocks of blistered lava, and here and there pieces of petrified wood. There was no regular path, and we had to pick our way carefully amongst the scoriae, some of which was as sharp as knives ... if the approaches to the lake were so barren and naked, we might well tremble for the fate of our animals.' The Samburu on Mount Nyiru had laughed openly when they had heard that livestock would be taken to the lake. Teleki now understood the reasons for their incredulity.

The day of 5th March 1888 was to become an important date in the annals of exploration and discovery in East Africa.

The good spirits with which the thought that we were nearing the end of our long tramp had filled us in the morning had long since been dissipated, and our hopes had become restricted to finding some little pool with slimy green water at which to quench our thirst, when all of a sudden, as we were climbing a gentle slope, a grand, beautiful, and far-stretching scene was spread out before us ... As we got higher up, a single peak gradually rose before us, the gentle contours rising symmetrically from every side, resolving themselves into one broad pyramidal mountain, which we knew at once to be a volcano ... On the east side of the mountain the land was uniformly flat, a golden plain lit up by sunshine ... We hurried as fast as we could to the top of our ridge, the scene gradually developing itself as we advanced, until an entirely new world was spread out before our astonished eyes. The void down in the depths beneath became filled as if by magic with picturesque mountains and rugged slopes, with a medley of ravines and valleys

Above) Mount
Kenya, at 17,058 feet
the second highest
mountain in Africa.
Teleki was the first to
reach its snowline.

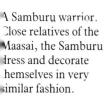

A Samburu warrior.
Close relatives of the
Maasai, the Samburu
dress and decorate
themselves in very
similar fashion.

(Right) Turkana fishermen using wicker traps to catch fish in the shallow waters of the lake now named after them.

(Opposite) Sirima, an important water pan in the arid countryside near Lake Turkana.

(Below) Lava boulders close to Lake Turkana, typical of the country through which Teleki and his men trekked.

A Turkana girl standing on a fishing raft made from doum-palm logs.

An old Turkana woman, as weather-beaten as the country from which she hails.

A Turkana elder in his leopard-skin cape and wearing a decorated nose plate.

(Opposite) A Turkana girl bedecked with beads. She has inserted in her pierced underlip a brass ornament.

(Right) Pokot girls carrying water home in hollowed-out logs. The brass earrings of one signify that she is married.

(Below) A Pokot woman in tanned goatskins. Cicatricial body scars are not unusual as a form of decoration.

A Pokot warrior in all his finery.

which appeared to be closing up from every side to form a fitting frame for the dark-blue gleaming surface of the lake stretching away beyond as far as the eye could reach.

For a long time we gazed in speechless delight, spell-bound by the beauty of the scene before us, whilst our men, equally silent, stared into the distance for a few minutes, to break presently into shouts of astonishment at the sight of the glittering expanse of the great lake which melted on the horizon into the blue of the sky. At that moment all our dangers, all our fatigues were forgotten in the joy of finding our exploring expedition crowned with success at last. Full of enthusiasm and gratefully remembering the gracious interest taken in our plans from the first by his Royal and Imperial Highness, Prince Rudolf of Austria, Count Teleki named the sheet of water, set like a pearl of great price in the wonderful landscape beneath us, Lake Rudolf.

When the explorers got back to Austria they found that the neurotic prince had committed suicide – an omen, perhaps, of the violence that has frequently enmeshed life around this lake. Almost ninety years elapsed before the government of independent Kenya changed the name to Lake Turkana after the people who live along its western and southern shores.

'Haya, Pwani! Let's go to the seaside!' the Zanzibaris exclaimed joyfully; but this first impression of a tranquil lake within easy reach turned out to be wholly misleading. There was a veritable hell still to be overcome, necessitating a night stop at a small water-hole, the Laisamis, whose pools of green tinted water nestle beneath sheer walls of jagged lava rock. Its well concealed location has made it a favourite rustlers' staging post in modern times. Steep precipices blocked the porters' way forward and a gale blew with unabated fury, whipping sand in their faces and unbalancing their heavy loads. The whole area was a sea of inhospitable lava, pock-marked with volcanic cones. Clouds of yellow sulphorous smoke rose from a prominent slag heap, indicating that it was still active, and a partially submerged crater of perfect circular form – Nabuyatom (Naboiaa-Etom, the elephant's stomach) – jutted into the ruffled waters of a jade sea.

Almost at our last gasp, we hastened on towards the slightly rippled sheet of water – the one bit of brightness in a gloomy scene. Another hour of tramping through sand or over stony flats, and we were at the shore of the lake. Although utterly exhausted, after the seven hours' march in the intense and parching heat, we felt our spirits rise once more as we stood upon the beach at last, and saw the beautiful water, clear and crystal, stretching away before us. The men rushed down shouting, to plunge into the lake; but soon returned in bitter disappointment; the water was brackish!

This should not have been altogether unexpected, for Thomson had made mention of a great salt-water lake. The alkaline water is faintly slimy to the touch and even disguised as tea is rather unpleasant to drink, though it does one no harm.

This fresh defeat of all our expectations was like a revelation to us; and like some threatening spectre rose up before our minds the full significance of the utterly barren, dreary nature of the lake district . . . No living creature shared the gloomy solitude with us; and far as our glass [telescope] could reach there was nothing to be seen but desert – desert everywhere. To all this was added the scorching heat, and the ceaseless buffeting of the sand-laden wind, against which we were powerless to protect ourselves upon the beach, which offered not a scrap of shelter, whilst the pitching of the tents in the loose sand was quite impossible.

We now realised to the full that the lake districts were uninhabited, and terrible forebodings assailed us of days of hunger and thirst, when we remembered that the same conditions were pretty sure to prevail till we reached Reshiat [the Samburu name for the Dassenech tribe, more commonly known as the Merille or Shangilla]. *We had provisions for ten days only; and when we subjected Lembasso to a searching cross-examination as to how we could improve our position, and how long it would take us to get to this Reshiat, his unchanging reply was fifteen days. He also said that Mount Kulal was inhabited, but that the people there were themselves suffering from famine, and that the wretched Elmolo, living by the lake, supported themselves entirely by fishing.*

Fishing! We had never thought of that; and immediately lines and rods of every size and variety were got out and distributed to the men. But hour after hour passed by and nothing was caught.

This is inexplicable. The lake teems with nile perch, tilapia and tiger fish and catching them from the shore is comparatively easy. Seven years later Arthur Neumann, an English hunter, followed in Teleki's footsteps with only thirty-five men, preferring the risk of hostilities to that of starvation. He recorded excellent fishing all the way up the east side of the lake. A strange, moody man, he too died by his own hand.

Throughout this terrible day one trouble, one disappointment succeeded another, until at last the sun went down, when our position became a little more tolerable. The parching heat was replaced by a tepid coolness; the wind blew less strongly, and finally sank altogether, whilst the sand-storms ceased. A bath in the clear lake refreshed us, and later we actually managed to quench our burning thirst with its water . . .

Sunset was succeeded by a beautiful night; the canopy of heaven was spread out clear and bright above our heads, gleaming with twinkling stars, and the veil of night hid the dreary surroundings from our sight. Our men began to pick up heart again, and sat chattering or cooking around their fires, whilst we discussed the chances of the future with Jumbe Kimameta and Lembasso. When later we sought our beds beneath the open sky, we had begun to hope again, but one anxiety troubling our rest; two more men, Mpunga and Saadalla, both quite healthy, had not yet come into camp, whilst another had succumbed by the way to the hardships he had endured.

Mpunga Balosi had fallen asleep several miles short of the lake and was lucky to be found alive by a search party the next morning but Saadalla, a bright young man of eighteen, was never seen again. This brought the death toll to eight since their departure from Baringo a month earlier.

Teleki did not underestimate the gravity of the situation; he realized that decisions had to be made – and made fast. Though aching in every limb, he set off at a cracking pace at the head of the column along the eastern shores of the lake. They trudged for two days through a desolate lunar landscape – a sort of hell-on-earth scorched by searing gale-force winds which howled monotonously from the east and flecked the jade waters with a white spume. Many porters were lame from their long tramp over sharp volcanic rocks in bare feet and, to add to their discomfort, the lake waters had a purgative effect. With no sign of animal life and not a scrap of firewood to cook on, Teleki made up his mind to go straight to Mount Kulal where conditions were unlikely to be any worse. They turned inland during the morning march on the third day and their spirits rose as the countryside became less austere.

We saw no big game except a single specimen of the gazelle Grantii, *until we reached at midday a little streamlet which issued from the base of a perpendicular wall of rock. The Count here surprised a small herd of zebras and Beisa antelopes [Oryx beisa] under the shade of some bushes, and, with five shots fired in rapid succession, he brought down five animals, one antelope and four zebras, one of the latter of the Greyvi [sic. Grevy] variety. This unexpected stroke of luck, combined with the finding of a shady sheltered camping-place near fresh clear water, where we could once more put up our tents, cheered us all immensely. We concluded that there must be many such streams issuing from the base of Mount Kulal, and game would therefore not be wanting, so, as Lembasso thought it very unlikely that the people of Mount Kulal would have anything to sell, we abandoned the idea of visiting them.*

The previous isolation of the area is today considerably diminished and the lake attracts venturers in ever-increasing numbers to view nature in the raw. As scenery it is an acquired taste. The spring that Teleki came across was the Mowoelkiteng spring – the spring of ox horns – four miles south-east of Loiengalani. His route took him inland from Loiengalani, now the principal town on the eastern shore-line; take away its spring and it is an uncommonly beastly place, where winds of quite extraordinary violence are an indelible nuisance and give one little rest. They are caused by currents of cold air being drawn down off the nearby mountains to replace hot air which rises from the low-lying lands of the lake basin. The sun burns and scorches in spite of these winds but when the air stills, the heat is almost sufficient to addle the brain.

A day later, after a short march, the expedition reached another fresh-water spring, the Laredapach, with a rhino falling prey to Teleki's gun *en route*.

'Our pool of water was bordered by fresh green rushes and grass, and near to it rose a little wood of doum palms. The eyes of all our men were at once directed to the gleaming fruit hanging on these trees, and very soon they were all happily gnawing the brown rind which tastes more like bark than anything else.' One small bite was sufficient for Teleki but, properly ground, the flour is an edible substitute for cornflour. The milk in the centre of the ripe nuts is just as refreshing as the coconut and the kernel, though very small, is soft and tasty. By chance, a stray goat appeared at the waterhole and the very next day gave birth. It became an expedition mascot for the rest of their journey north, supplying a bowl of nourishing fresh milk every day. At this point the expedition had rations to last a further five days and was in real danger of perishing; that it was sustained for three grim weeks was almost entirely thanks to Teleki's prowess with the gun. It was no longer single-minded dogma, but hunger, that drove the explorers relentlessly on, because the caravan had reached a point of no return and it was impossible to do otherwise. The thought of being consumed in this vast no-man's-land was horrifying, and the dangers unmistakable, as Teleki urged his weary men forward with a new urgency – just hoping that reports of a Dassenech granary would turn out to be true. By the time they sighted the first Dassenech village at the north-east corner of the lake, another thirteen men had lost their lives attempting to penetrate this accursed land.

The only people they met on the way were the El Molo, who are related to the Maa-speaking pastoralists. At one time they were said to be the smallest tribe in Africa and in danger of extinction. In the last thirty years intermarriage with their Samburu, Rendille and Turkana neighbours has boosted their numbers very considerably, at the same time wiping out many of their original customs and most of their own language. They suffer from a high fluoride intake and a protein-rich fish diet which induces rotten or discoloured teeth and, more occasionally, badly deformed bones. Teleki estimated that there were 200 to 300 people living on the barren, windswept islands off El Molo Bay who supported themselves by hunting and fishing. He hunted hippos close to the bay itself.

Fifty miles beyond El Molo Bay stands Moite Mountain, which falls vertically down towards the lake in a chaotic jumble of coal-black lava boulders. Here there is a stretch of several miles where it is almost impossible to follow the shore. Lembasso persuaded the count to turn inland and avoid the obstacle, though he had no idea of the way or whether water would be found. The scheme contained all the elements of disaster and Teleki made a bad mistake in listening to him without first making a reconnaissance. By cutting the caravan off from its life-line, he very nearly added his expedition to the list of those that had set out into the interior of Africa, never to be seen or heard of again.

It was stifling inland and Teleki's porters, who had grown accustomed to drinking from the lake whenever they were thirsty, were ill-prepared for the gruelling conditions. At the end of their first march they dug in a dry river bed to a depth of six feet and found a little moisture seeping through the sand. This proved cold comfort, though, for much worse was to come the following day.

Crest after crest was scaled, each one in the hope that we would come to a pool, or at least to the dried-up bed of a brook, with some green about it. But one undulation succeeded another, midday came, the sun was at the zenith and poured down its scorching rays upon our heads. It was one o'clock now, and a third of our worn-out men lay stretched exhausted on the ground, here one, there another. Our own cheery 'Haya twende! Let's press on!' no longer had any effect, and many loads without owners lay scattered about. At last at two o'clock we began to descend a gentle slope which led down to the sand-choked, dried-up bed of a stream, where we caught what we took for the gleam of fresh green grass. But when I reached it, it was only to meet with fresh disappointment. Half the men were lying about staring vacantly before them; loads and animals were in the most hopeless confusion; donkeys and sheep wandering aimlessly about, the former either without their saddles or with those saddles under their bellies or round their necks. Not an askari or donkey-boy was to be seen anywhere. All discipline was at an end, and the men were utterly demoralized.

Teleki had shot two rhinos and pressed on with the vanguard. One of the dead animals lay close to the path but everyone was too worn out to bother with it. They had no way of knowing that their companions had found a trickle of water at the base of a rocky precipice two hours ahead.

As even the first to get to the pit could not satisfy their thirst, it was a very long time before any water could be obtained to send back to the poor fellows who had fallen by the way. Late in the evening and during the night the stragglers gradually came in and flung themselves like wild vultures upon the water. Each one was eager to be first, so that the dark ravine was soon the scene of a bitter struggle. Not until after a great deal of trouble, and with the help of the Somal mercilessly wielding their whips, were the combatants separated, and something like order restored.

It was a very disorganized and shaken band of men that cut back to the lake a day later. In three and a half hours they arrived at Allia Bay and encountered the northern settlements of the El Molo, which have since disappeared without trace. Between 150 and 200 people were living on two sandbanks rising just above the level of the lake. At first they were diffident of

the strangers whom they supposed were all women because, unlike any other men they had seen, loin-cloths and *khanzus* covered their nakedness.

They lead a kind of amphibious existence, scarcely differing from that of the crocodiles which, with their wild animals, they kill and eat. The two islands are not more than half or one square mile in extent. On the larger are from thirty to fifty, and on the smaller about fifteen brown huts, of the hayrick shape, huddled closely together . . . Their sole possessions are one or two cows, a dozen sheep, and perhaps a couple of dozen dogs. A third uninhabited sandbank nearer the beach serves, with muddy bank, alike as storehouse for fuel, and mooring ground for canoes . . . The men are circumcised in the Mahomedan manner. The hair is dressed in various fashions, either dragged up into a short thin tuft which is thickly smeared with red fat, or combed back flat, and, with the help of some greasy green or violet coloured clay, moulded into quite an artistic-looking chignon. The latter style is peculiar to young men, and is sometimes finished off with two short ostrich feathers . . . Rings are worn in the lobe and sides of the ear, but the lobes are very slightly distended. Other ornaments are bracelets worn on the upper and the lower arm, made of brass or iron wire or of hippopotamus hide. A round knife is also sometimes worn as a bracelet, the edges being protected with a leather case . . . I must add that all the men, but none of the women, carry a little two-legged stool to sit upon, which also serves them as a pillow at night.

Both settlements had three- or four-man dugout canoes made of doum palm logs which were propelled by crudely fashioned double-ended oars. Tents were pitched half a mile back from the lake in the shade and shelter of *Mswaki* trees, *Salvadora persica*, whose fibrous wood is used as toothbrushes by many country-folk to this day.

Elephants have not been seen on the shores of Lake Turkana for over fifty years, yet less than a century ago they roamed its entire length. Teleki made his own small contribution to their eventual disappearance by hunting there, although one wounded monster which took refuge in the lake had its revenge.

As Teleki had his canvas boat made ready, intending to shoot the elephant from the boat or drive it ashore, he was distracted and Dualla took over the hunt. Dualla calmly approached his motionless target, paddled round it and fired at it a dozen times with his Henry-Winchester rifle, but it took not the slightest notice of boat or bullets. He then changed his weapon for a heavy Express rifle and circled it once more, firing two shots and boldly venturing closer. All of a sudden, the elephant spread its ears and charged furiously, at which Dualla and his companions quickly leapt overboard in fear of their lives. 'In the twinkling of an eye he was upon the fragile craft, which he first shoved before him for a little distance, and then seized with his trunk. He shook it, crushed it, tossed it about, and then contemptuously flung it aside. Finally, without taking the slightest further notice of the men, who were diving close to him, he marched with slow and stately steps through the water, and disappeared behind a peninsula.' Such was the ignominious end of the second boat which Teleki had brought with him from Europe!

Teleki passed right through Koobi Fora without the slightest idea that it was to become the world's richest known treasure-trove of fossils of early man. The area to him was 'a chaotic medley of blocks of rock making walking most arduous'. In the past twenty years, Dr Richard Leakey, the renowned palaeontologist from Kenya, and a team of international scientists have caused experts to revise radically their long-held views on evolution. A skull of *Homo habilis*, or 'handy man', more than two million years old was found in 1972 and a discovery of even greater significance was that of *Homo erectus*, one of man's oldest-known ancestors who walked upright over 1.6 million years ago – 1 million years earlier than previous estimates for man's evolution. There is strong evidence to indicate that the region was once a well-watered, fertile area with large forests and abundant game. The process of transformation into the harsh desert environment of today has taken place over several hundred thousand years and still continues.

Teleki had no idea how the Dassenech would react to such a large caravan invading their country. 'The first meeting with natives unaccustomed to caravans is always a most anxious and exciting time. The too sudden appearance of a large party will often induce flight, or ignorance of the language and customs of the natives will lead to hostilities.' The expedition had trudged through sparsely populated districts for fifty days and Teleki's half-starved men were desperately in need of food. The grain they had brought with them from Baringo had long since run out. The count had absolutely no doubt in his mind that Dualla was the only man who could be relied upon to negotiate with the Dassenech; so, nearing the end of the lake, the shrewd Somali set out early one morning with a party of hand-picked men, while the rest of them lurked morosely beneath stunted thorn scrub with the heat hovering around forty degrees Centigrade. As the hours ticked by and darkness fell, a sense of foreboding gripped the protagonists and silenced them. At length distant shots rang out and Dualla, skirting the lake shore, reappeared at ten o'clock that night. He had wandered about for a long time before finding traces of human habitation, then had great difficulty conversing with the Dassenech, who spoke no language known to him. At first they had been suspicious of his intentions but, as usual, he was adept in his dealings. Before long they responded positively to his overtures of friendship and, in so doing, impressed him no end, for the sight of forty men who might just as well have dropped from the skies perturbed them so little. Teleki was delighted with the report; he could move forward again confidently.

After the brooding silence of a windless day, huge cumulonimbi massed ominously over the lake. That night loud peals of thunder rang out disconcertingly as bolts of forked lightning dashed the troubled waters with an unrelenting fury. After months of dry weather the parched soil ached for rain, greedily soaking up the first scattered drops, which heralded a deluge lasting twelve hours. Most of the porters slept in the open and were thoroughly demoralized by the wild wet night as they shivered in numbed discomfort, their complexions ashen-grey or dull yellow. Flash floods turned the dry river beds into raging torrents carrying all before them. An attempt to cross one at daybreak almost ended in disaster. Several valuable loads were swept 1,000 yards downstream and the carriers would have drowned had the Somalis not taken bold action to grab hold of them. By late morning the turgid waters had shrunk to a trickle but it took Teleki another day to sort out the chaos and approach the Dassenech settlements.

Soon we were once more on the beach, here over-grown with rushes and flanked by the low sandy hills at the northern base of which we knew, from Dualla's account, we should find the Reshiat village. And there, sure enough, some 1,100 yards off, it lay, rising up distinctly against the gleaming white sand, surrounded by crowds of natives. Most of them were warriors, armed with spears and long narrow shields, who watched our movements as eagerly as we did theirs . . . This was perhaps the most interesting day of our whole journey, for we were now for the first time face to face with a perfectly unknown people. And the way in which these natives, who had hitherto lived quietly far away from the rest of the world, received us on this first day of our arrival was so simple, so utterly unlike anything related in the accounts of their experiences by African travellers, that we could not get over our astonishment. First came a party of ten or twelve warriors, and behind them a group of some sixty or eighty men, who advanced fearlessly towards our camp. They paused every now and then, but evidently not from nervousness, for they allowed the women laden with food to approach a good bit nearer to us. We gazed at the dark, supple forms with eager curiosity, but drew back when the first group squatted down at a distance of some 200 paces from the camp, lest the sight of our white faces should upset the negotiations.

Kimameta, Dualla and Lembasso went forward to make peace. 'We are glad that you have come to us,' the Dassenech spokesman said. 'We will remain your friends and the only struggle shall be between your beautiful goods and our products. And in this you will get the worst of it, for our food supplies are inexhaustible.' A closer scrutiny of the trade goods, however, disappointed the villagers. Iron was worthless, they did not care for cloth and the little beads were taken as seeds. Not until the women had had their say were the red and blue 'Maasai' beads accepted, one string equalling two pints of sorghum. With fifteen loads of grain bought in, Teleki and von Höhnel appeared on the scene but the Dassenech looked at them askance.

We approached them in a friendly manner, to find that even the warriors shrank from us with the greatest dislike, not apparently from fear of shyness, but from disgust. Some prime tobacco, which I offered to one man, was indignantly refused, although the Reshiat are very fond of chewing tobacco and taking it as snuff. The feeling of repulsion, however, soon wore off, and in the afternoon some two hundred men and women crowded into and about the camp, touching and staring at all the things new to them.

These were the encouraging signs to a break in their journey that was to last nearly six weeks.

Camp was sited a short distance from the Dassenech village close to a clump of shady acacia trees under which a daily market was established. With the coming of the rains, the overcast skies kept daytime temperatures at a tolerable level though mosquitoes were an unwelcome nuisance at night. Numerous scorpions had been driven out of their holes by the rain and posed a much greater threat to the barefoot porters. However much the depredations of crested cranes, *Balearica regulorum*, kept their numbers in check, there was always a risk of someone falling victim to their poisoned tail stings, which can be excrutiating but not lethal. Fortunately, the chief, a bearded patriarchal figure, spoke fluent Samburu which solved the communication barrier. 'He was about 50 years old, very slim, and more than six feet high. He wore no ornaments, and his only clothing was a coarsely woven sackcloth-like garment several yards long, made of sheep's wool, such as we had already seen on Mount Nyiru. He wore this either like a shawl over his shoulders, wound round his body like a girdle, or draped in various ways.' He carried in his right hand the indispensable *karro*, a two-legged stool which was used as a seat or pillow. Women came daily to camp bringing fresh milk in wooden vessels, and sorghum, once dubbed by his men as asses' fodder, was eaten with relish. The porters caught fish in the lake, gathered mussels in its shallow waters and picked soft, sticky red berries close to its shores as a welcome change to their monotonous diet. Only the purchase of cattle, sheep and goats proved to be an insurmountable problem. It was not that the Dassenech were unwilling to sell them; rather that no trade goods of sufficient value took their fancy.

Unlike the Maasai, Teleki found the Dassenech unhelpful in parting with reliable geographical information. Questions were often evaded or deliberately ignored, and outright opposition to his plans to return down the west side of the lake was never fully explained. 'There is but one way for you and that is back the way you came,' the obdurate chief used to say. 'Fly over the lake, swim over it if you can, but if you can't, then go back! That is the decision of all the Reshiat.' Teleki had a feeling in the back of his mind that Lembasso might have put the chief up to saying this, because it was only natural for a Samburu to prefer a route close to home. But when Teleki enquired about the route to Empaso Naibor, the white lake, the chief's answer was the same. 'There is no way. What do you want to do there anyway? It has been dried up for a very long time.' Every attempt at a friendly discussion about their route ended in a similar manner. Opposition to their wishes had become a state of affairs. If the chief was pressed further, he would seize his long staff and turn his back on the travellers, who paid not the slightest attention to his antics. If he would not agree to let them go their chosen way, they would go by force if necessary. Be that as it may, they were not yet ready for a showdown because their half-starved men had first to be better nourished and rations bought in for the journey back home.

As the days turned into weeks, the attitude of the chief towards his guests

thawed a little. In the end 'El Moruo Torono' – Teleki had nicknamed him the wicked old man – gave tacit approval for them to make a short safari to Empaso Naibor, though he still refused guides to show them the way. He did condescend, however, to look after eleven sick men as well as the ivory and trade goods they wished to leave behind. Intermittent heavy rain had solved the main obstacle of finding water *en route*, so Lembasso was elected pathfinder, although he had never before been this far north. Teleki had been assured by Lembasso and the Dassenech that Samburu *manyattas* would be found near the lake; he therefore left laden with his iron wire in readiness to buy cattle. Much to his disappointment the lake region was uninhabited and the few deserted *manyattas* his party did come across had not been occupied for about three years. Wild animals were everywhere, but the seasonal lake presented an uninteresting and unattractive spectacle. Her Imperial Highness the Archduchess Stefanie, wife of Crown Prince Rudolf – a loud-voiced woman at the best of times – would not have been amused at having this 'newly discovered sheet of water' named after her, had she known what it looked like. 'On the beach and in the air were thousands of scavenger birds including vultures, marabou storks and crows glutting themselves with the fish which lay about in great quantities in various stages of decomposition . . . The water of the lake was very brackish, and but for the rainpools it would have been impossible to remain where we were.' The fish were probably lung fish which, as the rain-water evaporates, worm their way into the thick mud at the bottom of the larger pools. There they curl themselves into balls and, as the sun bakes out the last of the moisture, the mucus with which they line their holes turns to parchment. Thus sequestered, their hibernation may last several years until the rains eventually return, when they come to life again, wriggle free of their cocoons in the softened mud and swim away.

Except for the southern tip of the lake which Teleki visited, Stefanie lies in Ethiopia and its name changed a number of years ago to Lake Chew Bahir. To this day there are no roads, no villages, no power lines and no telegraph poles in the area; there is nothing, in fact, except rock and scrub. Rain-water rarely puddles in the lake bed and the wild animals vanished long ago. The explorers took it upon themselves to hold a party and celebrate as an outward manifestation of their success. 'We brewed ourselves a bowl of foaming liquor, made, it is true, of nothing but honey, water, tartaric acid and doubly-distilled carbonic acid, but which tasted delicious, and we emptied it with an enthusiastic "Hip, Hip, Hurrah" [anglicized] in honour of the royal pair whose names it is our proud privilege to associate all the geographical results of our arduous undertaking.'

Teleki and von Höhnel returned to their base camp on the shores of Lake Turkana very undecided which way to go home but, in the fullness of time, a plan was carefully worked out. For a start, Dualla reconnoitred the Omo delta to check on the state of the river. But scarcely had he left than he was back again with the unsettling news that it was in spate and formed an impassable barrier. The Omo rises in the southern highlands of Ethiopia and is the only permanent source of water for Lake Turkana, which has no outlets. As such, the level of the lake is largely controlled by the duration and intensity of the rainfall in Ethiopia, which is normally at its peak in April and May – the very months when the explorers happened to be there. It is of passing interest to know that the lake level has fluctuated over a range of sixty-five feet this century, an extent greater than any other lake of natural origin in the world.

With plans under way in Ethiopia for drawing water from the Omo to irrigate large tracts of arid land, it is destined to drop much more.

At least Dualla's bad news was better than no news at all, and it forced Teleki to concentrate on the only routes now open to them down the east side of the lake. The next stage of the plan was to buy in food. As it was not being brought to them, they had to go and fetch it. So von Höhnel set off with Dualla and another fifty porters to make the necessary purchases. Torrential rains were a major cause of concern and in places where Dualla had passed dry-shod three days earlier, von Höhnel and his men had to wade through water up to their waists. They came across a people whose women disfigured the lower lip in a very remarkable manner, boring it first, and then gradually widening the opening till a piece of ox-horn, almost the width of the mouth, could be inserted. The lower incisors were removed to expose the tongue – an appearance that was altogether singular and rather revolting.

After foraging in their villages, two tons of sorghum and dried beans were purchased, with Dualla hitting on the bright idea of using a measure which held twice as much as the usual one. While these tribesmen may have puzzled at this ruse, the Dassenech got their own back by maintaining a defiant posture over the sale of their cattle. The porters could not understand why their leader allowed hundreds of sleek animals to pass their camp each day without taking measures to acquire some – by force if necessary.

Of course the possibility of a forcible solution of our difficulties underlay all our discussions, but we did not mean to resort to it till all other means had failed. The Reshiat had received us kindly and dealt honourably with us; we did not want them to repent having done so, or to turn their first coming into contact with civilization into a curse. On the other hand we had to remember that the lives of two hundred faithful and devoted men depended on our decision, and that our first duty was to them.

Von Höhnel was plagued by millions of vicious mosquitoes and hurried back to camp on his third day of absence in fear of being cut off by the fast-rising floodwaters. All the while Teleki had pondered the dilemma alone in camp. Would he take his men back via Marsabit Mountain or retrace his steps down the east side of the lake – a route which neither he nor his men wished to follow? With only twenty charges of ammunition left for each gun, a major consideration had to be the choice of the safest passage. Eventually, he realized there was no alternative but to backtrack and, if all went well, he would explore Turkana and Pokot country to make up for the disappointment at not being able to reach the western shores of the lake.

Smallpox was spreading southwards among the Dassenech and the explorers wasted no time in the division of loads. 'Every man, whether porter, *askari* or guide received, in addition to his load, sixteen days' rations of sorghum. No load weighed less than 110 lbs and the heaviest weighed 148¼ lbs. Then there were the weapons, ammunition, cooking utensils, sleeping-mats etc.; in a word, our men were expected to make such efforts as nothing but a case so desperate as ours would have justified.' The men saw it very differently. 'Takufa yote, Bwana. Why should we all die just because the pig-headed Merille refuse to sell us cattle?' they grumbled. 'Leave it to us and we will soon drag hundreds of the finest oxen here by their tails.' But Teleki would hear nothing of it so, on 14th May, they tottered out of camp beneath their massive burdens, heading for a very uncertain fate.

CHAPTER 15

A critical situation

Kujikwaa si kuanguka, bali ni kwenda mbele
To stumble is not to fall down, but it is to go forward

Swahili proverb

THE CHARACTER OF THE LAKE environs had changed greatly with the advent of the long rains. Wild flowers, lilies and fresh green grass had sprung up everywhere, bringing welcome life to hitherto barren areas. Although winter migrants had already taken flight to northern latitudes, weaver birds were busy building their exquisitely woven nests in acacia trees laden with golden flower balls, which had suddenly burst into the most lovely and delicate pale green foliage; like orchards in Europe when the harsh cold of winter has passed on, so it was here when the hard grip of drought conditions had been broken. Teleki lost no time shooting several rhinos and zebras to supplement their dry rations. But the annual migration of elephants back to Marsabit Mountain had already begun and not a single one was seen on the march. 'We now realized that it had only been the quantity of elephant meat obtainable at the time of the greatest drought which had enabled us to make our way to the northern end of the lake. Had we attempted the journey at the present time of year, we should probably have lost nearly all our men.'

Despite the porters' heavy loads, they covered the 235-mile trek down the east side of the lake in the remarkable marching time of ninety hours spread over sixteen days. This was twelve days shorter than their outward journey, which had taken place under more favourable conditions. Fate had been much kinder to them than they had dared hope. The expedition still had a little sorghum in reserve though several porters had used up their rations recklessly. Only three men had died on the march, one of them, Matchako, a sturdy young fellow, having contracted smallpox. Knowing that he would be driven out of the caravan when the disease was discovered he had, of his own free will, kept away from his companions. Food and fire were left at a safe distance on every halt but, after a day, he was never seen again. It is a milestone in medical history and an outstanding tribute to the profession that this highly infectious disease has been eradicated. The last-known case of smallpox was reported in Somalia some years ago and was quickly isolated. Little do we now realize the untold misery and suffering it brought to the peoples of Africa and Asia. Almost half the population of some districts in Kenya was wiped out towards the end of the last century, when an epidemic swept south from Ethiopia.

Teleki ordered camp to be pitched in exactly the same spot at the southern end of Lake Turkana whence their safari began eighty-five days before; only now, everyone was in better spirits, with the explorers indulging in a little mutual admiration. While von Höhnel named the active volcano 'Teleki's volcano', Teleki named the God-forsaken, wind-swept bay beside which they halted 'von Höhnel Bay'. With the area still completely inaccessible except on foot and looking the same as it did a century ago, no one has given a thought to changing those names. The features remain today, as then, a silent reminder of the historic journey undertaken by the two pioneering travellers.

Teleki and von Höhnel made a half-hearted attempt to climb Teleki's

volcano – as smooth and straight as a chimney – before they finally left the district; but sulphur fumes and pitch-black lava flows, in which there were dangerous holes up to sixteen feet deep bristling with stalagmite-like spikes, forced them back well below the orange-tinged rim of the crater wall. With their exploration of the lake at an end, they hurried away west towards Turkana country. They had to pick a way through a confused tapestry of coarse, porous volcanic boulders which, in places, had to be shoved aside or rolled into the depths below. Sharp-edged rocks, the size of a man's head, made walking insufferable for the barefoot men who soon complained loudly of their wounds. The monotony of the landscape was relieved here and there by gaunt, weather-beaten trees which eked out an astonishing existence for ten months in every year against impossible odds. An occasional eagle or vulture could be seen soaring high overhead; otherwise, the land was sterile with no sign of life. It was as if the Creator had tired of his efforts in other corners of the globe and left his work in this district unfinished.

Once the travellers had gained the Loriu Plateau, the going became a little easier and nature seemingly more benevolent. The bare black rocks gave way to bare black men tending their sheep and goats. They reached the banks of the Kerio River two days later, where tents were quickly pitched beneath shady acacia trees. Within the hour Turkana of every age group had flocked into camp, 'these people being the very noisiest we ever met ... whilst the way in which a dozen warriors advanced to greet us resembled the charge of an enemy, rather than the peaceful welcome we knew it to be'. With uplifted shields and flashing spears they dashed towards the startled Europeans. Teleki observed with equanimity that the Turkana were very different from any other tribe he had come across.

Circumcision is not practised amongst the Turkana. Most of the men wear nothing but an ornament round their waists, consisting of home-made iron and brass beads. The young men, or, to speak more correctly, the warriors, for some of the married men here take their share of fighting, also wear a loin-cloth of kidskin some three inches broad in front and six behind, the edges being very prettily decorated with metal beads. Nearly all the Turkana ornaments are made of iron. The bracelets consist of a number of loose rings of wire, and the neck ornaments of six strong iron clasps resembling armour, the wearer being compelled to hold his head up very stiffly. From the upper arm droops a plaited leather ornament generally ending in a cow's tail, and the legs are often adorned with rings of plaited leather from which hang iron chains, or simple leather bands. In the pierced underlip of both sexes is worn a little brass rod or plaque, and from the nostrils is suspended an oval brass plaque. In the lobes of the ears are inserted a number of little rings.

As a rule, people who disregard clothes pay great attention to their hair. This was certainly true of the Turkana whose curious hairstyles were unique. The warriors plaited their hair into a large bun and decorated it with ostrich feathers, whereas the older men matted theirs with the hair of their ancestors until it hung down their backs like a narrow sack up to three feet long. This extraordinary creation was also adorned with ostrich feathers.

Turkana girls wear a little leather apron which is prettily decorated with a broad band of ostrich eggs pierced and strung together. Down the back of the waist hangs a second longer apron made of brown dressed kidskin tastily finished off at the edge with iron or brass beads. Older women wear long aprons in front as well as behind. The ornaments of the women consist of several rows of beads worn round the neck, girdles made of iron and brass rings or goats' teeth, and ear, nostril, lip, arm and foot rings or plaques of various kinds. The hair of the women is always twisted into a number of thin strands which hang straight down, short in front and long at the back. Tattooing is often practised, and consists of raised scars in parallel curves, in the men on one or both shoulders, and in the women on the abdomen.

The pain borne during cicatricial disfiguration made up for their lack of a circumcision ceremony to signify manhood. Not much has changed among the Turkana this century, except for the hairstyles and ornaments of the men. No other people seem to survive with fewer possessions, which is probably just as well, for their igloo-shaped shelters are the poorest of any in East Africa and give them practically no protection from the elements. Life in this harsh and unyielding land is sustained on remarkably little; almost anything with four legs is eaten and, in season, small berries add nourishment to a spartan diet. It is hardly coincidence that the countless wild animals of

Teleki's day have disappeared for ever, leaving one of the largest districts in the country deprived of its faunal heritage. All ages and both sexes of the Turkana love chewing quids of pungent tobacco and it follows that the indelicate yet frequent habit of squirting gobs of brown spittle through a gap in their teeth has become second nature to them. The Turkana language is reputed to have more swear words than any other language on earth and it surely typifies the tough, fiercely independent character of the people who speak it.

Timid travellers would have been anything but comfortable in Turkana country, but Teleki and von Höhnel were not troubled by nerves. Mock hostile charges, endless shouting and grotesque dances accompanied by erotic gestures were all taken in their stride. Dualla, however, had never before in his life seen such wild people and quite lost his temper with them over endless and, more often than not, fruitless hours of haggling over oxen. He was also taken aback by their belligerent attitude. 'You are downright fools not to know that good manners requires you to exchange assurances of friendship with us before you begin trading,' they chided. 'And how dare you take water from our river without permission. Anyway, who asked you to come at all?' If their uninvited guests really wanted to trade, they would have to offer the Turkana medicines for bringing rain, winning wars and making their cattle fertile. Lembasso had assured Teleki that the Turkana would sell any amount of livestock, but he failed to mention that tobacco and not beads would be their most favoured medium of exchange. Teleki had no tobacco in his stores so his attempts to buy cattle and camels were futile. Thereupon von Höhnel started out for Logatham accompanied by Dualla and seventy porters in a last effort to replenish their dwindling supplies. Following dry river beds fringed with fan palms, *Hyphaene thebaica*, they reached the Turkwell Delta where their pleas were once again met with a blunt refusal. Moreover, sorghum was unobtainable in the only area in Turkana country where it was known to grow.

Von Höhnel rejoined Teleki four days later near the Katirr *lugga*, a few miles west of the Kerio River, having brought with him one ox, fourteen donkeys and ninety sheep and goats. It was a disappointing and motley collection which pleased no one. Under way again, they crossed over the Katigithigiria Hills – von Höhnel's Ol-doinyo Orok or black hills – to the Turkwell River where, according to the Turkana, they would find large herds of cattle and wild animals as numerous as grains of sand on the sea-shore. The promised land had an all too familiar ring to it, and proved to be yet another instance of the travellers being told what the locals thought would please them rather than the bitter truth. It was rather like Swahili etiquette which required the initial answer to a question to be good in all circumstances; only in later conversation is bad news communicated. When Teleki enquired from one of his guides, Ali Schaongwe, how things were going, Ali answered, anxious as usual to please, 'Habari Njema, Bwana, watu wawili wamekufa! Good news, sir, two people have died!'

Unfortunately, the Turkana were more interested in disposing of their ivory than in parting with their livestock; only two donkeys and two sheep were offered for sale. Teleki had reason to believe that elephants lived in the riverine forest, but it would have been folly to hunt them in the tangled undergrowth where winds eddied dangerously. The countryside was bare beyond the dense thickets and, try hard as he might for two days to shoot something for the pot, not a single wild animal was seen. Meanwhile their food reserves had dwindled to two small lean oxen and a handful of sheep. Again and again the fatal necessity of sacrificing their remaining animals had been averted at the last moment, but this time there was no way out. Teleki gave orders for four donkeys to be slaughtered; yet, hungry as his men were, they would not touch the meat. In support of their conviction, they related how an entire caravan had died after eating their donkeys. This fable would have been spread deliberately by traders whose interests would not have been best served by allowing half-starved men to eat pack-animals.

With no time to lose to avert starvation, the expedition pushed south along the forest line of the Turkwell River. Teleki carefully avoided the wide sandy *lugga* due to the many obstructions caused by uprooted trees, which told eloquently of the mighty force of the current during the rainy season.

For seven days they lived off berries and fruits from wild fig trees, supplementing this unappetizing diet with a warthog and two crocodiles which were shot on the banks of the river. But this was merely a foretaste of the hardships that came later. First, they passed through Ngaboto, situated near the confluence of the Suam and Weiwei Rivers, where fields of corn waved tantalizingly in the breeze. 'Allah Akbar!' one wag exclaimed. 'I never thought we would ever see *dhurra* again. The perpetual grass diet we have had to put up with lately had made me think it really would have been better to have been born an ass!' This first impression of a land flowing with milk and honey was, alas, grossly over-optimistic, as they soon found out to their cost. In fact, the sorghum was barely half-ripe and the further south they moved, the greener it became. They found the harvest in progress in just one place. 'The natives cut off the ears of corn and then pluck them to pieces with their fingers, throwing them on to an open place of flat ground where they are left to dry in the sun after which they are lightly thrashed with a stick. Grain is packed in baskets some six inches in diameter made of plaited branches and hung up in trees at a height of over 35 feet from the ground.' The locals had suffered a crop failure the previous year and had very little food to offer passing caravans. Much of the surplus had already been bought by another caravan which happened to be there in search of ivory. This brought about an unhealthy competition, disrupting the traditional markets. At the end of a day's hard bargaining Teleki failed to add significantly to his men's rations, so they were once more reduced to foraging in the woods, ravenously devouring fledgelings from weaver birds' nests and surreptitiously 'borrowing' sorghum from the cornfields to keep body and soul together. Teleki had forbidden them to steal, but he turned a blind eye to their night excursions so long as there were no complaints from the farmers.

Our position was now pretty well desperate. Our men had supported life with the greatest difficulty for weeks; many had succumbed to their privations, and all were terribly pulled down. Buoyed up with the hope that when we got to Suk we should find plenty of food, they had struggled bravely on, and here, at the very threshold of the promised land, we were face to face with the fact that it too contained nothing for the support of the caravan.

An idea was mooted to plunder their way through to Baringo, but that would have closed the district to traders indefinitely and was not taken seriously. Their only real hope of buying cattle was to make contact with the nomadic stock-owning half of the Pokot tribe – von Höhnel also called them the Suk – who lived east of the Kerio valley. It was a vile journey. The rain lashed down in torrents, making movement treacherous across the sodden ground. No sooner had they forded the Kerio River at a point due east of the Cherangani Hills than their 'helpful' guides promptly decamped and were never seen again. Within hours, a cloudburst on the hills turned the sluggish chocolate-brown waters into a furious deluge which prevented anyone recrossing to the other side. This was precisely what the Pokot had hoped would happen to their unwanted and unwelcome guests whose plight was now desperate.

We felt that the time was approaching when our caravan would be converted into a mere horde of reckless plunderers. But after all, we were to learn of what heroic stuff many of our men were made in this time of trial. Makatubu and Muhinna Wadi Kidiwa especially distinguished themselves. They suggested flinging a rope across the river to keep up a connection with the dhurra *plantations. A dozen times they tried to swim across the rushing torrent, taking a thin line with them to begin with; but again and again they were swept down by the strength of the current, or sucked into some whirlpool, so that we almost gave them up for lost. At last, however, they succeeded in their bold attempt. A strong line was made taut, and after many hours of hard work a few of the bravest of our men were got across the river, and we were able to console ourselves with the thought that if everything else fails we should at least be able to get some unripe* dhurra.

Two days later Teleki knew that he had to move on. No contact had been made with the nomads, while the health and morale of his half-starved men, continually drenched by heavy rains, grew rapidly worse. Besides, the Pokot farmers had detected the plundering of their corn fields, which made food supplies even more uncertain.

Ten men were missing when the caravan set out on 19th July towards the Chepanda Hills, and twenty-four hours later Teleki planned drastic measures to save the lives of his dispirited men. Although they had met up with the nomads and lavished gifts on them to stress friendship, the cattle owners were no more favourably disposed to the travellers than their farming cousins. Whichever barter goods were offered to them, they stubbornly refused to part with their livestock.

Our powers of self-denial were exhausted at last, and we had to save the lives of our two hundred men at whatever cost to ourselves or others. There could no longer be any doubt as to what we ought to do. We must take the cattle we needed from the natives by force, and the only thing to be considered was how to do so in the least offensive manner. We finally decided upon the following plan. To begin with we shifted camp higher up the mountain and nearer the village, discovering in so doing that one-third of our men were almost too weak to move. The caravan was then divided into two parts, the strongest of the men, nineteen in all, were to be left in camp with Dualla, who was to make a raid upon the natives, whilst the rest were to go on with the Count.

Dualla supervised the stitching of thirty Somali-style pack-saddles so as to transfer as many loads as possible to the donkeys. Then Teleki, to get well clear of the Pokot in case of revenge, set out with his suffering and disabled men. The party included von Höhnel, who was laid low by a severe attack of malaria and had to be carried in a hammock. They struggled slowly up the Kito Pass before camping beside a little stream on the rocky eastern slopes of the Chepanda Hills. Not for the first time did everything depend on the wily Somali who was carefully laying down his plans for the raid while the others waited anxiously for him to show up. He attacked the *manyatta* under cover of darkness and found no difficulty in driving away the herds, for the inhabitants were taken completely off-guard and fled. Anticipating reprisals, he formed a well-armed rear-guard to protect the drovers. Then, as dawn broke to the sound of war-horns, he left the area as quickly as possible. Before long, 200 ferocious warriors flung themselves with reckless bravery at his little force, but were unable to withstand the withering barrage of fire coming from his deceptively harmless-looking 'fire spears'. The inglorious battle lost, they turned tail and ran for their lives. 'Towards evening the joyful sound of signal shots reached us from the distance, and a little later we saw cattle, goats and sheep filing down the mountain slope towards us. Soon the valley echoed with the lowing of cattle and the joyful shouts and friendly chatter of the men as they exchanged greetings and news.'

At last there was plenty of food for the caravan, but relief came too late for many of the porters who had gradually weakened and passed away. It had been by far the worst part of their journey but in his diaries von Höhnel did not reveal the full extent of their misfortune. Since everyone had lived for weeks on end on a starvation diet of berries, weeds, half-ripe figs, acacia resin, fledgelings, fungi and unripe sorghum, the death rate was tragically high. Even the nickname the porters had given to the corpulent count 'Dachi tumbo', German belly – was no longer appropriate, for he had shed his Teutonic paunch, losing ninety-seven pounds to become an almost unrecognizable 141 pounds. Teleki had an iron constitution and never fell ill but he and von Höhnel were by then worn out both physically and mentally; they had finally lost the urge to travel any further. In any case, there was no food in the area and their stolen stock 'melted away like snow beneath the midday sun'. After resting up for nine days at the Njemps' village near Lake Baringo, they turned for home. For the sake of their brave little body of men, they chose the easiest route back to Taveta through Naivasha and Ukambani. On 9th August, they bade the Njemps farewell and wended their way south on familiar tracks past the hot springs and brooks of Lake Bogoria. In areas where Teleki had hunted six months earlier, the animals were now just as numerous. 'As before, thousands of buffaloes were roaming to and fro, rhinoceroses were standing or lying about in the grass, elands, zebras and gazelles were grazing in charming groups at the edge of the leleshwa jungle, while ostriches were marching proudly about in the open steppe and crested cranes were standing in a rain pool or, with much shrieking, taking short flights and re-alighting.'

The Maasai offered no resistance to the expedition's passage past Lakes Nakuru, Elementeita and Naivasha. Indeed, they were delighted that Teleki's men had dealt a blow to their arch-enemies, the Pokot, readily exchanging eight fat oxen for twenty-four sheep and goats. Von Höhnel found time to take bearings of Lake Naivasha from thirty-six different positions because he had surmised, quite rightly, that it had been placed incorrectly on the maps of those who had preceded him. He also commented on the leleshwa scrub growing on the Ang'ata Oolkeek, the firewood plains, between Naivasha and Gilgil, which Thomson suggested had died of natural causes; he saw clear signs of damage by bush fires and not by any change in climate. The Maasai use the fragrant leleshwa leaves as a perfume, often putting them under their beds at night or under their armpits when travelling. They are most particular about body odour, which is largely a matter of diet. To this day, the smell of one of their *posho*-eating neighbours is so repugnant to them that they call them 'Iloongu' – the bad-smelling people.

Teleki was amazed at the welcome his men received from the Kikuyu. It could not have been more friendly or more genuine, even if the medicine men believed that their aggressive treatment of the travellers the previous year had led to poor rains and a crop failure which now had to be redressed.

We chose a site for our camp near a village. Young and old at once set eagerly to work to collect brushwood, whilst others made holes in the ground with their swords, and in next to no time our fence was up. What a change had come over these people! . . .

We passed three delightful days amongst our Kikuyu friends who came from far and near bringing plenty of poultry, honey, sugar-cane, potatoes, fresh beans and tobacco for sale. They also offered us slaves, including a pretty young woman with a baby at her breast, leading a little three-year-old boy by the hand. The owner was willing to sell the mother and baby, but wished to keep the boy for himself. Silently, and apparently indifferent to everything, the young woman awaited her fate, but the tears rolled down the little boy's fat cheeks on to his yet plumper body. Jumbe Kimameta, to whom these beautiful wares were offered, had not the heart to separate the child from his mother, and he had not goods enough to spare to bid for the boy too. Now as we had noticed that our Jumbe was always very good to his slaves, Count Teleki presented him with the balance necessary to buy the whole

party, making it a condition that the family should be kept together. The total price was twenty rings of iron wire and twenty strings of Maasai beads, of the value altogether of only about one dollar.

The little boy made a first-rate goatherd of his own free will and became a firm favourite of the expedition for the rest of their journey home.

When Teleki and von Höhnel left Kikuyu district for the last time, they saw Mount Kilimanjaro in the far distance, standing out in majestic splendour against a pale blue sky freshly washed by heavy rain. Von Höhnel was quick to realize that the bearing he took of it was the most important of the many thousands he had recorded in the course of their travels, since it enabled him to connect his maps of the northern districts to those of the coastal region.

The borders of Wakamba country were closely guarded against surprise attacks by the Kikuyu and Maasai, so when the columns reached the frontier, scouts came down from the hills to check who the travellers were and where they were going before allowing them to pass. 'We were now in the north-west corner of Ukambani, in the district of Iveti, also still sometimes called Machako, after the recently deceased chief of that name.' Machakos was then a few shacks which housed a dozen Swahili traders. Within two years, it had become an outpost of the Imperial British East Africa Company and the major market east of the Rift Valley. It even boasted a rough stone house with a trench round it, where a lone European was responsible for victualling the company's caravans travelling to Uganda. Several years later the railway line was laid twenty miles to the south of Machakos and its strategic importance rapidly diminished as the Nairobi railhead grew. The highlands of Iveti are a rugged treeless area but, like so many other places, were well-wooded in the distant past.

But for their ornaments, which are numerous and pretty, the [Wakamba] *men go almost naked, wearing round their loins only a number of rows of* mikufu [fine wire] *or thin brass chains, or a girdle about a quarter of an inch thick made of fine twisted brass wire. On the legs, beginning at the ankles, are wound rows of white Maasai beads from four to six inches deep, looking like socks. Bracelets and necklaces are also worn. Suspended from necklaces or fastened on the forehead we also noticed a few finely chiselled round metal plaques of different sizes, resembling medallions, and betraying an artistic skill and taste far exceeding anything we had noticed elsewhere in Africa . . .*

Very effective and tasty is the dress of the women and girls of Ukambani. They cut away the hair except from the top of the head, what is left looking like a close-fitting skull cap. Every superfluous hair is removed with the aid of some little pincers worn round the neck. But for the various necklaces, the upper part of the body is left uncovered; round the waist is worn a girdle made of some fifty or sixty rows of blue beads of the size of a pea, and below this girdle hangs a little apron of gleaming home-made brass and iron beads, the whole forming a striking contrast to the velvet-like chocolate-brown skin, and giving the young girls a most picturesque appearance.

The Wakamba were first-rate archers and made well-flighted arrows whose steel heads were barbed and dipped in poison. These weapons were used as much for hunting as for self-defence and to this day the Wakamba are noted for their hunting and tracking skills. For many years, they formed the backbone of Kenya's army, serving with distinction in India and Burma during the Second World War. The expedition's progress through Ukambani was uneventful, since most of the local people had become quite accustomed to trading caravans passing through their territory. They were always pleased to sell their surplus food for barter goods and even more delighted when traders reached Ukambani without any trade goods left. On those occasions, they demanded ivory in exchange for food, which they subsequently sold at the coast. It was a tough journey with little reward. Even if they managed to run the gauntlet of highway robbers, the unscrupulous merchants at Mombasa fleeced them. There were very few animals left in northern Ukambani but they were still abundant in the less-populated, poverty-stricken areas to the south. At Kikumbulyu, Teleki shot his eighty-third and last rhino of the trip. Add to this the ones that von Höhnel shot and the tally reached more or less 100.

The rest of their journey took them over well-worn footpaths back to Mombasa, where they arrived on 24th October 1888 to an emotional welcome. Among the many delights of their return to civilization was the luxury of a cake of soap – an important little item of personal hygiene which they had not had for ten months. The Maasai may have reasoned with some justification that, like their *posho*-eating neighbours, all white men were 'Iloongu' too!

Forty-eight hours later they set sail for Zanzibar, with those married men who had survived the painful ravages of these uncompromising lands

Teleki shoots his last rhino of the trip

anxiously speculating whether their wives had remained faithful during their long absences and whether there had been additions or changes to the family circle. Teleki and von Höhnel spent eight weeks on the island recuperating, until they left for Aden towards the end of the year. From there, they made a brief excursion to the walled city of Harar in Abyssinia before returning to Europe after an absence of two years.

They had completed one of the last great African expeditions of travel and adventure, enabling geographers to add significantly to their knowledge of Mount Kenya and the lacustrine chain of the Great Rift Valley. Cartographers were delighted with von Höhnel's most detailed and painstaking observations which almost completed the map of East Africa, while scientists were fascinated by the comprehensive collection of flora and fauna they had brought with them. Among the many items new to science were three chameleons, sixty beetles, fifteen butterflies and moths as well as locusts, spiders, mosses, lichens, flowers and a beautiful lobelia, *Lobelia telekii*, which is found in Kenya's mountain regions above 10,000 feet. Most of Teleki's hunting trophies and the African artefacts he collected were lost during the Second World War.

Teleki travelled to Indonesia in 1893 and later to India but left no account of these hunting trips. Little is known of an unverified report of a second visit he is said to have made to East Africa with the sole intention of becoming the first person to conquer Kilimanjaro; in this, he apparently failed again. He remained a bachelor all his life and spent the rest of his days running his stud farm and family estates. He died in Budapest on 10th March 1916 after a long illness.

Von Höhnel received an unexpected letter in 1892 from William Astor Chanler – a wealthy young New Yorker – inviting him to join another expedition to Africa. Chanler had set his sights on exploring the unknown country lying north of the Tana River, between Lake Rudolf and the Juba River, but most of the porters deserted him, causing the collapse of the expedition. By this time von Höhnel had returned to the coast on a stretcher having been badly gored by a rhinoceros.

Soon after resuming his naval duties, von Höhnel was appointed aide-de-camp to Emperor Franz-Josef. Later he visited Abyssinia at the head of a trade delegation and met Emperor Melenik. Later still, he was promoted rear admiral before retiring from the service in 1909. In the succeeding years his pension was almost wiped out by inflation and only through the generosity of Chanler – who became a staunch friend – was he able to make ends meet. He died, almost destitute, in Vienna on 23rd March 1942 aged eighty-four. Unfortunately, the Nazis removed all his personal papers, which have never been seen again.

It is true that the two lakes which Teleki and von Höhnel revealed to the outside world have both had their names changed in recent years. However, they still bear witness to this remarkable journey and to the porters, who were the backbone of any expedition. While some travellers termed them lazy, mutinous and inveterate liars, others praised their tremendous powers of endurance and sense of humour. Those who suffered most thought that the only way to make a porter show a sense of respect was to flog him. Of course, the men were not paragons of virtue and a firm hand was often needed; but treated fairly, they would follow their leader, whatever his foibles, with unswerving loyalty and even risk their lives in the endeavour. The porters were the unsung heroes of every successful safari. Without them, the geographical exploration of East Africa a century ago would have been impossible.

SELECT
BIBLIOGRAPHY

PART I

Burton, Sir Richard F., *First Footsteps in East Africa*, 2 vols, Longmans, Green & Co., London, 1856.

Coupland, Sir Reginald, *East Africa and its Invaders*, Oxford University Press, London, 1938.

Krapf, Rev. Dr Johann L., *Travels, Researches and Missionary labours during an eighteen years' residence in Eastern Africa*, Trubner & Co., London, 1860.

Kretzmann, Paul E., *John Ludwig Krapf*, The Book Concern, Ohio.

Miller, Charles, *The Lunatic Express*, Macdonald, London, 1971.

Moorehead, Alan, *The White Nile*, Hamish Hamilton, London, 1960.

New, Charles, *Life Wanderings and Labours in Eastern Africa*, Hodder & Stoughton, London, 1873.

Paterson, J.H., *The Man-Eaters of Tsavo*, Macmillan, London, 1907.

Speke, John Hanning, *What led to the Discovery of the Source of the Nile*, Blackwood, Edinburgh and London, 1864.

Wakefield, E.S., *Thomas Wakefield, Missionary and geographical pioneer in East Equatorial Africa*, London, 1904.

PART II

Dawson, E.C., *James Hannington, first Bishop of Eastern Equatorial Africa*, Seeley & Co., London, 1887.

Rotberg, Robert I., *Joseph Thomson & the exploration of Africa*, Chatto & Windus, London, 1971.

Thomson, Joseph, *To the Central African Lakes and back*, Sampson Low, Marston, Searle & Rivington, London, 1881.

—— *Through Masai Land*, Sampson Low, Marston, Searle & Rivington, London, 1885.

Wray, Rev. J. Alfred, *Kenya our Newest Colony (1882–1912)*, Marshall Bros, London, 1913.

PART III

Höhnel, Lieut Ludwig von, *Discovery by Count Teleki of Lakes Rudolf and Stefanie*, Longmans, Green & Co., London, 1894.

INDEX

PICTURE SOURCES

Line engravings are taken from the following sources: *Discovery by Count Teleki of Lakes Rudolf and Stefanie* by Lieut Ludwig von Höhnel (Longmans, Green & Co, 1894); *Documents sur l'histoire, la géographie et le commerce d'Afrique orientale* by Capt. M. Guillain (Paris, 1856-7, 2 vols); *The Graphic* (22 March 1873; 13, 20 and 27 June and 11 July 1885); *Men and Creatures in Uganda* by Sir John Bland-Sutton (Hutchinson, 1933); *Narrative of Voyages to Explore the Shores of Africa, Arabia and Madagascar . . .* by Capt. W. F. W. Owen (London, 1833, 2 vols); *Reisen im Ost-Africa in dem Jahren 1859 bis 1865* by Baron Carl Claus von der Decken (Leipzig and Heidelberg, 1869-79, 4 vols); *Through Masai Land* by Joseph Thomson (Sampson Low, Marston, Searle & Rivington, 1885); *Travels, Researches and Missionary labours during an eighteen years' residence in Eastern Africa* by Rev. Dr Johann L. Krapf (Trubner & Co, 1860).

The endpaper, showing Rebmann's rough sketch map of the Kenya region, is taken from the *Church Missionary Intelligencer* (no. 1, vol. 1, May 1849) and is reproduced by kind permission of the Church Missionary Society.

All colour photographs are the copyright of the author.

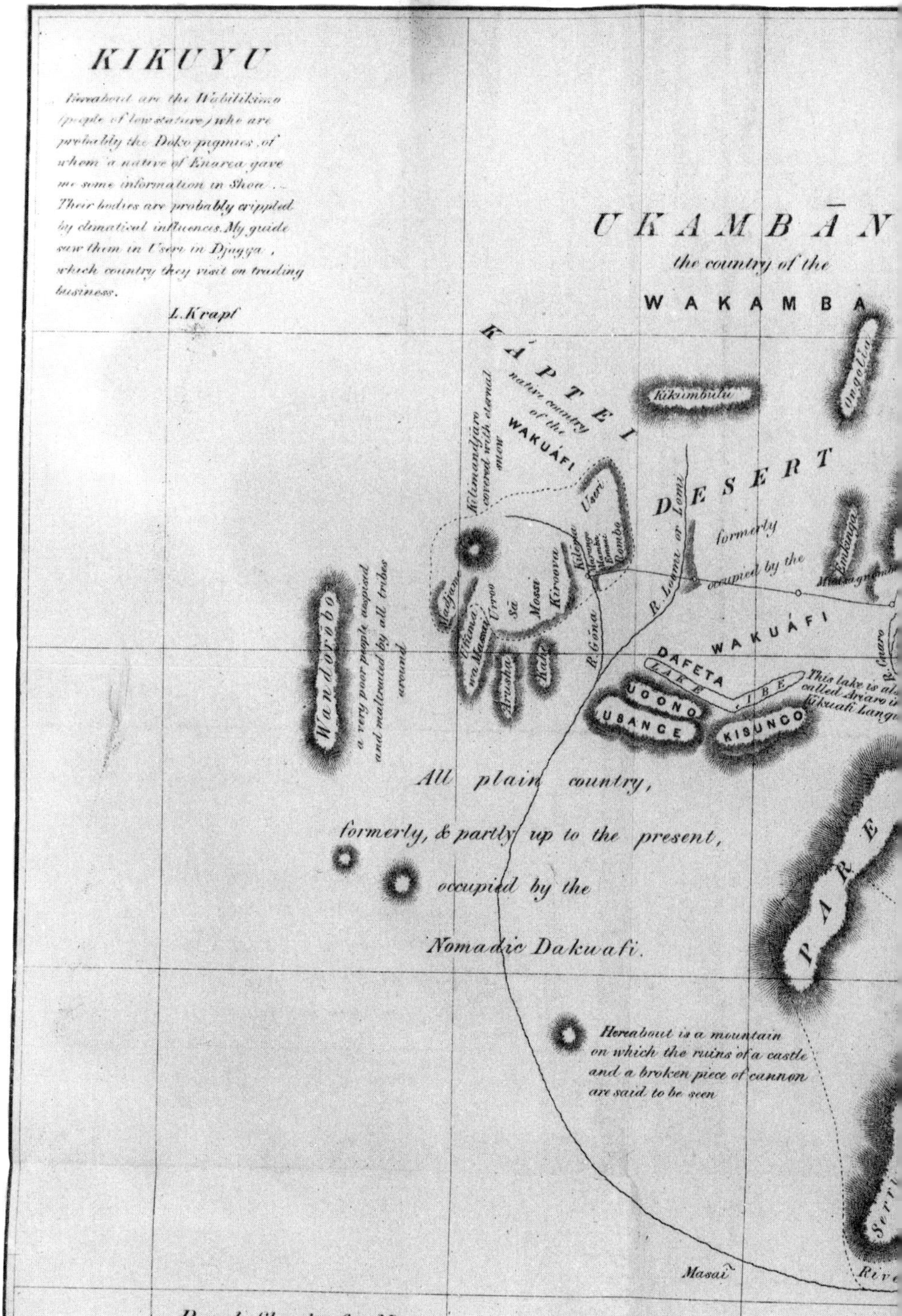

KIKUYU

Hereabout are the Wabilikimo (people of low stature) who are probably the Doko pigmies of whom a native of Enarea gave me some information in Shoa. Their bodies are probably crippled by climatical influences. My guide saw them in Useri in Djagga, which country they visit on trading business.

L. Krapf

UKAMBÁN[I]

the country of the

WAKAMBA

KÁPTEI

native country of the

WAKUÁFI

Kilimandjáro covered with eternal snow

DESERT

formerly occupied by the

WAKUÁFI

Kikumbuliu

Ongáta

Endáagga

R. Jehore or Leoni

Wandorobo

a very poor people despised and maltreated by all tribes around

Maûyou

Mbumi
Masai Usseo

Masai
Séi

Kirooru

Kilombe
Lambe

Régóna

DAFETA

LAKE

JIBE

This lake is also called Saváro in Wakuáfi Language

UGONO

USANGE

KISUNGO

Chara

PARE

All plain country,

formerly, & partly up to the present,

occupied by the

Nomadic Dakwafi.

Hereabout is a mountain on which the ruins of a castle and a broken piece of cannon are said to be seen

Serr[...]

River

Masai

Rough Sketch of a Map,

from 6° to 2° South Latitude &

from 35° to 41° East Longitude, for the

illustration of our Journeys in

the Year 1848.

J. Rebmann.

Mombas, Sep.t 22.nd 1848